A Year
in Our
Gardens

OTHER BOOKS BY ALLEN LACY

In a Green Shade: Writings from Homeground (2000)

The Inviting Garden: Gardening for the Senses, Mind, and Spirit (1998)

The Gardener's Eye and Other Essays (1995)

Gardening with Groundcovers and Vines (1993)

The Garden in Autumn (1990)

The Glory of Roses (1990)

Farther Afield: A Gardener's Excursions (1986)

Home Ground: A Gardener's Miscellany (1984)

Miguel de Unamuno: The Rhetoric of Existence (1967)

EDITED BY ALLEN LACY

The American Gardener: A Sampler (1988)

Gardening for Love: The Market Bulletins,
by Elizabeth Lawrence (1985)

TRANSLATED AND EDITED BY ALLEN LACY
(with Martin Nozick and Anthony Kerrigan)

The Private World, by Miguel de Unamuno (1984)

Peace in War, by Miguel de Unamuno (1983)

EDITED BY NANCY GOODWIN

A Rock Garden in the South, by Elizabeth Lawrence
(1990)

A Year
in Our
Gardens

Letters by

Nancy Goodwin

and Allen Lacy

Illustrations by Martha Blake-Adams

The University of North Carolina Press

Chapel Hill and London

© 2001 The University of North Carolina Press

All rights reserved

Designed by April Leidig-Higgins

Set in Monotype Centaur by Eric M. Brooks

Manufactured in the United States of America

The paper in this book meets the guidelines for
permanence and durability of the Committee on
Production Guidelines for Book Longevity of the
Council on Library Resources.

Library of Congress Cataloging-in-Publication Data

Goodwin, Nancy (Nancy Sanders)   A year in our
gardens: letters by Nancy Goodwin and Allen Lacy /
illustrations by Martha Blake-Adams.   p. cm.

ISBN 0-8078-2603-0 (cloth: alk. paper)

1. Gardening—North Carolina—Hillsborough.

2. Gardening—New Jersey. 3. Goodwin, Nancy
(Nancy Sanders)—Correspondence. 4. Lacy, Allen,
1935—Correspondence. 5. Gardeners—North
Carolina—Hillsborough—Correspondence.

6. Gardeners—New Jersey—Correspondence.

7. Goodwin, Nancy (Nancy Sanders)—Homes and
haunts—North Carolina—Hillsborough. 8. Lacy,
Allen, 1935—Homes and haunts—New Jersey.

I. Lacy, Allen, 1935– II. Title.

SB455.G62 2001   635.9'09756'565—dc21   00-044734

05 04 03 02 01 5 4 3 2 1

For Craufurd and Hella

Contents

Acknowledgments

I want to thank Catherine McConnell and Adrianna Weaver Vargo for helping to plan, plant, and maintain the gardens at Montrose during 1998. Their help gave me more time to write and more to write about. I am grateful to Arthur O. Tucker, Research Professor in the Department of Agriculture and Natural Resources at Delaware State University, for his advice on botanical names. Most of all, I thank Craufurd Goodwin for encouraging me to attempt this and for his continued support and advice.

Nancy Goodwin

My letters already abound—and properly so—in expressions of gratitude to many people who have enriched various stages of my life, including musicians like Glen Johnson and teachers like Mrs. Harkey. My indebtedness to my wife, Hella, is constant. But, for what they have done from late 1997 until today, I must acknowledge—and gladly!—special debts to my family physician, Dr. William E. Hooper Jr.; to two surgeons, Dr. Larry Kaiser and Dr. Keith Calligaro; and to my pulmonary specialist, Dr. Susan Gregory.

Allen Lacy

Introduction

My husband, Craufurd, and I moved to Montrose twenty-three years ago. We had spent the previous ten years looking for it. At first we wanted a place with more room for a garden. We lived near the edge of the campus of Duke University in Durham, North Carolina, and within two years of moving there, I ran out of space. I never thought twice about making a garden. My grandparents had gardens; my parents had gardens. I thought that everyone with any land at all cultivated it. I made my first garden in 1963 and never got over the thrill of growing plants well, combining them because of their forms or the color of their flowers. I believe I inherited my love of flowers from my mother and my appreciation for trees and shrubs and the quality of the land from my father. Horticulture was an endless world to explore: more plants to grow, different conditions to experience, and the need for more land led Craufurd and me to investigate properties in the surrounding area.

We settled on Hillsborough, North Carolina, primarily because of the quality of its dirt. It is a lovely old town, first developed because native Americans and later European settlers needed fertile land to support themselves. My father spoke in hushed tones about the quality of the soil in this area. We knew of several attractive properties on the edge of town and waited until one came on the market. I often wondered what lay behind the fence separating Montrose from St. Marys Road. We saw it first the day we came to meet the son of Alexander H. Graham, the third generation of the Graham family to live on the property. Mr. Graham had recently died, and there was a chance that his sons would sell it.

The property was first subdivided from a nearby plantation in 1799. In 1842, William A. Graham, later governor of North Carolina and secretary of the navy under Millard Fillmore, moved to the property. Susan Washington Graham named it Montrose, after the town in Scotland from which the Grahams originally came. The Grahams began the gardens, planting trees that still remain on the property, and, we believe, laying out the kitchen garden, now our main sunny garden.

For me it was love at first sight. I liked the large, bright Victorian house and loved the little law office behind the main building, but I immediately wanted to work in the garden. The soil in the kitchen garden had been freshly tilled and was a rich red-brown clay loam. I had never seen anything like it.

On August 4, 1977, Craufurd and I moved to Montrose, and my life took on new meaning. At last I could make the garden of my dreams. I would run out of time, never run out of land.

For the first year I did very little gardening. I noted the way the shadows fell, explored the terraced woodlands, and greeted each season with excitement. Masses of bulbs appeared in unexpected places near the shrubs that bordered a field. I had brought from my first garden old bulbs that I thought I could never replace. But then they were what emerged from the soil here. There were old forms of narcissus, wood hyacinths, and fall-blooming crocuses. It was the most exciting year ever. I was on the ultimate Easter egg hunt.

I began in a tentative way to make my own garden here, at first feeling like an intruder but gradually feeling accepted. I honored the shape of the garden. For the first three years we, too, grew vegetables in the large kitchen garden. We grew beans, corn, spinach, melons, lettuce, beets, potatoes, carrots, and three dozen tomato plants planted in cages built by Mr. Graham that we purchased from the estate. What we couldn't eat or give away, I froze. We had tomato juice from our property every single morning during those years.

Gradually a feeling of discontent crept over me. I didn't want to grow vegetables and spend every evening of the summer freezing them. I was curious about other plants I might grow. I was more interested in flowers, shrubs, and trees than in vegetables or cooking. In addition, I found it increasingly frustrating to have to come in out of the garden on beautiful sunny days to teach children piano and harpsichord—as I had done since college days.

In 1984 I began a small mail-order nursery to give me a further excuse to be outside. I had discovered the precarious position of cyclamen in the wild and learned that there were few opportunities to purchase nursery-propagated plants in this country. I thought that developing a nursery would enable me to give up teaching music and devote my time to the garden.

I began by offering cyclamen, boxwood rooted from the plants on this property, and a vigorous strain of *Primula* × *polyantha* I had discovered at a nursery nearby. For the first time in my life I had perennial primroses that returned year after year and set seed. I had no trouble germinating the seed and had developed a fine strain of heat tolerant, fragrant flowers. For two years I ran the nursery in the morning and taught music in the afternoon. The nursery grew in every way. I needed help with propagation and packing.

I first became aware of Allen Lacy when Craufurd reported that he was enjoying the column by a garden writer in his daily *Wall Street Journal*. How could this be? What was a Wall Street gardener? I had visions of J. P. Morgan in a high collar with a long cigar, giving orders to his estate staff. Craufurd then started bringing the *Journal* home, and I read Mr. Lacy's columns during my lunch. What a surprise! Here was a garden writer who did not just write about plants or gardens. He wrote also about philosophy, religion, history, and current events. He embedded his horticulture in the wider world, not just on Wall Street but on any street. And he had style—the power to entertain, to amuse, and to inform.

Then, to my amazement, I began to note in these columns small references to Durham, North Carolina, and even to an old school and college friend, Martha Bell (as she was when I knew her). How could this be? Was the *Wall Street Journal* pursuing its regional strategy to the extent of providing its columnists with references they could add for local color? At a party one day, I learned from a friend, Joanne Ferguson, that the answer was that Allen was "one of us." He was a Duke graduate twice over and was even at that time editing Elizabeth Lawrence's book, *Gardening for Love: The Market Bulletins*, which Joanne had acquired for Duke University Press, where she was executive editor. "Write to him," Joanne said. "He's civilized and will certainly reply." And so, in 1985, I wrote my first letter to Allen, telling him about my new little nursery specializing in endangered cyclamen. He wrote back quickly, as Joanne had suggested he would.

Allen came to Montrose in May 1985. I thought he was charming. We wandered around the place. I won't ever forget that day. We discovered some mutual interests and shared values. I discovered that we had similar backgrounds. Our first gardening experiences had been with bearded irises. Mine never bloomed; Allen still remembered that the first plant he ever bought was an iris called 'Happy Days', a yellow cultivar that he first got in full bloom. What was really important when I met Allen was that it was the first time in my life anyone had asked about my interest in gardening and actually seemed to listen to my answer.

Allen wrote an article on Montrose for *American Horticulturist* and then for the *New York Times* when he became garden columnist for the "Home" section of that paper in 1986. We quickly discovered the power of his praise. One day while Craufurd and I were eating lunch, someone from Dun and Bradstreet called. It seems that after one of Allen's columns mentioning Montrose Nursery appeared, someone contemplated buying the nursery but couldn't find any record of its existence. We had to inform the caller that the business was still only at the "mom" stage, with "pop" engaged elsewhere, and that the venture capitalists would do better to spend their time on other prospects.

I had just come to the point where I felt enormous pressure at running this nursery alone. Allen called one morning, and I said I didn't know where to turn. Quickly he responded, "I know just the person—Martha Bell Blake-Adams. I'll call her now." He did, and she came to work with me within a week. About this time I also hired Douglas Ruhren and Katia Wolf, who did much of the propagation for the nursery, and Ruth Batchelor, who weeded the garden and helped with shipping. These people were the nucleus of my tiny staff.

The nursery grew beyond my hopes and dreams and eventually became a burden, finally taking every minute of my time and energy. I hadn't time to look at the garden, much less work in it. In 1992 we had a series of tragedies that affected everyone working here. First, the large old *Magnolia acuminata* that was a hallmark of the property fell crashing to the ground. Then my mother died. Two close family members of my staff died. And finally, and most tragically of all, a dear young employee, Johanna Petty, was killed in an automobile

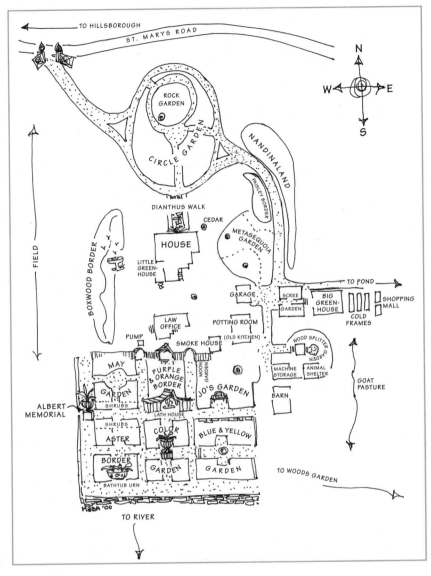

Montrose

accident shortly before her twentieth birthday. It brought me to my
senses. I realized that we don't always exit from this world in the
order in which we enter it. I still didn't have my garden. I made the
decision to have one final year with the nursery and then devote the
remainder of my life to the horticultural development of the land at
Montrose.

It was the second-best decision I ever made (the first was when I married Craufurd Goodwin). The garden blossomed. We turned the old kitchen garden into a series of gardens unified by the color or peak season of the plantings. The aster border came first, then the purple and orange border, and then the blue and yellow sunken garden. The old grape arbor was replaced by a magnificent lath house designed and built by Wayne Hall and underplanted with shade-loving plants. We made a memorial garden for Jo Petty. It peaks in July and August, her birth and death months. We turned the circle in front of the house into a foliage garden, with interest primarily in fall, winter, and spring. We rejuvenated the old rock garden that had probably been originally planted in the nineteenth century. We made a scree garden by tilling masses of stones into an area that was formerly lawn and planting small plants and those requiring excellent drainage. We ripped out the ivy lining the walk leading to the house and planted a collection of old dianthus cultivars I had been accumulating for years. We developed walks through the woods, where the land had been terraced in the 1930s for erosion control. In 1998, the year of the correspondence reproduced here, we began planting the final third of the kitchen garden, making a May garden, a new aster border, and a double shrub border. We dreamed and planned and planted. We explored plants of all sorts, buying no more than one plant of each cultivar or one packet of seeds and saving the best seeds from each year for the next. It is my great adventure.

Craufurd works with me, advising me and controlling my exuberance and desire to have plants everywhere. He makes most of the stone walls, prunes and thins out the woods, and keeps the fields and lawns mown. He also does the grocery shopping, and during the nursery years he did almost all of the cooking. Together we have a vision for the future of the land we care so much about. We want to protect it and all the creatures that share it with us. We continue to work to realize that dream.

In December 1997, I wrote to Allen Lacy to ask whether he would be interested in writing to me and hearing from me for a year, possibly resulting in a book. He had recently had surgery and was about to undergo surgery again, and I thought such an exchange of letters might distract him. I was also curious about how we could both live in the same USDA Zone, Zone 7A, and not be able to grow all of the same plants. I wanted to hear about his weather, the light, and the constant wind he had to cope with. I wanted to tell him about my joy in winter, the sounds of the woodland birds and animals, and my distress in summer. I knew we would have to do this with the possibility of others reading over our shoulders, but I wanted the letters to be personal—and Allen and I both tried to forget about potential future readers.

Neither of us could have predicted everything that happened in the year of our letters. Looking back over it, I don't believe I would have attempted such a thing if I had known what I had to deal with. I also think the letters were, for both of us, the most constant element of the year.

Nancy Goodwin

Nancy has made a good start in her introductory comments, but I'd like to fill in some blanks, starting with 1985 and her letter to me about her new nursery specializing in endangered hardy cyclamen. I had just written a column for the *Wall Street Journal* praising a mail-order nursery, now long since defunct, that was offering several species of these plants. In rather overheated prose, the nursery reported in its catalog that the cyclamen tubers it peddled had traveled long distances on camel trains with brass bells all ajingle. Nancy writes above that she had been enjoying my pieces in the *Journal*, but she tactfully omits any mention of my cyclamen column. It proved that I was terribly ignorant of something I really ought to have known. Hundreds of thousands of many species of wild cyclamen were being collected illegally from rocky hillsides in Turkey and the Middle East. These lovely little plants, with flowers like tiny pink or white butterflies, were consequently endangered in their native habitats. One of Nancy's purposes in starting Montrose Nursery and raising cyclamen from seed was to enable American gardeners to grow them in good conscience. I don't think she said it to me outright, but she probably felt strongly that I should not use my horticultural pulpit to publicize nurseries that traded in illegally collected plants.

Shortly after I received Nancy's letter, my wife, Hella, and I drove through the wonderful gates of Montrose and up the long, winding driveway to its beautiful white house set in the midst of white oaks, pecan trees, a fine deodar cedar, and one of the largest specimens in the eastern United States of *Magnolia acuminata*, the cu-

cumber magnolia. There were many subsequent visits, at every season of the year.

Montrose Nursery quickly became legendary among American gardeners, not only because of its conscience-friendly cyclamen but also because of its wide offerings of choice, often rare, perennials that could withstand the horrendous summer heat and humidity of the North Carolina Piedmont. It also introduced a number of plants, such as boltonia 'Pink Beauty' and heuchera 'Montrose Ruby', that have become staples of American horticulture.

On a couple of occasions, Nancy visited the garden Hella and I were making near the Jersey Shore, in the southern part of the state. We occasionally chatted by telephone, but we also wrote long letters to each other at sporadic intervals. If I recall them correctly, they were more like parallel garden monologues than like dialogues with the real back-and-forth quality of true conversation.

In December 1997, when Nancy proposed that we revive our correspondence, but on a more regular and systematic basis, I was more than agreeable. There were some major differences between us. She gardened on deep and fertile clay loam. I gardened on a thin layer of acid sandy soil sitting on top of 3,500 feet of gravel. She tended a large and ever-expanding series of gardens that were reckoned in acres, while our house and garden at the Jersey Shore sat on a suburban lot just 100 by 155 feet. Winter, she often said, was her favorite season; I would be perfectly content to leap right from Christmas to St. Patrick's Day.

There were also similarities between us. Nancy and I had both gone to Duke University in the mid-1950s. We had not known each other, perhaps because I majored in English literature and she in music. Music was another bond between us, as we shared a passion for classical music—Bach, Handel, and Mozart in particular—a passion equal in both longevity and intensity to our love of green and growing things. And, in a really remarkable coincidence, Dr. Richard Sanders, Nancy's father, had in my senior year been my professor in a course in Victorian literature. Nancy and Craufurd also shared with Hella and me the fact that the real estate we occupied had considerable history to it.

When Nancy wrote me to propose an exchange of letters, I had just had surgery to open and replace a carotid artery that was 95 percent occluded. A routine chest x-ray prior to this procedure (the second endarterectomy on the same artery within five years) had disclosed a spot on my right lung, and more surgery was scheduled very soon. Nancy had undergone surgery herself a few years earlier, so she knew well the territory I was just about to explore with a great deal of anxiety.

There is obviously less to tell readers about our garden than about the gardens at Montrose, because there is less of it. Hella, our two sons (Paul and Michael), and I moved over a quarter of a century ago to our bit of sandy earth in Linwood, New Jersey, at about 39° N latitude and 74° W longitude. Our old house, originally a farmhouse, part of it dating back to 1812 or so, now lay, with its much diminished land, on one of the most well traveled roads in our county. Suburbia had grown up around it; it had lost all traces of its agricultural beginnings. When the property became ours, it was landscaped in the familiar American pattern of foundation plantings around the house and a front lawn open to the street. We had no visual privacy from the constant traffic. To achieve some privacy, we began planting hedges of bamboo, bayberry, holly, vitex, and many other woody plants all around our lot. Today we have an enclosed garden. We grow a great number of annuals and perennials in a cottage garden where part of the old front lawn used to be. Shade-loving plants grow in another spot in front of the house in a small woodland garden. We have also installed extensive decks and pergolas in back of and to one side of the house, where we constantly experiment with gardening in containers.

Montrose is a historic piece of property, and so is our bit of earth on Shore Road, although it has no name. We do feel, nonetheless, that our occupancy here is an act of stewardship, not ownership. We hope to pass the property on to its next occupants in much better condition than it was in when we obtained it.

This hope is now assured, incidentally. In one of my letters to Nancy, I describe our old house and speak of it as sound. Not exactly, it turns out. And, writing now in early 2000, I have revisited a letter from early 1998 with a delicious sense of irony. Shortly before lung surgery, I wrote about a dream in which workmen discovered rot in one part of our house and then repaired it. I took the dream to have symbolic meaning only and to refer to my preoccupation with whatever that spot in my lung might turn out to be. Two years later, Hella and I have just been through the experience of rebuilding one-third of our house. We meant only to remodel the kitchen, but when Jim Brightly, our young builder, opened up the walls and floor, he discovered extensive termite damage. The oldest part of the house was, in fact, sound, having been built with well-aged,

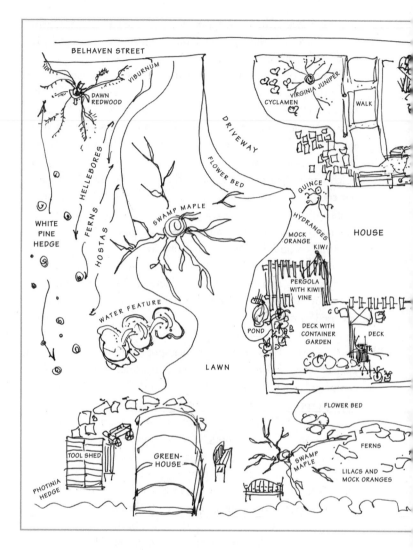

sturdy, first-growth oak. But the lumber used in an addition built sometime between 1910 and 1930 was inferior stuff. Termites had made a fine meal of it perhaps forty years ago. The construction, moreover, was flimsy, with mere two-by-fours as floor joists, some of them nailed together in the middle. "Allen," Jim said, "the back of your house has been held together by paint and a lot of good luck." The house is now held together by much more, for Jim and his crew have rebuilt it entirely, from the ground up. It should be good for another century at least.

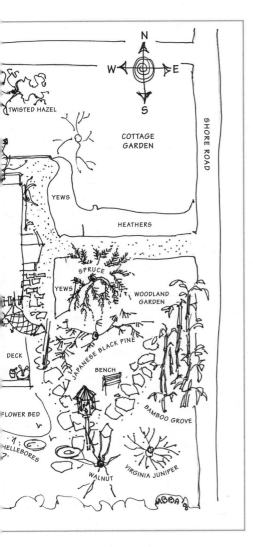

Linwood

A final thing Nancy and I have in common is that we do not garden alone, but with a companion who also happens to be a help-mate. Hella and I operate in somewhat different spheres, horticulturally speaking. I am better at identifying plants than Hella is, and I know more botanical Latin, but she has a far better eye and a much greater understanding of design, form, and color. Believing that I am absolutely incompetent at pruning, she handles most such chores, discouraging my use of saw or lopper. We confer increasingly on ways to improve our garden, particularly as regards plant combinations. Over the years, I have come to trust with absolute certainty her judgments of both plants and people.

In closing, a word is in order to explain that, as our letters reflect, Nancy and I have slightly different approaches to horticultural nomenclature. I resort to common or popular names, despite their undeniable ambiguity and lack of precision in many instances, far more often than she. This stylistic preference is partly a matter of inclination and partly a matter of habit in writing about plants and gardening for a general audience, including some people who may (wrongly) regard the use of scientific plant names as snobbish or worse. I also confess to at times getting weary of taxonomists telling us that the right name of the sweet autumn clematis is *Clematis paniculata*, then changing their minds and saying that it's really *Clematis maximowicziana*. Then, hardly have we mastered those seven syllables than there's another change, this time to *Clematis terniflora*. Nancy, quite sensibly really, doesn't allow irritation over a trifling number of instances of nomenclatural instability to affect her commitment to precise scientific terminology as it applies to plants. She and I also differ stylistically in treating scientific plant names that have also become common names. I am more likely to write dahlia 'Bishop of Llandaff', and she to write *Dahlia* 'Bishop of Llandaff'. What's really important, however, is what we both agree on: it's unquestionably a marvelous plant that everyone should grow.

Allen Lacy

Winter 1998

Saturday, December 20, 1997

Dear Allen,

Craufurd told me of your call, and I apologize for not calling you back. I am sad about your next ordeal. I certainly think you are right to go ahead and do it sooner rather than later. What did the doctor say about the prognosis?

We loved Hella's Christmas cookies, thought of you both, and spoke of you after lunch each day until they were gone. But I thought of you most when I walked through the garden. I remembered your first visit many years ago when we walked across the stubble of a newly mown field to the cyclamen woods where I had to keep an eye on your feet. Now it is impossible to walk there without stepping on cyclamen, and I no longer caution visitors or shriek at them.

January jasmine is blooming now, and I am excited about what I will find on my Christmas walk. I always make a list of what is in bloom. There will be cyclamen, I know. In fact, we have been to 22° and I have perfectly happy *Cyclamen persicum* in the woods toward the pond. These came from seed collected in the coldest parts of Israel. It took a long time for me to get up the nerve to plant them in the garden. I have *Primula* × *polyantha* and *P. vulgaris* blooming in the woods. The usual johnny-jump-ups and *Phlox subulata* are blooming in the dianthus walk.

I see flowers of *Narcissus romieuxii* and *N. cantabricus* in the rock garden and at the woods' edge. A precocious *Helleborus niger* blooms near the driveway and *H. cyclophyllus* in the scree. I keep hoping to find a hepatica some year, but I don't think it will be this one.

Winter is truly my favorite season of the gardening year!

Love,
Nancy

Tuesday, December 23, 1997

Dear Nancy,

About winter, we solidly disagree. It is, to be sure, the season of bloom for some of my favorite plants—the fragrant hybrid witch hazels like 'Arnold Promise' and 'Jelena', the various winter heaths, snowdrops, and of course the long procession of hellebores, which would be beautiful in any season. But I have a confession. All of these plants are placed where I can see and enjoy them from inside the house, without venturing outdoors.

As for winter itself, I dislike it, and the longer it goes on, the more I dislike it. I regard the winters I grew up with in Texas to be just about right. A blue norther would bluster in from Canada, we would all get excited about the nasty weather, and two days later it could be warm, almost balmy. Christmas was generally mild. (I think we may have had just one of the white kind.) Winter, real winter, took place mostly in January. If it snowed, the snow generally melted by noon. That still strikes me as its proper behavior.

New Jersey winters are highly variable. They can be fierce or mild. One year we may have blizzards, the next hardly a snowflake.

January, this year, will not be a time for wandering around the garden enjoying it, even were that my wont. My second go-round with a surgeon in Philadelphia is scheduled for January 13. It's going to be different from the carotid surgery I had last month. So far, no doctor has said anything about my prognosis, but I won't go home the next day, for sure. There's going to be pain (which I like even less than winter). But I have a lot of confidence in Dr. Kaiser, the surgeon, and I'm no stranger to the idea that pruning can be highly beneficial.

Getting back to the topic of winter, I accept it intellectually. It's just a matter of the tilt of the earth on its axis. That's not within my control or anyone else's, and if almost sixty-three years of life on this earth have taught me anything, it's the folly of worrying about uncontrollable things. Furthermore, I know that if I lived where there was no winter or where winters were so mild as to be almost negligible, I would have to forgo many favorite plants that insist on winter dormancy. And this part of New Jersey has far too many greenhead flies and other biting insects as it is. I shudder to think how many more there would be without freezing weather.

Still, I don't like winter. (Hella does, but then she was born in Berlin.)

The new greenhouse is of course going to alter my experience of this season. (Our granddaughter Anna calls it "Opi's playhouse.") The greenhouse wasn't finished until after Thanksgiving, but it's already half filled with plants, especially fragrant ones. The best right now are the jasmines. Two Sambac jasmines—the delicate 'Maid of Orleans' and the double 'Grand Duke of Tuscany'—look happier at this time of year than they ever were when they had to struggle for existence in a corner of my study. The Grand Duke's blossoms are far from lovely (Hella says they look like curds of cottage cheese), but the sweetness and intensity of their fragrance exceed those of any other jasmine. The flowers of a calamondin orange and a Meyer lemon also perfume the greenhouse air, likewise an occasional flower on our potted banana shrub (*Michelia figo*), which smells exactly as its common name promises.

I've also put a good many plants with scented leaves in the greenhouse. Their scent doesn't rise up to greet me when I open the door, but they please my nose when I brush against them. There are several scented pelargoniums, including peppermint, my favorite for the brilliant light green of its velvety leaves as well as its fresh, invigorating, summery smell of mint. Star anise is delightful for its delicious odor of licorice when its foliage is crushed. I've also got a pot of holy basil. Its scent is unlike any other. Sweet and spicy in equal measure, it pervades the air if it is touched even lightly, and its delectable odor stays on the hand for hours. And I have a pot of pineapple sage, too. It is a curious plant; or, rather, people respond to it quite oddly. Give them sprigs of it to sniff and tell them it's pineapple sage, and they always say, "Oh yes, it smells just like ripe pineapple." Give it to them without the name, however, and ask them what it smells like, and see what happens. They always say that it smells delicious but never come up with a comparison to pineapples.

At the moment, although there are plenty of plants in the greenhouse, there's room left over for two chairs and the table at which Hella and I like to have lunch, enjoying the warmth and the sound of water splashing from a little fountain made of cedar and bamboo.

Fondly,
Allen

Friday, December 26, 1997

Dear Allen,

Yesterday we went to Durham to visit my father, from whom I got absolutely no response. I can only think this will be his last year. Craufurd and I came home and cleaned the pantry. Or rather we began cleaning the pantry. Just before dark I did my annual Christmas walk and found a splendid number of flowers for my list. Here it is—but remember, I counted only those on which I could see the anthers: *Helleborus foetidus, H. niger, H. cyclophyllus* (this is an early-blooming form from Corfu); *Pulsatilla patens; Jasminum nudiflorum; Narcissus romieuxii, N. cantabricus; Cyclamen coum, C. cilicium, C. graecum; Erica × darleyensis* 'Silberschmelze', *E. carnea* 'Springwood White', *E. c.* 'King George'; *Phlox douglasii* 'Boothman's Variety', *P. nivalis* 'Camla', *P. subulata* 'Tamaongalei'; *Iris unguicularis; Chimonanthus prae-cox; Crocus laevigatus, C. longiflorus; Asarum megacalyx; Isopyrum biterna-tum; Erysimum alpinum; Clematis cirrhosa; Galanthus caucasicus;* some vi-olas, a splendid dandelion, the old red quince (*Chaenomeles × superba* 'Crimson and Gold') from my Durham garden, and, finally, *Primula vulgaris* and one *P. veris.*

That's as large a list as I have ever had. I believe the difference this year is that though it has been colder than normal during the day, we have not had colder than normal nights.

I stopped writing to go to the post office and now have your last letter. I can almost smell the delectable humid smells of your green-house and see you sniffing the jasmines. I have most of the ones you do—primarily because I read an article you wrote on jasmines in the *Wall Street Journal* long before I met you. You listed Logee's as the source, and I promptly ordered every one they had that I didn't. Last winter they died, and this past summer I replaced them. I would hate to go through winter without seeing the swelling buds of *Jasminum polyanthum* or enjoying *J. nitidum* with its fragrant white stars. We can grow a few outside, and even now I have a vase of opened *J. nudiflorum* on the coffer in the living room. I pick them when the tips of the flower buds turn red.

You mentioned the tilt of the earth at the beginning of winter. I don't understand why winter begins after we have had nearly a month of cold weather and leaves us after nearly a month of warm, but I accept that there is a gardener's winter and an astronomical one. Craufurd and I went to a Winter Solstice party at the home of an academic couple. The invitation included the following dates for it:

Gregorian: Sunday, 21 December 1997
Mayan: Long count = 12.19.4.13.19
tzolkin = 9 Cauac
haab = 17 Mac
French: Décade I, Primidi de Nivôse
    de l'Année 206 de la Révolution

Islamic: 20 Sha'ban 1418
Hebrew: 22 Kislev 5758
Julian: 8 December 1997
ISO: Day 7 of Week 51 of 1997
Persian: 30 Azar 1376
Ethiopic: 13 Takhsas 1991
Coptic: 12 Kiyahk 1714
Chinese: Cycle 78,
    year 14 (Ding-Chou),
    month 11 (Wu-Chen),
    day 22 (Ding-You)
Julian day: 2450804
Discordian: Setting Orange,
    The Aftermath 63,
    Year of Our Lady of Discord 3163.

I found it very academic, but in copying it out for you thought it interesting.

Elizabeth Lawrence's *Gardens in Winter* was the first book to open my eyes and mind to all that we might grow here in Zone 7A at this time of year. I found it in a secondhand bookstore over thirty years ago and proceeded to try to find seeds or plants of everything she mentioned that I had never grown or heard of. *Iris unguicularis* was the last one found—at Loleta Powell's nursery, after Craufurd and I moved to Montrose. I read that it took three years after planting to bloom, and sure enough it took every day of that. I now know that if you plant it in fall just as it recovers from summer dormancy, it will bloom in fewer than three years.

Tell me more about Opi's new playhouse. Why did you want it? What do you want to grow there? How do you plan to manage it? What will you do when pests discover it and decide it is their new playhouse? What kind of floor does it have? How do you get to it from the house? Can you enter it in your jammies and slippers? Do you go in there the first thing every morning?

Here's more on why I love winter so much—and one reason may come as a little surprise. Only in winter do I get an occasional day out of the garden. Don't misunderstand. One day is enough, two just bearable, and by the third I feel desperate to get back to it.

Also in winter I love the openness that comes from our deciduous trees. I love the view of the terraces in the woods. I can see from the big rocks all the way to the overlook, a place you may never have been. It is at the highest point on our land, and from there I can look down on the flood plain and occasionally see the river. Would you believe this lovely spot is where generations of Grahams dumped all of their garbage? We finally hired Mr. Huskins to come in and take away twenty-seven tons of wire, bottles, old stoves, etc. He told us that before there was garbage collection everyone selected the highest spot for a garbage dump. They could simply drive to the edge and throw it over. Now the perimeter has cyclamen growing near the hemlocks and beneath some of the trees felled by Hurricane Fran. I hope this spring to find young trilliums here and there from seeds I scratched into the ground two years ago.

I wonder whether the wind in your New Jersey garden prevents your loving winter as I do. I remember your commenting on our still air in summer. In winter that still air is quickly warmed by the sun. Right now we are foggy in the mornings because even the nights are warm. It is in the upper 50s or lower 60s when I walk down to get the paper at 6:30 A.M.

Love,
Nancy

Monday, December 29, 1997

Dear Nancy,

Opi's playhouse? I wanted it because I have always wanted one. In my early life in Texas, I didn't need one because of the short winters. But when I moved north, where winters are real, the desire to keep plants flourishing year round got stronger. What do I want to grow there? Mostly tropical and subtropical plants—hibiscus, passiflora, jasmines, mandevillas, and so on. I'll propagate from cuttings the coleus worth keeping from year to year. I'll grow from seed mostly those annuals that aren't easily available at every garden center hereabouts in the spring. I want to keep some open space, for a table and a couple of chairs. At the moment, I think of the greenhouse as a mini-conservatory.

The greenhouse floor is red brick pavers, laid in a basketweave pattern. Originally it was to be gravel on a base of sand, but I changed my mind. Brick retains the heat of the day well toward evening. It can be hosed down to keep humidity up. Those are my ex-

Linwood

cuses for changing from gravel. My reason is that brick looks nicer.
It also helps explain why a greenhouse estimated to cost no more
than $6,000 ended up costing more than $12,000.

I do not know yet what I will do about the pests that will in-
evitably and quickly decide that it's their greenhouse. I lean toward
tiny nonstinging wasps, lacewings, ladybugs, and other beneficial
insects. We've used these on occasion successfully with houseplants
indoors to rid ourselves of scale, mealy bugs, and other problems.
Our friend Anita Beckwith manages both her large greenhouses
with only these and other biological controls. Rachel Carson is one
of my saints, but I have never quite been an organic gardener of the
Strict Observance. I shall probably spray from time to time, but not
the very first time I touch a lantana and white flies flit up.

I get to the greenhouse by walking across the west part of the
deck; then it's only ten or twelve feet to the door. I don't go there in
my pajamas because I almost never wear any. I also don't go there
first thing each morning—not before I've had two cups of coffee
and checked the news on TV.

The wind here does figure in my antipathies toward this season.
This morning at 8:00 the temperature and the windchill factor were
both 31°. This coincidence is uncommon during winter, because of
breezes from the nearby ocean and bay that are pretty much constant all year. Winter's discomforts find their equivalent in sum-

mer's pleasures: the only room in the house that's air-conditioned is my study, but that's for the benefit of the computer.

The catalogs have started arriving—so far just the seed catalogs from mass-market companies like Burpee and Gurney. I read them from cover to cover as soon as they appear in the mailbox, for they are the first sign that a new growing season will soon be upon us. I also spend hours poring over the odd little catalog of Totally Tomatoes in Augusta, Georgia, which sells nothing but tomato and pepper seeds. We can't grow either vegetable, as our garden is too shady, but Michael has sun and grows both for our two families. This year I will start our tomatoes in the greenhouse. Michael has instructed me to order his favorite, 'Carmello', from Shepherd's Seeds. From Totally Tomatoes I'm ordering seed of 'Mortgage Lifter' and 'German Johnson', the two heirloom varieties Hella and I got last summer at the farmers' market in Chapel Hill. If Plato could have known tomatoes, he would have proclaimed that these two perfectly embodied the Idea of Tomato-ness!

The catalogs I take seriously haven't come yet—the ones I devour, study, and restudy for weeks, the ones listing and describing plants I've never heard of, much less seen, as well as new cultivars of more familiar plants. In the ten years that Montrose was a nursery, its catalog was the touchstone of all the rest. I still miss it, but I console myself with the catalogs of Heronswood, Olympic Coast Garden, Canyon Creek, Coastal Gardens, Plant Delights, Woodlander's, and a few other favorites. They have in common private ownership by one, sometimes two, truly far-gone plant nuts. A personal voice sounds through the pages of all their catalogs.

Such catalogs frustrate me, but they also excite me. They frustrate me because there's so little room left in our garden that I can grow only an infinitesimal fraction of the tempting plants they describe. They excite me because they testify that with every passing year American gardeners have a greater and greater number of choices in the plants we can grow. Take the genus *Arisaema*, for example (which I'm writing about in the next issue of *Homeground*). A decade ago any gardener aspiring to grow them would have been pretty much limited to the tiny number of North American species, starting and maybe ending with our jack-in-the-pulpit. Now, increasingly, many of the quite wonderful East Asian species are becoming available from our best nurseries, like Heronswood. Last spring I reckon I could have acquired eighteen species from comby patches of darkness from the clouds scudding across the sky, in the aftermath of last night's coastal storm.

Love,
Allen

Friday, January 2, 1998

Dear Allen,

What a splendid letter. In many ways I am glad that my favorite catalogs haven't come yet. For one thing, I am still recovering from fall. The enormous but delightful chore of putting the garden to bed takes every moment my tiny staff and I can give to it. And now there are the leaves. This year Craufurd and I are happy and grateful recipients of nearly all of Hillsborough's leaf collection. The town bought a fine new truck with a vacuum and grinder, and we have thus far received over fifty loads of ground-up leaves — pure gold. The problem is that we can't just leave it lying around; no one would be able to get around the driveway. As it is Craufurd can't get his truck out of the garage, so we just keep hauling cartload after cartload. We have done most of the beds and are reclaiming the parts of the woods we planted or hope to plant. A twelve-inch layer of leaves will discourage microstegia at least for a year or two.

We agree on the best tomatoes. Craufurd and I tasted 'Radiator Charlie's Mortgage Lifter' last summer for the first time, after finding it in Hillsborough's tiny farmers' market. We liked it and 'German Johnson' tomatoes equally well.

I like some of your favorite nurseries. I don't know Olympic Coast Garden or Coastal Gardens. I really like Primrose Path and We-Du, the new reincarnation as well as the original. Have you explored Mt. Tahoma Nursery? I discovered it just as I closed Montrose Nursery, and I often order from Rick Lupp. He has mostly small plants with small prices. The woodies are good and inexpensive. These are three small nurseries with small ambitions but all are owned by one or two people who care about plants and who produce what they sell. For woodies, I think the best nurseries are Fairweather Gardens and Roslyn Nursery. The owners are real plants people, rather than entrepreneurs. (I still recoil at the memory of the large nursery I visited in Norfolk ten years ago. When I mercial sources. As regards plant availability we are closing the gap between us and our British counterparts, but we've still a long way to go. On the Internet I just ran across the huge catalog of Crûg Farm Plants, a private nursery near Bangor, Wales, whose proprietors, Bleddyn and Sue Wynn-Jones, have been plant collecting (seeds only) in East Asia for many years on various expeditions. I'm sending along just part of its online catalog, the eighteen pages of plants with names starting with "A." Please note the arisaemas— over fifty species or forms, starting with *Arisaema amurense* and ending with *A. verrucosum*. Knowing that you are growing a fair number of species, I'd be interested in hearing where there's an overlap between what you're growing and what Crûg is offering to British gardeners. (I also wonder if you can account for the strange appeal that these extraordinary plants have for some of us. Most plants are sexual, but these seem almost pornographic.)

I'm not at all disturbed, by the way, that some of these arisaemas aren't available to us at the moment. Our friend Barry Yinger just keeps bringing us one superb East Asian plant after another. We can, I think, count on him to keep it up. (Am I correct in my suspicion that some of your own arisaemas came into your garden via Barry?)

Now to another matter. During my highly enjoyable four days at Montrose last August, I couldn't help noticing the great number of ornamental species of *Solanum* growing here and there, mostly in pots. I recall the name of just one, *S. quitoense*, which I think was the rather fierce and paradoxical plant growing in a mixed container by the archway and steps leading to the purple and orange border. If the picture in my head is right, it has large, succulent, jagged leaves with dangerous spines here and there and centers of velvety purple. How did you come by so many of these eggplant relatives? Which of them have promise or merit as garden plants? Are we on the verge of a huge surge of interest in solanums, such that they may be in the first decade of the new millennium what salvias have been in the closing years of our own? And—impolitely, perhaps—do you worry that some may escape from your gardens to become vicious weeds we may come to curse?

It was very dismal and gray this morning. I went out to the greenhouse to turn on the halide lights for some approximation of sunshine. I've not looked out the window since I sat down here at the Macintosh, but I now see that we have bright sunlight broken asked the owner the difference between two cultivars of grasses, he proudly told me, "One costs $14.95 and the other $16.95.")

Crûg Farm Plants is tempting, indeed. I cannot resist arisaemas (or arums, either) and remember being offended when one nurseryman on the West Coast described them as "oddball plants."

There are oddball people, yes, but no oddball plants! My first association goes back to my childhood when my mother found some jack-in-the-pulpits in the woods and brought them home to her wildflower garden. In those days no one had a conscience about collecting plants in the wild, but I'm not certain that would have deterred her. I believe in responsible collecting of seeds, but I see no need to collect tubers of anything.

Back to Crûg Farm's catalog. I have plants of *Arisaema amurense* and *A. a.* var. *peninsulae* but they aren't old enough or happy enough to bloom yet. Last summer I saw my first blooms on *A. candidissimum* grown from seeds sent by Wayne Winterrowd and Joe Eck. I don't know *A. ciliatum* but it sounds wonderful, perhaps a bit hairy? Both *Aa. consanguineum* and *concinnum* grow here, but only the first has bloomed for me. As for *A. dracontium*, Mother told me that "nice people don't allow it in their gardens." It is a gross *A. triphyllum*. The problem is that it is so vigorous that it can crowd out the more elegant, smaller forms; also, every seed germinates. I grow it anyway, not wanting to be all that nice! No, I don't have *A. exappendiculatum* but I do grow *Aa. erubescens* and *flavum*. *A. flavum* is something of a challenge. It has a cute little fat flower, comes up late, and is easily overwhelmed by some of the more vigorous hellebores that grow near it. I sometimes miss the flowers because I am distracted by visitors and duties in the main gardens. No, I don't have *Aa. formosanum* or *galeatum*. I have young seedlings of *A. griffithii* and am more excited by the prospect of seeing that great cobralike hood than any other. I sold *A. heterophyllum* when I had the nursery and now have enough seeds just to step them into the woods where I hope they will naturalize. And, your hunch is correct—my tubers came from Barry Yinger, the best source of many fine arisaemas and gingers. I think of him when I see this one bloom. The flowers look like graceful, green birds on tall, skinny legs. *A. jacquemontii* grows and blooms well in the lath house, and *A. kiushianum* grows but doesn't bloom in the woods. I don't know what each one wants, alas. *A. ringens* is an eye-catcher, with glossy leaves and splendid flowers that look somewhat like great snail shells. So far I can't get seed set, but I always get flowers. I think longingly of one a friend had in her garden in Chapel Hill. It bloomed two months before mine, and I suspect might have been *A. r.* forma *praecox*. I don't have *Aa. robustum* or *sazensoo*, but do have *Aa. serratum* and *sikokianum*. I have *A. thunbergii* subsp. *urashima* and saw my first flower last spring—this after nine years of waiting. I love the little flowers of *A. triphyllum* and have many forms, some with fat little flowers striped with maroon or with green and white. The variety of flowers is enormous, some having dark, nearly purple stems. No, I don't have *A. verrucosum*, but I do have *A. tortuosum*.

I agree with you that these are sexy plants. But they can be very shy about reproduction. I couldn't get seed set one year on *A. sikokianum*, so I rolled back the base of the spathe and found the male and female flowers at the base of the spadix. It was then a simple matter to brush a little pollen onto the females. I could have hired a gnat or a fly to help out but didn't want them breeding in the greenhouse.

I like these plants because they have flowers I have to look for. They never shout "Look at me," the way daisies, roses, and all the other more popular flowers do. They are there for those who make the effort to look. I feel the same way about asarums, with their little brown juglike flowers sometimes hidden under their leaves.

Solanums have come one by one into the garden at Montrose, usually from friends who come and see that we are fascinated by plants of all sorts. Some are frightening. Certainly we are on the verge of declaring *Solanum atropurpureum* a weed. It turned out to be hardy; it doesn't spread underground *but* it seeds about everywhere, and since the stems are covered with thorns that get tougher as the plants age, no one wants the job of weeding them out. *S. jasminoides* is a beauty and thus far presents no problem of control, probably because it is somewhat tender. We haven't gotten the display from it that we dream of. *S. quitoense* arouses great interest here. It is frighteningly beautiful, notable for its hairy leaves tinged with purple and its round seed pods, also covered in fur. I learned from a visitor that the fruits make a splendid drink, but I am afraid to experiment with eating or drinking solanums. Did you notice *S. pyracanthum*? Splendid orange thorns grow along the veins of its blue-gray leaves. As for whether I worry about their becoming weeds, yes sir, I worry every minute!

Today is my birthday. I hope to spend the rest of the day cleaning off the rock garden. I still feel like I did when I was in college, but it is a shock to look in the mirror. Happily, I don't care about that anymore.

Love,
Nancy

Tuesday, January 6, 1998

Dear Nancy,

Yours of the 2nd appeared in our mailbox today and was eagerly devoured. I picture you knee-deep in those fifty loads of leaves. After years of composting, we have managed here to turn our sandy soil from blond to brunette, but some time ago we started leaving autumn leaves out in the street (by the curb) to be picked up by the county recycling authority, which sells finished compost very reasonably indeed. Still, it takes the trucks some time to complete the cleanup. Even now, in some neighborhoods there are huge piles of leaves, fairly crushed into pieces by automobile traffic. I'm always tempted to scoop some up in a big plastic bag and add it to our kitchen-waste compost pile. But, a question: you write that a foot of leaves "will discourage microstegia at least for a year or two." What is—what are, perhaps—microstegia? It's not in my dictionary, nor in *The New RHS Dictionary of Gardening*, where I find only "microsorium" and "microstrobus." I see in my mind's eye some very small rodent, or maybe a pestiferous plant related etymologically if not botanically to *Physostegia*.

It is sad about your father's decline. I don't like to use the word "tragic" for things like Princess Di's death in an automobile accident, but Alzheimer's is tragic, for sure and certain. From the time my mother started getting lost while driving around her neighborhood and tried to give her diamond jewelry to strangers, to the time she knew I was someone but not exactly someone she could identify, was perhaps a matter of two years. First she went absent from us, then from herself. I first noticed that something was terribly wrong when my parents visited us and Mother seemed to think she was in Dallas. Then other things happened, like serving my father ice cream in a dirty ashtray. One day I called home and she spoke of redbirds, so pretty, and red lights flashing in the driveway, so pretty. That was how I learned of my father's next-to-last heart attack. When my father died, I found the little appointment book she had been keeping. Every day for months, she wrote her Social Security number at the top of that day's page, followed by "My name is Jetta Surles Lacy. My children are Allen, Bill, Johnny, and Bobby." Then, suddenly these entries ceased, shortly before the pretty redbirds and flashing lights in the driveway. She spent over ten years of unconscious existence in a nursing home.

I have not seen your father since my senior year at Duke, when I took his course in Victorian literature. He seemed to embody his topic, always reserved and dignified, slightly unapproachable perhaps. (I think I got B's from him.) I was taking Bill Blackburn's writing class the same year, 1955–56. By the end of the year, just before graduation, Bill invited me to call him by his first name. I would never have called your father "Richard," and certainly not "Dick." My students all call me Allen by the way, unless it's just "you." If I insisted on something more formal, I would be elitist, violating the code of our supposedly egalitarian institutions of higher learning. But none of my students will ever have the great thrill of being invited, *eventually*, to use the first name of one of their teachers.

I did notice *Solanum pyracanthum*, and it scared me! As far as drinks made from *S. quitoense* are concerned, I just looked it up. Sometimes called the golden fruit of the Andes, this plant is also known as *lulo* and *naranjilla*. I don't know what *lulo* means; I presume it's a word in one of the indigenous Andean tongues. *Naranja* is orange, *naranjilla* the somewhat deprecating diminutive form of the word. (If it ended in *-ita* instead, greater enthusiasm would be conveyed.) Its acidic, gelatinous fruits are used in juices, sometimes combined with unfermented sugarcane squeezings, and also in pies and preserves. *Solanum* is a tricky genus as far as food goes. We eat potatoes and eggplants, but at least one species is used to poison cockroaches. In the history of humankind's long effort to discover what's safe to eat and drink, there must have been many mistakes and many martyrs.

More catalogs came yesterday—Wayside, White Flower Farm, and Heronswood. I have bought little from the first two, but since I was a boy in Texas, Wayside and its catalogs have figured strongly in the education of many gardeners. wff has the more elegant catalog, with spectacular garden photography. Heronswood—well, now that Montrose Nursery has departed, this has the most tempting catalog of all. Seven whole pages are devoted to the genus *Geranium*—with an offering of thirteen cultivars of *G. oxonianum* alone, starting with 'A. T. Johnson' and ending with 'Walter's Gift'!

Anita Beckwith and her mother, Lucy, just dropped by, giving the greenhouse their entire approval. Three weeks ago Lucy had the same surgery I'm having at Pennsylvania Hospital next Tuesday—same surgeon too, Dr. Larry Kaiser. She's doing fine. I was glad to be able to ask her some of the things I forgot to ask the surgeon before Christmas. And I got some results of medical tests back; Monday's echocardiogram and stress test turned out okay. Even better news came when my family doctor's nurse called about the report on the bone and body scan. "It's negative," she said. I thought "o *shit*," but then remembered that in these things negative is good news and positive isn't. One more test tomorrow, but it's just blood work.

Cheers,
Allen

Tuesday, January 6, 1998

Dear Allen,

I want you to know how very happy I am to learn the result of your bone scan. (Martha called and told me.) I was so afraid the spot on your lung might be a small indication of greater problems. Now I can relax a little and worry only about the surgery itself. I am counting the days now until your operation. I hope you have a fine birthday tomorrow, but I won't stop worrying altogether about you until I hear all is well after the 13th. I believe in pruning too, but prefer to be the doer rather than the done to!

I have a plant that you need in your greenhouse, or do you already have *Parochetus communis*? The common names are blue oxalis and shamrock pea. It has cloverlike leaves with the most beautiful intense blue flowers ALL winter. I looked up the meaning of the name in hopes of remembering it more easily and found that it means "near a brook," and that is just what it wants—water every day plus full sun. That's fun, a little like patting a dog every time you pass it. It is frost tender, so I can't send it until summer, but do let me know if you want a piece.

I'm hoping that this year we can exchange a few plants with each other. You certainly have some I covet—for example, *Hosta* 'Sum and Substance'. I think if I plant it in the middle of some hellebores and spray it regularly with an egg, pepper, and detergent spray, I can deter the deer. I will send you some things you expressed interest in last summer—seeds of Barry's perilla, a tuber of *Dahlia* 'Bishop of Llandaff', and *Momordica charantia* seeds.

We are having what they call around here the January Thaw. It's a joke because we really haven't had the January Freeze yet. We've been down to about 18° but only one night, and the *Cyclamen persicum* I am testing outside still look good.

Other plants are in flower now. One is a tiny colchicum, *C. burtii*, with white flowers and dark purple-black anthers. I hoped to have more flowers this year than last, but still have only one plant growing happily by the driveway near the metasequoias. *Crocus imperati* subsp. *suaveolens* blooms nearer the house but also beneath the metasequoias. Here I do have a clump, in fact a clump large enough to divide. This is a delightfully fragrant crocus, but the fragrance doesn't come up to me—I must kneel to it.

It isn't true that the growing season ends when winter comes. Besides the plants that I have mentioned in active growth, even in bloom, bulbs that won't appear until March are making their roots. And think of the growth on chick, wild onions, and that weedy little cress Gertrude Jekyll used to eat.

Love,
Nancy

Saturday, January 10, 1998

Dear Nancy,

I got your last letter yesterday. There are a jillion things to do before driving to Philadelphia Monday. I'll start this letter this morning and probably finish tonight.

Yes, I would like to get your *Parochetus communis*, and it's good to find out what its name means. I had assumed it had something to do with the Holy Spirit, but of course that's Paraclete. I had this plant some years ago, never saw a flower but liked the foliage, and then lost it in its first winter—didn't know it was tender.

Hosta 'Sum and Substance' will come your way this spring as soon as it breaks dormancy so I can make sure I dig the right one. There was one large clump I could identify for sure by location, but I moved it somewhere else to make room for the greenhouse. I have another idea for deer-proofing it, besides your detergent and pepper spray. Put it in a suitably large container—this is the biggest hosta I grow—and put it on your shady screened porch, where Bambi can't get at it. I had some hostas in pots on our deck last summer. We don't have deer, thank God, but we do have slugs to spare. They have so far not discovered the deck as a feeding place, or perhaps it's just too high for them to venture up from the moist ground.

We have had a balmy week, with record high temperatures. Thursday and Friday there was dense fog all day—gloomy, but warm. Saturday around noon the fog lifted and brilliant blue skies and sunshine returned. Usually at this time of year there's not much difference in our weather and most of New England's, but thanks to El Niño, we're basking in comfortable temperatures while northern New England is still in the grips of the worse ice storm in a century, with millions of people still without electricity. (We do get bad ice storms here too from time to time. The kerosene heater in the greenhouse is controlled by a computer that requires electricity. I need to think about some kind of backup—maybe a small propane stove—just in case.)

We are supposed to return today to more seasonable weather. But the interlude has been marvelous. Yesterday, in shirtsleeves, I picked winter jasmine. We slept last night with the back bedroom window half open. When I woke up this morning, birds were singing as if it were April!

Yesterday a nurse from the anesthesia department at Pennsylvania Hospital called, explaining everything that will happen next week. They'll set up several IVs. The one in my hand will be used to give the drug that will put me under. That will be the last thing I remember until I return to semiconsciousness, with lots of tubes and catheters sticking out. I'll be heavily sedated for twenty-four hours after the operation but occasionally awakened to check on my responses to various stimuli. When I've regained consciousness more fully, I'll have some little button or whatnot to push that will provide instant relief from pain. I'm due at Penn at 6:00 A.M. Tuesday, with surgery scheduled at 7:00. Some of these details sound grim, but it's better to know in advance part of what I will experience.

Hella and I are going up to Philadelphia Monday afternoon to stay at the Holiday Inn near Independence Hall. She'll probably stay there Tuesday and Wednesday nights, then commute from here. Paul and Michael will come up very early Tuesday to be with her during the surgery.

I usually forgo reciting dreams to others, for one's dreams are seldom of much interest, but I had the same dream repeatedly last night. It was about our house, except that in the dream, the house had a basement. I was familiar with the basement, I thought, but then workmen discovered a room we didn't know about. It was a lovely room, Victorian in arrangement and furnishings, but in one corner the wooden floor was rotting away, badly enough to endanger the entire house. One of the workmen said he would fix it. I came back sometime later and there was a brand-new floor. The house was safe. It's perfectly clear, don't you think, what the dream was about?

Martha sent two boxes of the most wonderful gifts for Anna and Sarah, who both got dollhouses for Christmas. She sent dollhouse furniture—her mother's, from the early 1920s, and her own, from the 1940s. There was a miniature set of china and silver, also Oriental carpets, typewriters, Toby jugs, maybe a hundred different pieces. The girls were delighted. I like to think about the connections between their childhoods and Helen Bell's and Martha's that come into being through the transmission of physical artifacts down through four generations. There is something sacramental here.

I woke up jittery this morning, but the black mood passed quickly.

It is a beautiful and cloudless morning, but our warm interlude is over. The windchill factor this morning was in the low teens. *Aucuba japonica* 'Marmorata' was at half mast.

Monday night, both Hella and I will have our last cigarettes. Dr. Kaiser told me that considering the amount I smoke, I should probably not even think of stopping until right before surgery.

Love,
Allen

Tuesday, January 13, 1998

Dear Allen,

I keep waiting for the phone to ring, to hear the news of how it went. I can't seem to concentrate on anything else. I guess the best news from you is that you are giving up smoking. I know it will lengthen your life, and, heaven knows, you have more to do and more to say than any of the rest of us. Martha said she would do it, too. I hate to push her any more than I already have, but I hope you will persuade her and Hella and anyone else you know and love. I might also give you a list of people to encourage to keep on smoking, but I won't.

We received another load of leaves yesterday and spread them onto the old dog pen area. You may remember the first bit of the nursery was there. Belle, never acknowledging that she was a dog, refused to stay there. After she ate her doghouse, we concluded that the space might be inhospitable to deer and so put potted plants there. It worked until we produced so many plants in the nursery they wouldn't fit and had to be set in mulch at the south end of the vegetable garden.

About the microstegia (it may be "microstegium"), it is a major weed here. We also call it annual grass or bamboo grass. It has jointed stems, and it roots where it touches. The only good things we can say about it are that it is annual and is easy to pull up. It is also easy to mow and self-sows into the lawn. The problem there is that it is cleistogamous, with fertile flowers appearing in September, when they quickly go to seed. We have controlled much of it by spraying with a grass-specific herbicide in September, but we find that this thick, heavy mulch of ground-up leaves works as well, and I feel happier about using it.

Wednesday, January 14, 1998

Late yesterday morning the sun came out, and I thought, I'll bet it is over for Allen and the operation went well. I am certain you are uncomfortable and will not feel like yourself for a time to come, but I am so relieved because I trust my intuition that you'll be around next January 14 and many more to come. Intuition isn't evidence, of course, so I called Martha and found out that you were in the recovery room.

Later that morning, I went to see my father and had the curious experience of seeing a nurse feed him. He has a bit of plastic tubing of some sort tucked up along one side. She straightened it out, poured in a little water, then a can of something and some more water. She bent the tube and fastened it shut with a rubber band. He actually spoke the name of the liquid she fed him, and she assured me that he knows exactly what she is doing and why. He and I had little dialogue. About the only thing I can get him to do is salute. So we saluted with one hand and then the other, and blew kisses, and I left. I am sure you can imagine what an emotional drain each of these visits is to me—and also why I must go.

I, too, think it an extraordinary coincidence that you actually had a course from him and that we would meet for the first time thirty years later. Victorian literature had nothing to do with our meeting. By the time we met, we saw nature in twentieth-century terms, not nineteenth.

As for calling professors, much less parents or grandparents, by their first names, I agree completely. I feel uncomfortable with it. Craufurd says he likes it and doesn't care. I keep asking myself why I do care and can't explain it. Certainly I don't consider myself superior to those younger than I except in the number of years I have survived on earth. The only person who calls me Mrs. Goodwin is the hardware store owner.

I want to know how you feel now that the operation is over. I remember my own so well. You kindly sent me books on gardening to read, and I saved them with the same delicious anticipation I used to have when I saved the icing from the cake until last. But when I felt well enough to read, I couldn't read about gardening. I knew I was really myself again when finally I could return to it.

By the way, I saw the perfect bumper sticker for you to put on your new car: AIN'T SKEERED!

Today I walked in the woods, studying the new *Helleborus niger* seedlings blooming for the first time. I am excited about them. One has gray leaves veined with a lighter gray-green and several flowers to a stalk. They are tinged with pink and have slightly grayed backs. I feel certain that this is a chance hybrid with *H.* × *sternii* as one parent. Some of the others look more like they have a bit of *H. argutifolius* in them. All of these grow near each other, so the bees must have done the cross-pollination.

I have several pots of *H. lividus* in the greenhouse and am trying to cross them with *Hb. niger, argutifolius,* and × *sternii.* Last year I successfully made the cross with *H. niger* and I have about four full flats of seedlings coming along. They will have to be called *H.* × *ballardiae,* since Helen Ballard did it first and courtesy and convention require that anyone else who makes the same cross should use that name. The important thing is that I can dream now of a great, long path lined with them in the year 2000. (I used to say that and laugh, thinking that's the next century, but now it is just around the corner.)

I will probably call you before you get out of the hospital. I have hesitated because I remember how few and brief were the moments when I felt like talking to anyone. I remember that you called me during one of those moments. There is something so basic and demeaning about being in a hospital. One is concerned primarily about staying alive or getting a bit of oneself to stop hurting. The most routine bodily functions become enormous worries and chores. I also remember my excitement about getting my back fixed forever. I will be happy for you when you can go home and at least see your new greenhouse from the outside.

Love,
Nancy

Wednesday, January 21, 1998

Dear Nancy,

Hella picked me up yesterday morning at Pennsylvania Hospital. I was back home by 1:30. For most of the past twenty-four hours I've been asleep. Dr. Susan Gregory (Duke, A.B., but decades after us), who was just added to my retinue of physicians—she's a lung specialist—says, "In all things, listen to your body, and it will tell you things." My body has not, surprisingly, had much to say yet about being being entirely deprived of its beloved and accustomed Carlton 100s since midnight, January 12; it has, however, bitched a whole lot about lack of sleep. "Complete hospital bed rest"—perhaps there once was such a thing. I remember the flu one year at Duke and a week or so in the West Campus infirmary, and the memory is of quiet . . . muffled voices, no radio and of course no TV blaring, just the kind of silence that comes in late evening when snow that has been falling all day comes to a stop. The quiet days in hospitals are long gone. Today noise is almost constant where hospital patients try to rest and sleep. Almost everything beeps, and what doesn't beep whistles or rings or makes some other disturbing noise. And, oh yes, the nurses talk loudly, even at night.

If I ever go through anything remotely like the last ten days again, I shall insist on a private room, not go along with semiprivate. In the intensive care unit, where I spent about twelve hours, an old man in the bed adjacent to mine yelled obscenities nonstop.

The orderlies shouted right back at him. After hours of this noisy solo with chorus, I was finally moved to a private room in ICU, but had hardly settled in to enjoy it than I was moved upstairs to the semiprivate room where I spent the next five nights and six days. Here, the gods did not smile on me in giving me my roommate. He was unpleasant in every imaginable way. I was not displeased when he was released and I had the room all to myself for five or six hours. My next roommate was something of an improvement, as he slept most of the time, but the luck of the draw still argues strongly for a private room.

I'm fading now . . . back to you later.

Love,
Allen

Saturday, January 24, 1998

Dear Allen,

Yes, by all means insist on a single room next time, but it would be better not to have a next time! It is bad enough to be in a hospital when you'd rather be in a garden. If I feel awful, I don't want to have anyone around, not even Craufurd. The details of your ten-day ordeal seem very real to me. I was fortunate to be in a room alone, so I didn't have to have the television on every minute, but my room was outside the nurses' station, where there was laughter and talk and occasionally arguments all day and all night. I think the shrill, rhythmic beeps with an occasional long trill from various machines were the worst of the uncommon sounds that became all too common before I came home. For one thing, I didn't know what they meant, and, for another, I couldn't seem to work their rhythm into a comforting pattern. One reason I love riding on trains is the reassuring rhythm of metal wheels on rails. And here in Hillsborough, when the wind comes from the west, I hear that same rhythmic noise, always accompanied by the pleasant dissonance of train whistles.

Love,
Nancy

Tuesday, January 27, 1998

Dear Nancy,

Two weeks ago right about now I was just coming to at Pennsylvania Hospital after five or so hours of surgery. A week ago at this time—midafternoon—I had just gotten back to Linwood, proceeding then to sleep, sleep, and sleep. Every day since, there are new signs of progress toward recuperation, although subjectively I have felt about the same every day.

When I left the hospital last week, the word from the surgeons involved was that: (a) what they removed was cancer, a carcinoma; and (b) no chemotherapy and no radiation would be required. I assumed that this medical opinion, like any other, needed to be confirmed or countered by a second opinion, but yesterday Dr. Leonard Galler, the lovely man who was my surgeon for the initial carotid artery surgery a few years back, called to see how I was doing. He had gotten the latest medical reports from Penn. I don't need a second opinion in this case, he said. Instead, he said, we are fully able to speak of a cure.

I am still very tired. One day I try not to nap but to do things out in the greenhouse, and the next day I crash.

Love,
Allen

Monday, February 2, 1998

Dear Allen,

Your medical news is splendid, and I am thrilled to know that you are no longer smoking. I think about you now in your recovery. I hope that you soon feel like you should. I remember feeling impatient with my body. I thought it should have healed long before it did.

Groundhog Day. It is no surprise to me that we have six more weeks of winter forecast by those poor, tortured woodchucks dragged from their long winter's sleep. I saw a red sky this morning when I walked down to get the paper, and the forecast is for another storm sweeping up from the Gulf. I guess it goes from us to you, intensifying as it moves over water. We lacked about one drop of breaking the record for rainfall in January. We had over seven inches. I bless the Graham that terraced this hillside, for we have almost no erosion.

Groundhogs notwithstanding, this is the winter that wasn't. The garden is delightful with *Cyclamen coum* in bloom all through the woods. All of the colors blend, and with them blooms *Crocus tommasinianus* from Elizabeth Lawrence's garden. Seedlings sprouted in the paths, and now I have new color forms, some darker than my original ones and others nearly white. Why is it I feel such a bond with her knowing that the parent of a plant here may have grown in her garden? I believe also that many of my seedling hellebores came via Miss Lawrence from Carl Krippendorf's garden. Plants bring with them their own stories. We sometimes have trouble reading them, partly because we don't take the time. I think about Mr. Krippendorf, discovering his new patches of aconites in his woods.

I remember my first January at Montrose. We had snow and ice beginning at the New Year. Our dearly beloved cat, Thomas, died early in the year, and we buried him at the north end of the vegetable garden as soon as we could dig in the soil. The bluebirds came and sang throughout our sad little ceremony.

The bluebirds always return in January. I saw them weeks ago, perched on the roof of the little greenhouse and in the pecan trees just beyond. I saw and heard them again this morning. The pair of geese that nest there came again to the pond about two weeks ago. I haven't seen them yet, just heard them. White-throated sparrows sing their sad, wavering songs every evening, and the little Carolina wrens fuss every time a cat walks by. The cedar waxwings are here too, with their shrill squeaks. There are lots of juniper berries left, so I hope they will stay a while. What birds brighten your winter?

Now I have three different species of cyclamen in flower — *Cc. coum, trochopteranthum,* and *pseudibericum.* A year ago I planted my most special forms of *C. coum* in a brand new part of the garden. I want to keep the seed strain as pure as possible. These are all from wild-collected seeds from Turkey, and the leaves are spectacularly marked with silver and green. I have a few solid green ones, and they have the darkest flowers of all. Yesterday I found my first *Iris reticulata* blooming in the woods with cyclamen, hellebores, and crocuses.

Thursday, February 5, 1998

Time passes! It was lovely hearing your voice this morning. I haven't been out in the storms but have instead recovered from my flu inside. Today I have no staff because they have finished most of their inside work, and it is very satisfying. I heard Fred McGourty once suggest that no one should have a garden larger than his wife can tend. He had a point! I love it when I have the garden to myself.

We've changed our visiting hours this year, eliminating Wednesday, when people might arrive without an appointment. No one came. The town asked us to do it, and during the past two years we've had about a dozen people arrive that way. Instead we have added Saturday afternoon, but by appointment. Already there have been about two dozen visitors, even at this cold season. I had a memorable tour last weekend. A couple came from Winston-Salem on their way to Apex to see their daughter. They were making a new garden that would be terraced and wanted ideas. I asked the appropriate questions, trying to discover whether they would have sun or shade. "A bit of both," they replied. So I gave the grand tour, even taking them to the woods to see our terraces. The garden has seldom looked more beautiful in winter. In addition to the cyclamen and crocuses, the later hellebores are blooming ahead of schedule. The woman commented as she left, "We'll come back when there's something in bloom." I believe she expected to see roses.

Love,
Nancy

Thursday, February 12, 1998

Dear Nancy,

It's been a while since I wrote! But, as you wrote last month about my sending you books you couldn't read right after your own surgery, we learn about ourselves after the experience. Also, there's surgery and there's surgery. An endarterectomy is in no possible way preparation for thoracic surgery. There's also a difference between getting better from day to day and feeling better. The operation, they say, was a success. Obviously I can do more from day to day, certainly from week to week. But feeling better? Not yet, not really! The only person who accurately described in advance the way I would feel was my cardiologist. She said to get ready to feel like I'd barely survived being hit by a Mack truck. She was right, but she didn't tell me how long I would feel this way. (I'd like to know now, but suspect that the answer isn't "till tomorrow.")

But there may be good signs. Suddenly I feel like Rip Van Winkle. One moment it was early January, with plenty of time yet to order seeds and start them in the greenhouse, and now February is well under way, with no seeds ordered yet and just a few things checked off in catalogs.

Practical arrangements here are that I (try to) sleep upstairs at night but spend the rest of the day, from early morning on, in the living room of this old house. When we moved in a quarter century ago, it would not have been especially pleasant. A dead-end room, it had and still has ample east windows, but niggardly ones on the south side. The room was good for listening to music, but there was no way to see outside or get there. Now there are generous French doors opening onto one corner of the deck—at its lowest level, so that the realities of dirt are within view. I can lie on my side on the sofa, looking at plants I set out years ago that have done what I hoped (hellebores, although their bloom is still some time off), those that came up on their own (a black walnut, now a tall tree, that sneaked in as a seed brought by a forgetful squirrel and that now thoroughly poisons the soil), and those that were planted for our reasons but then developed according to their own hidden agendas (English ivy, intended as a groundcover, now an aerial shrub).

Snowdrops are starting here. We have one kind only, unless a different sort that Hella brought last February from her mother's place in Tennessee has made an appearance. I'll bet you have over ten, maybe more. I'd love an account of each and every one, where you got it, how it differs from all its fellows, and all the rest. And, oh yes, would you be willing to write about your dianthus walk for the spring issue of *Homeground*?

Love,
Allen

Wednesday, February 18, 1998

Dear Allen,

You asked about snowdrops. I like everything about them. First, the time they bloom. I wonder if all gardeners are like me, always anticipating the next season. The snowdrop season begins in late October with *Galanthus reginae-olgae*. By Thanksgiving I have a pretty good display of *G. caucasicus* near the metasequoias and one or two days later have more than I can count. *Gg. nivalis* and *elwesii* follow shortly. I feel guilty about having the latter but in self-defense plead that I didn't know they were disappearing from the wild when I bought them so many years ago. Now I am glad I bought the ones I did, because I never see snowdrops in garden centers any more. They are happy in my soil and have multiplied and seeded about. The latest one to bloom here is *G. ikariae*—mine came from a customer in the old Montrose Nursery days. It is different from the others, with broad green leaves rather than the silver gray ones. I find the flowers as variable as cyclamen, but the variation demands more effort to see in this species. The cups are fascinating, with green spots at the base, sometimes at the base and the tip, sometimes with an "x," and occasionally completely green. Galanthuses emerge from the soil with their leaves wrapped tightly about the flower and with a slender bract folded over the white bud as if to hold it all together and form a strong tip to push through the earth. Gradually everything expands and relaxes. Some scillas do the same thing. I weeded the rock garden yesterday and could see the blue tips of *Scilla bifolia* flowers expanding faster than their leaves.

We have endured incredible rains—three and a half inches night before last. With a tin roof magnifying every sound, I imagined it was even more. I saw the river from the compost piles. Late yesterday afternoon I walked down and saw that although the water spread across a large area, none of it came to the lowest terrace.

Love to write about the dianthus walk; it is one of my few gardens for all seasons.

Love,
Nancy

Thursday, March 19, 1998

Dear Nancy,

Tomorrow is the first official day of spring, but so far in this advancing year the seasons are very mixed up—almost as unsettled as has been my life, with its alternations between home and hospital.

As you know from Martha, as February wore toward its conclusion, I felt worse and worse, not better and better, as my surgeon had predicted. I was wracked with a horrible cough and could barely breathe. Finally, on the 26th, the second day of Lent, I went back to Philadelphia to see Dr. Gregory. She took one look at me and packed me off in a wheelchair for immediate hospital admission. I was back in Philadelphia Hospital for twelve days, in bed and hooked up to tubes and machines. I had serious pneumonia and a very nasty strep infection.

After two days with another unpleasant roommate, I took my own advice and got a private room, which was worth every penny. I could talk freely on the phone or with visiting family members, even if I didn't feel like saying much . . . and even if I was pretty doped up on morphine.

Ah, morphine, the gift of poppies! I stayed on it for days and days, until my doctors took me off it on Friday, the 6th of March. The next night I woke in the wee hours with hallucinations of jungle cats in my room. They seemed friendly, purring and rubbing against me, and one licked my hand with its large, raspy tongue, but I was worried they might escape to the hall and attack a nurse. That would have been okay if they'd gotten the right one, a bouncy little ball of cheer named Brandy or Candy, something like that, whose wont it was to approach me saying, "Now, let's take our medicine," or "take our temperature," but other nurses were less expendable. So I called Michael (it was 2:00 A.M.), explained the cats to him, and asked him to . . . I don't know, call the Philly police for a SWAT team, something. He said later that I sounded extremely lucid, even persuasive, but still he called the nursing desk instead, which sent someone in to ask if I was having a bad night. The next morning one of the attendants said that post-morphine incidents of the kind were not all that unusual: earlier that week a woman just down the hall had called the desk asking for a nurse to come right away to make the iguana stop eating her left leg.

I was discharged Monday, March 9, somewhat to Hella's surprise, with a small chest tube (it's still there now) for drainage, and with no strength at all. It was all I could do to get out of the car and drag myself inside to the living room, where I stayed pretty much immobile for three days. Friday I had my first visitor, a friend and colleague from the college, and that afternoon I even drove to the bookstore in the little shopping center a couple of miles away. I parked on the curb, walked a few steps into the store, and then had to sit down, meanwhile wondering how on earth I was going to be able to do a lick of gardening anytime soon, maybe ever.

Recovery comes quickly, however. Every day I've done more and more: yesterday Hella and I were out for almost five hours, doing various errands.

I do have help in the garden, however, in the form of a student who did some work here early last fall. He's strong and burly and, best of all, he's worked for a garden center, a local nursery in northern N.J., and a landscaping service. In September he pruned back and transplanted some fair-sized, overgrown clumps of *Cornus alba* 'Sibirica' in no time flat. I got in touch with him yesterday, and he's agreed to come work here as soon as the heavy rain lets up.

It is now a time of reckoning. There are too many woody plants in our small garden, so there are choices to be made. A large *Viburnum plicatum* f. *tomentosum* at the front corner of the house must go. It's never been happy anyway—I suspect that beneath it there's plaster and other rubble from God knows how long ago. In its place, Marc, that student, will move a supposedly dwarf crape myrtle that has outgrown its allotted space nearby. Not far from the viburnum there's another unwelcome choice, between a fastigiate ginkgo and a volunteer sassafras now over fifteen feet high. The ginkgo is the winner, but I will mourn the sassafras.

There's more for my student to do. I have a list: mulch the paths in the front garden and the work area between shed and greenhouse with recycled bark from our country composting authority; prune severely a vitex, several privets, and a large cotoneaster; remove the tumbledown fence along the front sidewalk; mow back and rake up quite a lot of *Liriope muscari*; and much, much more.

Throughout my latest hospital stay, as during most of the winter up till then, the weather was warm. The drive home started out springlike. In Philadelphia's Society Hill, cherry trees and forsythia were in full bloom, as was *Prunus* × *incomp* 'Okame' in our own garden. Also in flower were *Iris reticulata*, *Cyclamen coum*, many hellebores, snow crocus and hybrid crocus, early and even a few midseason sorts of daffodils, and *Anemone blanda*. A huge carpet of fairly weedy violets beneath the *Lagerstroemia faurei* next to the driveway, violets that had never really bloomed much, was this year almost covered with flowers. En masse, they were the darkest purple imaginable—almost enough to convince me that they were worth growing, not weeds at all. But we had no sooner pulled into the driveway than the sun disappeared behind some very nasty black clouds sweeping in from the west, and the temperature dropped from the 60s into the low 20s. The weather has been miserable ever since.

Love,
Allen

Spring

Thursday, March 26, 1998

Dear Nancy,

We've had two calm, cloudless days with deep blue skies—the look of spring, anyway, but cold temperatures have belied appearances. (Average temperature this year was lower the first three weeks of March than in January or February!) Today may approach the real thing, in the 50s, and tomorrow we're promised the high 60s . . . and not a moment too soon. The main floral extravaganza is yet to come, but one of the truest delights of early spring is wandering about the garden and noting which herbaceous perennials have broken dormancy and been spurred onward into another growing season. Hemerocallis have been evident for two, maybe three weeks. *Dicentra spectabilis* has just broken ground; likewise the *Aquilegia canadensis* that self-sowed serendipitously a few years back in the midst of *Deutzia crenata* 'Nikko'. The two bloom together in perfect harmony in early May. I would like to take credit for contriving this marriage, but of course cannot.

I hope to get my brawny ex-student Marc here shortly, but in the meantime, despite the immediately foregoing praise of the accidental elements in gardening, I have been thinking a lot about revising the most neglected part of our small garden, the northeastern corner, where Belhaven Avenue runs into Shore Road. Our gardening efforts began here a quarter century ago, as the front lawn started to be transformed gradually into a cottage garden. It's heavily planted in spring bulbs, including the anemones and grape hyacinths and other so-called minor bulbs that have accommodatingly sown themselves everywhere. I've already mentioned the small trees and flowering shrubs that must be reduced in number this year, but I haven't said much, if anything, about the perennials that dominate this part of our garden. Many date from the time when I was writing a regular newspaper column—when our garden was my laboratory to try out new plants. Many of these have either long since disappeared (lavatera 'Barnsley') or barely hold their own (*Solidago odora*) against competition. The competition consists of rather-too-successful spreading perennials, highly invasive beasts like *Macleaya cordata, Campanula takesimana, Fragaria* 'Pink Panda', *Aster tataricus*, and so on. The tartar aster, I might mention, is one of several perennials whose season of bloom is particular to autumn, part of a group that also includes several New England aster cultivars, *Helianthus angustifolius*, and many late salvias, especially the tender *Salvia leucantha*. Another treasure is the top-notch soapwort gentian (*Gentiana saponaria*) that came years ago from Montrose. It is truly splendid for its teal blue bottle flowers and its late fall foliage, which is a fine shade of apricot pink. But back to the beasts: I should also mention *Asteromoea mongolica*. I love it for its great crop of elegant little double white daisy flowers from late summer through most of autumn. It looks shy, but is anything but; it spreads relentlessly and insidiously by a network of stolons. Oh yes, I know its real name is something else, but Elizabeth Lawrence's name is the one I can remember.

I plan never to touch the bulbs when I get around to redoing the front garden. The great virtue of bulbs, anyway, is their "plant us and then forget us until our time rolls around again each year" behavior. Some perennials—those that don't spread and bloom for a long time (particularly another Montrose treasure, *Calamintha nepeta*)—are unthinkable to live without. I want to keep the autumn perennials, also some others with a restricted but spectacular season of bloom, like crocosmias 'Lucifer' and 'Solfatarre'. Everything invasive, however, must go this year, except maybe for a few plants of the tartar aster (just about the latest-blooming plant in our garden and also, unlike most asters, a decent cut flower). It will take about a week to purge this part of the garden and replace it with . . . what?

For once in my life as a gardener, I'm guided in making this decision by an idea about design, not just thoughts of "here's a gap, now quick, what can I stick in it to fill it up?" A couple of years ago Cynthia Woodyard, who designs gardens as well as photographing them, explained to me that one of the design principles she honors consistently is the principle of repetition. A garden may embrace great variety and diversity, but without repetition—a sense of familiarity and of being at home—it arouses in us a feeling of restlessness. Repetition within a garden of the same plants or combinations of plants or of plants similar in form, color, and texture, however, brings a sense of repose. Increasingly, I've honored this principle here, especially in the shady places, with their hostas, epimediums, and ferns, and now I want to resort to it in dealing with that northeast corner, in this way. As you know, in recent years I've gone daft for container planting, on the extensive decks out back and spilling down into the rest of the back garden. In an astounding number of barrels, pots, troughs, hanging baskets, and so on we are growing a huge assortment of plants suitable for such cul-

Linwood

ture. There are lots and lots of subtropicals, foliage plants, long-blooming annuals, and so on. If you will, in these containers I'm using a certain plant vocabulary of things like *Alternanthera dentata* 'Rubiginosa', *Plectranthus argentatus*, many different cultivars of coleus, *Zinnia angustifolius* and *Z. peruviana*. What I now want to do is use these and similar plants in the front garden, too.

By the middle of July I hope to be able to let you know whether this idea is sound or a mere pipe dream. That's one advantage of using a lot of annuals or tender perennials! (Another is being able to do something entirely different next year . . .)

Here, however, is an item from my "nothing new under the sun" file. In a secondary source that gives the date (1892) but not the name of the work quoted, the influential British garden theorist William Robinson refers to "*Coleus, Alternanthera, Perilla, etc.*" as "mean little subtropical weeds that happen to possess a colored leaf" but still "plants without fragrance, beauty of form, or even the charm of association." A decade or two ago, I scoffed at coleus as beneath contempt (I knew only the seed-grown mixes, not the really sensational, vegetatively propagated clones that are now the rage. Then, I hadn't yet made the acquaintance of *Alternanthera dentata* 'Rubiginosa' or of perilla). Now I can't get enough of all these plants—and I have a lot of like-minded company. Taste, it seems, has reverted to the Victorian sensibilities that Robinson railed against, although, let's hope, carpet bedding is not due for a comeback.

March 27

Spring is truly here! There's bound to be another frosty night or two before the soil warms up, but for three days now it's gotten up into the high 80s. Tuesday Hella and I drove to Philadelphia for a doctor's appointment—adjusting the tube draining my chest, supposedly the next-to-last time before its eagerly awaited removal—and then took back roads home, stopping at various little roadside nurseries. Wednesday I worked in the garden all day . . . well, until 4:00 P.M. anyway. Did a lot of fairly heavy pruning with a dandy little handsaw, including cutting a multitrunked vitex back from twelve feet to about four feet. Doing this was probably not the brightest idea to come along this year, for the exertion, with both hands, may have caused the little postsurgical emergency that ensued when I discovered that the aforementioned chest tube was nowhere visible: it had worked its way back inside me somewhere. Hella called the University of Pennsylvania hospital and talked to one of my surgeon's residents, who suggested going to the hospital just down the street to see if a doctor there could extract the damned tube. I was in the emergency room for over four hours. One of the doctors there consulted by phone with the surgical resident in Philly several times before turning chicken about even touching the tube. Finally Michael drove Hella and me to Philadelphia, where the tube was easily restored to its proper place. We stayed the night (what was left of it) in a hotel, then came back yesterday morning, again stopping by several garden centers on the

way. Didn't buy anything. This is the time of my preseason recon-
naissance missions, trying to find out exactly what plants are going
to be available locally this year.

Oh yes, I should also report that one of the most striking plants
blooming now is a clump of yet one more piece of Montrose here
in our garden, *Ranunculus ficaria* 'Brazen Hussy'. It grows in the lee
of a purple barberry, where it could be overlooked were it not as in-
sistent as its name suggests. It shouts for attention, and I comply,
with complete admiration of its varnished-looking golden flowers
and its glossy leaves, of a dark shade that almost suggests chocolate.

Fondly,
Allen

Thursday, April 9, 1998

Dear Nancy,

This morning's tour of the garden—just in advance of the torren-
tial rains forecast for later—had a lesson about the difference between seasons as they unfold and seasons as they are remembered.
Daffodils were in their late glory (this year, thanks to El Niño, they
will overlap slightly with lilacs, whose clusters of buds are already
showing dark purple, two weeks ahead of their usual appearance).
Pulmonarias are everywhere, in furious bloom. Nearby, there's another plant I like, which may not suit your taste at all, a primula
named 'Mark Viette', which has double flowers of pastel pink and
powder blue. The flowers seem more like they belong on an African
violet than a primrose, but there you are.

There's more I could write, but the morning is wearing on, I've
got to drive to Philadelphia soon (let's hope for a final goodbye to
that chest tube), and Martha and Garry Blake-Adams should arrive
from Durham by nightfall, unless the rains detain them.

Love,
Allen

Thursday, April 9, 1998

Dear Allen,

Is the year really less normal than usual, or is it that I am writing to you more frequently and can seldom find a week that is as I had expected it? We had spring all winter, and when spring arrived, we had winter. I don't like spring best, but I can't help feeling a thrill of excitement as each plant returns from dormancy and first I find a tip and then a bud or leaf. I hope I never get over it.

What I don't like about spring is its violence. It isn't just the storms, with hail and winds that take the edge off that bit of warmth I might otherwise feel. Enticing and extensive periods of warm, soft air interspersed with intense cold make spring the cruelest season. This year I cut back my epimedium foliage before record cold that damaged the buds and flowers. That makes this a poor epimedium year for me—a major disappointment. We had the lowest temperatures of the winter just before the official first day of spring. Primulas were frozen and both flowers and leaves damaged. *Cyclamen coum* and *C. pseudibericum* withstood it all, and my spirits soar once again as I discover that this is a very good arisaema year. Many *Arisaema sikokianum* have survived without damage, although I admit to putting about a foot of ground-up leaves on their opened flowers. And I also admit that in general I believe that is cheating. I want plants that can take what they must in this climate. But I always want more, and to get more I must get a good seed set. I also have about a dozen *A. thunbergii* subsp. *urashima* blooming in the woods. This jack-in-the-pulpit has a broad brown spathe but with a splendid long tip that curls up and over it. I grew them from seed, and they bloomed for the first time last year—about nine years after germination.

Now that spring is really here—despite hail today and 35° forecast for tomorrow—I can see about six cardiocrinums producing stalks instead of leaves only, and that means flowers. Do you remember your first visit here in 1985? That was the first year I had them flower. These are almost all offspring from those original plants. I remember going round the garden with you and bemoaning the fact that they were on stalks so tall I couldn't smell the flowers.

I have had a completely new staff (of two people) for several months now, and the garden looks better than ever. We have planted many of the trees and shrubs that sat about in pots for a decade or so. We have removed almost all traces of the nursery that remained in view of the house. We hope to clear away the remains below the big greenhouse during this summer and put in gravel on which to set our tiny little nursery stock for visitors. All of this work and more besides is cooperative or collaborative. This is what Montrose is all about. Most people who come to work here bring with them ideas, many of which we try. That is how I hope the garden will continue long after I am gone. It should never be the same two years in a row. But there must also be coherence and continuity.

Friday, April 10, 1998

A small diversion. How well do you like daylight saving time? I absolutely loathe it! I feel angry for about the first two weeks after I have to set my clocks forward. I love getting up early, but I also love having a long morning, a short afternoon, and a long evening, coming in at or about dusk. Now I feel like I must come in during the middle of the afternoon, my morning is short, and I want to go to bed right after dinner.

We have cleared out the lath house. It had become a dumping ground for plants without a home. Now we are planting it with the coolest green ferns, a few hostas, polygonatums, and some *Pulmonaria officinalis* 'Sissinghurst'. We will have Mr. Huskins bring over a large iron vessel and set it into the ground. Finally, I will have a little water feature. I want a gurgle—no little boys peeing, no monsters throwing up into it, just the sound of water. We had our gardening seminar on the first day of spring. I called it "A Celebration of Spring." After this winter I thought I couldn't miss with the day, but mother nature has a mind of her own. We had a deep freeze— 17°—about ten days before, and the day itself was filled with showers. I had raindrops dripping from the tip of my nose and my ear lobes. My hair was sopping wet. But we did it anyway. We spent half the time in the garden and then had sessions on propagation in the potting room. It was a success. We sold more plants than ever on a single seminar day. Most people left in the early afternoon. Later we had tornado warnings all night. Several touched down near here.

Do you remember tornadoes in Texas when you were growing up? I never remember hearing of them in Durham. Weather forecasters say they were here, but because the area was so sparsely populated they most often damaged the woods and no one really cared. How many more people must we fit into our landscape before we realize there are too many of us? It breaks my heart to see trees cut, roads paved, houses built. No wonder the deer live in my back yard.

I have good news about deer. Finally I have a terrific spray that seems to deter them. I think I wrote you about it earlier, but it really does work. I still have hostas with leaves intact. I have daylilies with pointed leaves, not chopped off ones. And I have tulips in bloom. Maybe I will get some seed on the trilliums in the woods, and maybe this year I, too, will have flowers on *Gentiana saponaria*.

I sympathize with your need to revise your garden. I believe the two most difficult aspects of gardening are: (1) where to plant that plant that is so happy in its pot, and (2) how to keep the garden looking as it should while it ages. Garden maintenance here was out of hand. No longer could we see the urn in the aster border. The asters hadn't been reset for so many years that they were crowding themselves to death. We severely pruned most of the roses and tied all of them into the fences or onto the lath house. We cut away most of the ivy on buildings, fences, and trees so that it looks like delicate tracery instead of smothered decadence.

Aster tataricus certainly counts as invasive here but is easy to maintain in our heavy soil, and *Campanula takesimana* died. It doesn't surprise me that *Asteromoea mongolica* is pesky for you. (That was Elizabeth Lawrence's name for it, but I believe it must now be called *Kalimeris mongolica*.) I had it in many places in the sandy soil of my Durham garden, but I have trouble keeping it here. It doesn't seem to like full sun and clay soil. I don't know which condition is holding it back, but I cherish every bit of it. Also, I am beginning to view *Helleborus foetidus* as invasive, not underground but by seeding about. It worries me to find plants of hellebores uphill as well as down. I fear slugs carry the seeds that cling to their sticky bodies. Perhaps ants carry them, as they do cyclamen. Whatever the means of distribution, I find the results frightening. I propagate the best forms of *H. orientalis* vegetatively but dig out and compost most of their seedlings.

I wish I hadn't been completely overwhelmed by the nursery when I met Cynthia Woodyard. I certainly agree that repetition is an important element in design. It seems to me that design in a garden has as much in common with music as with painting. We need a unifying idea (color scheme or key) plus at least a little dissonance to enhance the harmony and, finally, the rhythm that ties it together and repetition to give it form. I certainly admit that design doesn't come easily for me. I get bogged down in the plants themselves. I

Montrose

love most of all finding those that are a little different—primroses with dark leaves and clear, intense flowers, tiarellas with pink flowers or variegated leaves. I want to reproduce them for mass plantings. I love it best when the garden begins to take over and seedlings (especially cyclamen) come up in unexpected places. The plants seem to flow from one area to another. I am well aware that a garden left to itself quickly reverts to wilderness, so I step in and remove or try to control the aggressors. It is not always easy to declare a plant long sought and admired a pest.

I am glad I kept records of propagation during the past ten years or so. We, like you, have to propagate and plant the many pots and urns that give this garden its character in summer. And we, like you, love coleus, even at the risk of being accused of neo-Victorianism. Certainly we can't have an exciting garden made up of pastels, without some plants with fully saturated colors in their leaves or flowers—not in North America, with its bright light, so different from the diffused, soft light in Britain.

I like thinking of a bit of Montrose in Linwood. *Ranunculus ficaria* 'Brazen Hussy' has been a star this year. We have it coming up through *Lysimachia nummularia* 'Aurea' and *Saxifraga veitchiana*. And I did plant that same lysimachia with *Ophiopogon planiscapus* 'Nigrescens' near the large rocks set at the corner of the driveway to deter automobiles and trucks from driving too close to the holly. You are here at Montrose, too. Do you remember sending seeds of a purple-flowered aquilegia with attractive glaucous leaves? We still have it at the edge of the woods garden. We call it *Aquilegia* 'Hella', and we also have *Scilla peruviana* grown from seeds you and Hella collected. That lives in the greenhouse.

Don't you dare go back to smoking!

Love,
Nancy

Tuesday, April 14, 1998

Dear Nancy,

Martha and Garry are about to depart for home after a splendid visit here over Easter weekend, so I'll take advantage of their courier service to send a few things, including a copy of *The Inviting Garden*.

The rest is plants.

1. Just sprouting in a pot, the tender, trailing, Tasmanian (how's that for alliteration?) violet, *Viola hederacea*. I gave this to you years ago, but you may have lost it over some winter or other. It's okay outside but very susceptible to spider mites in a greenhouse. Flowering almost constantly in white and purple, it's an excellent thing to drape on the outside of hanging baskets.

2. Also just beginning to leaf out, a clump of ramie (scientific name?). In the Nettle family, this plant from the tropics of Asia is a source of fiber sometimes mixed with linen or silk to produce fine, long-wearing fabric. I got it years ago from my friends Anita and Lucy and their herb farm. Despite its tropical origin it has proven

to be winter-hardy here in my neck of Zone 7. (Whether it will turn out to be as hardy in your clay soil as it is in my sand remains to be seen.) It's generally considered to be an economic plant, not an ornamental, but I admire its thick and pebbly leaves and its odd, green, wandlike inflorescences in late summer.

3. Dianthus 'Little Boy Blue', so named for its very glaucous leaves. (The single flowers are white.) I got this from Pierre Bennerup of Sunny Border Nursery. Now let's see if it can join your collection of garden pinks that can take high summer heat and humidity.

4. Two pots of a coleus I like, not for its middle-sized brownish leaves with green deckled edges but for its habit—low and extremely spreading by midsummer. I grow this in a pot with *Hakonechloa macra* 'Aureola'. The color combination is very fine, and I love the way the coleus surrounds this graceful grass on all sides like a flouncing skirt.

5. The large hosta, 'Sum and Substance', that you asked for some months ago is very late emerging. This clump may be it, but it could also be *H. sieboldiana* 'Elegans'. Sorry if it's not the right one, but if it isn't and you remind me next fall, I'll make amends.

6. Two little pots of fuzzy, pebbly gray plants. This is *Stachys* (species?) 'Hidalgo'. Twenty-four inches tall, orange-pink little flowers all season in whorls around leaf axils. Hardy to about 26°. Last year I grew it with *Asclepias currasavica*, an attractive combination, as the flowers of this subtropical milkweed are deeper in color (red-orange and gold) and the leaves smooth and slightly blue.

Love,
Allen

Tuesday, April 14, 1998

Dear Nancy,

Martha and Garry just left, heading back to Durham, accompanied by a quick note about a few plants I sent along for you.

Our friends arrived here in a ferocious thunderstorm Thursday, shortly after Hella and I (tubeless!) got back from the doctor. Martha presented us with your gifts. The pot of *Parochetus communis* went to the greenhouse right away. (I love its azure, pealike flowers!) The next morning Hella planted your fine assortment of primulas, nicely labeled according to color, beneath the old Virginia juniper by the driveway. It's a good spot for plants that appreciate dry shade during summer dormancy, such as the cyclamen that came from Montrose years ago. These have now grown to magnificent proportions. A couple of clumps of *Cyclamen hederifolium* are now so large that if the tubers were lifted they would probably be of that legendary size in British books, as big as pancakes. There is, incidentally, a mystery cyclamen blooming now. I thought it was *C. coum*, for the color verges on that bright carmine-magenta (is that the right descriptive word?) typical of the species. But Friday, when Hella was planting the primroses, I took a closer look. The leaves aren't rounded at all (not "coumish"). They look more like those of *C. hederifolium*, with beautiful patternings of pewter.

We had a marvelous Easter weekend with our friends. After Friday's planting was finished, we took off for Batsto, a restored industrial village (iron foundry during the Revolutionary War, glass factory thereafter until right after the Civil War, when it was deserted) on the southern edge of the Pine Barrens—a vast tract where you can drive and drive without seeing another car and hardly any houses or people. Saturday we drove farther up the Garden State Parkway to Wall Township, to see Paul and his family. Hella has been up several times since they moved into their new house, but Saturday was my first visit. The house, brand new in a brand new subdivision, is huge—Martha says a "starter castle"—and it sits on a five-acre lot. I don't quite understand why so much recently built residential real estate in New Jersey is so grand in proportion, but it seems to suit Paul and his brood.

The weather was warm, sunny, and calm all weekend. Sunday and Monday we mainly worked in the garden. I had to content myself with light chores, lifting nothing much heavier than a flower pot. The others put in some heavy labor, including moving one of our water features—a small fiberglass pool and a waterfall coursing down a pile of good-sized river rocks. This contraption originated three years ago, in the front garden. Neither Hella nor I was happy with its location. The next year, on one of their previous visits, the Blake-Adamses were inspired to help move it to the back garden, adjacent to the deck. On a subsequent visit, they left it in place but rearranged the rocks to transform the waterfall into something more ambitious. Now it's moved to the very back of our property, in front of the old shed in its new spot. When the Blake-Adamses come, things get moving, and I mean that literally, not figuratively—physical objects change their location. Garry moved a metal arch from its ludicrous position in the middle of a flower bed to a more suitable place at the head of a path, and also a red native honeysuckle and a nandina of substantial proportions. All these changes—dictated by Hella and Martha in concert—improved the overall appearance of the garden.

As ever,
Allen

Wednesday, April 15, 1998

Dear Nancy,

Now your good letter of the 9th and 10th has arrived. Yes, I do remember my first visit to Montrose in 1985—and those cardiocrinums. I have some vague recollection that we fetched a stepladder for a closer look at their white flowers, but wonder if I am right about the ladder. Sometimes we can remember things that we have not experienced, at least not in the form we remember them. (Ronald Reagan's movies sometimes were more real to him than Jane Wyman was.) Another example may or may not be that old *Magnolia acuminata* that came down in the drive at Montrose some years ago. I remember arriving early, right after it gave its final shudder and fell. Someone had decorated it with flowers, in memoriam. While she was here, Martha said I didn't arrive at Montrose until days after the magnolia's demise. You of course may remember my appearance after its fall in some third, entirely different way. (*Rashoman* is always with us.)

That magnolia came up in our conversation because the end is probably in sight for the swamp maple smack in the middle of the back garden. I don't know how old the tree is, and won't know until it's felled and the rings counted. It has surely been around for a century at least, and possibly might even have been growing here when the house was built, sometime prior to 1812. It is not a tree that I would have chosen to plant. Its shallow roots run everywhere in their greed for moisture and nourishment. It has been brushed by storms, once and maybe more by a hurricane. Tree surgeons have topped it twice since we moved here a quarter century ago. Early this spring, while the four main trunks were still bare, I looked up and saw that three were hollow, so almost certainly all four. One trunk must be amputated, and soon. If—*when!*—it falls in a storm, it will take the greenhouse with it, maybe the deck too.

Rationality demands that we call the tree surgeons in for one last operation—a fatal one—on our tree. Sentimentality suggests that we and our tree just take our chances. I have deep affection for that tree, despite those invasive roots, and despite the enormous crop of seeds that float down like little helicopters all over the garden every May. (Every last one germinates, I swear!) Our maple stays green very late every fall, weeks after others of its species are almost bare. When it turns, it starts out a warm shade of apricot, then flames cerise—a gorgeous sight at the day's end, when its leaves and the setting sun seem to make one single, glorious conflagration. Our sons and now our grandchildren have played in the shade of this tree, and—horrible thought!—when it is no more, our shady garden will be a sunny one. That means a lot of work, to find new places for pulmonarias, Solomon's seal, wild gingers, and other shade-lovers.

For the time being, we've decided to follow a path somewhere between rationality and sentiment. We'll call Big Pine, the tree folks, have them remove that one trunk or main branch, and then wait for the inevitable day that the rest falls, either by windstorm or by chain saw. The death of a tree that has been a character in the life story of a family is not happy to contemplate.

You asked if I like daylight saving time. It confuses me. I hate it when it starts and I have to set the clocks back and I feel that I've lost an hour out of the day (even though I get the hour back in the fall). For a few days after this change, I keep wondering what time it is, *really*. This question often pops to mind in what seems like the middle of the night, though in reality daybreak isn't far away and the birds have started singing.

Tornadoes in Texas when I was growing up? Lord, yes, except that then we called them cyclones. (Wasn't it a cyclone, not a tornado, that snatched Dorothy and Toto up over the rainbow?) When we were on a farm outside Irving, then a tiny town between Dallas and Fort Worth, a tornado brushed one corner of our front yard on Kit Lone Star Continuation Road, destroying the roof of a wishing well (a real well, with water in it way at the bottom somewhere) and most of a mildewed hedge of 'Dorothy Perkins' rose. The twister sounded like a freight train coming through, just as people say. Texas tornadoes, I think, mostly occurred during daytime, when you could see them. I found them scarier in Michigan when I was teaching at Michigan State, for they seemed to be nocturnal, with no visible warning.

I don't think I'll go back to smoking, or Hella either. It doesn't bother either one of us to be around smokers. I'm tempted with the first cup of coffee in the morning, also right after dinner. Sometimes when at the computer I reach for the ashtray that isn't there, also the shirt pocket that no longer holds a pack of Carlton 100s, but Hella pointed out constantly when I was a smoker that I didn't smoke while working so much as just light up and let the cigarette burn down (like incense?). My worst moment of temptation so far came at 6:30 the other morning. We were out of coffee, I drove to the Seven-Eleven to get some, and when I got out of the car, I saw somebody else's discarded, half-smoked cigarette, still burning. The sight made me want to go into the store to buy a pack of cigarettes as well as the coffee I came for. I didn't do it, but the urge was very powerful.

Still not smoking,
Allen

Wednesday, April 22, 1998

Dear Allen,

Martha is better than UPS. For one thing she brought the plants over the day after she left Linwood. I believe that's next-day service. What treasures you sent. The "tender, trailing, Tasmanian violet" is welcomed back. This time I hope I can do a little better by it during the winter. I noticed that you had cut it completely back. Is that how you prevent red spider? The ramie (it's *Boehmeria nivea*) is going into the new vegetable garden. Your beautiful blue-leaved dianthus 'Little Boy Blue' has gone into the center circle to help extend the dianthus walk north and help the transition between those two gardens. What a great idea for combining the coleus you sent — *Coleus pumilus*, I think — with that old "Hak grass," as some of my visitors call it. I have hakonechloa in a pot because it needs more moisture than is available in my garden, so I'll try it your way. I'm excited about the hosta and won't be too disappointed if it is *H. sieboldiana* 'Elegans'. That one is beautiful, too. *Stachys coccinea* 'Hidalgo' went into the center circle where I can see it in "dawn's early light." I mean that! I walk out to get the paper just at dawn on every morning except Sunday, when I am given a cup of coffee in bed plus time to read a little. The plants with gray or chartreuse foliage or those with hairy leaves all show up in dim light while greens and blues disappear altogether. We have, incidentally, just made a moon garden with gray or silver plants combined with purple. Instead of "points of light" it has points of dark.

El Niño is still with us. I had a day of tours planned, but because it's cold and rainy I now expect only a dozen hardy souls. We brought many plants out of the greenhouse yesterday just to receive some of this cold rain. I think it will be a better transition than if I wait until the heat really sets in.

The owls are better, that is, more loquacious than ever. In fact, they almost seem to speak in unison; certainly one begins before the other has finished speaking. We have them in the large oaks and metasequoias in front of the house and occasionally can see their silent flight. I always feel special when I see them fly. They are so secretive that it seems as if they decide when and if to allow me to see them.

As you remember, we have no lawn that should be properly called that. What we have are great expanses of mown areas, and this time of year is their peak. They are filled with the most delightful weeds. Although I like the velvety mown look, I also love the unkempt flowery look on the day before mowings. Buttercups (*Ranunculus bulbosus*, I think) grow everywhere, and now show their bright yellow flowers. There is a nice little pale yellow dandelion relative along the edge of the driveway. It may be *Krigia dandelion*. It has gray-green narrow leaves and flowers that are the most exquisite shade of primrose yellow. It doesn't crowd out anything but makes a mat in spring and then goes underground for the rest of the year. I even allow but don't encourage it in the rock garden. Even the common dandelion is a very beautiful thing and would be cherished if every seed didn't germinate. *Salvia lyrata*, as you may remember, grows all along the woods' edge in the former goat pasture. Dark purple leaves and medium purple flowers contrast with these pale yellow flowering companions. There are clovers in pink or white, and violets mostly in purple but some "confederates" (blue-gray and white) and even a few pure white ones that I occasionally move to more protected places. I have others in the garden proper, but these volunteers add to our meadow effect. Near the driveway I see hop clover, *Trifolium procumbens*, I think, with its pale yellow flower heads. We have penstemons along the road to the pond, and if

Craufurd falls behind in his mowing, they bloom in a delicate shade of red-violet. Daisies will bloom just a little later. We have other cultivated weeds, such as *Cyclamen coum* and *C. hederifolium* seeding about in the lawns here and there. I have other weeds to bloom in summer. Even the hairy-leaved plantains are charming. (I don't like the smooth-leaved ones as well.)

And, speaking of cyclamen, I believe your mystery species is *C. pseudibericum*. It blooms in spring, generally with leaves and flowers larger than those of *C. coum*. The color is usually carmine-magenta as you observed, and the lower side of the leaves is usually beet red.

Also, your memory of the visit to Montrose after the *Magnolia acuminata* fell is good. I was away in Norfolk, and you arrived the morning after the fall. I returned home that same evening and wept when I saw it.

The woods are closing in now, and I resent the new leaves obscuring my view. I know they give the shade-loving plants down there what they need, so will get used to it. It is my most special place, with the hill shielding me from the noise of the road and with seedlings of all sorts of treasures to discover as I crawl about weeding. As summer comes in with its heat, I will love the tree leaves and their cool shade.

Love,
Nancy

Friday, May 8, 1998

Dear Nancy,

I heard from Martha about your father's death. I am very sorry, but know that it must have come as sad, but also a relief. It was like that for me with my mother.

The reason that you haven't gotten a letter from Linwood in three weeks, you can probably guess, is spring planting, a rite preceded here by many visits to garden centers and local nurseries all over Atlantic County, also Delaware and one corner of Pennsylvania. You wrote in one of your letters this year that several containers give the gardens at Montrose part of their character. I agree—the molasses pot in the purple and orange garden, the urn above the aster garden, and all the rest—all are handsome. Here, things are somewhat different. We've got a tiny lawn, some perennial borders, a little woodland garden-in-the-making, but increasingly containers *are* our garden. On the deck alone, there are seventeen hanging baskets and seventy-six other containers, some very large, including seven urns of faux terra cotta that are thirty-six inches across and thirty inches tall. In advance of the long summer ahead, all must be planted by the middle of May.

We took one overnight trip in late April to Wilmington to visit Polly Hill, who is now in her nineties and very spry. Her sixty-acre farm on Martha's Vineyard is becoming the Polly Hill Arboretum. The official opening is June 25. I'm speaking then, but more on this later, for the topic at hand is filling up all those containers.

Wilmington and its vicinity are horticulturally much more active than southern New Jersey. I can always expect to find something new, unfamiliar, rare, or interesting, something beyond the usual garden center fare. So it was on this trip. I brought back some treasures. One was crossvine (*Bignonia capreolata*) 'Tangerine Beauty', I think a J. C. Raulston introduction. Damn it, I can't grow *Clematis armandii* up here. Crossvine lacks fragrance, but otherwise it is a reasonable substitute for that clematis—and the only evergreen flowering vine that's hardy in the North. I also came home with several fancy-leaf pelargoniums, and a phormium. The fancy-leaf geraniums are something I've meant to collect eventually. Finding seven named cultivars was a head start. I saw some phormiums last summer at Montrose and should have asked about their winter hardiness. I loved the one I got in Wilmington (enough to spend $50 on it!) Hella hates it and thinks that, like some of the carices, it looks dead. It's bronzy pink, with some yellow in it. I think the cultivar is 'Maori Sunset'. I surrounded it with a gaudy ring of another plant Hella dislikes, a red hypoestes.

We came back with some other new things. The golden potato vine, *Solanum jasminoides* 'Aureum' looks like a promising trailing vine for containers, especially if the species name pans out in the scent of its white flowers. We'll see—and sniff. Then there's a new plectranthus, 'Athens Gem', said to be a sport of *Plectranthus amboinicus* that turned up in Georgia in Allan Armitage's garden. The leaves are pale yellow green with a large, irregular blotch of deep green in the center. I put it at the edge of a good-sized pot together with *Hakonechloa macra* 'Aureola'. Their colors are almost a precise match, but their textures contrast greatly. The hakon grass is delicate, and its blades so slender they dance in the breeze, while the plectranthus is sturdier. Our planting chores, of course, are hardly begun.

Linwood

In your last letter you wrote of your loquacious owls. Some live near us, somewhere. We have never seen them, but we hear them calling at night. And I must tell you that the other day, driving back on Mill Road from Home Depot, we saw an eagle. Mill is pure suburbia. The eagle was sitting on the roadside, and then, with a mighty rush, it lifted itself on its immense pens. We were aston- ished with surprise. Its appearance was so unexpected, its flight up- ward so sudden. It reminded me of the time late one winter when I was watching a great many robins and cardinals, too, feasting on the final, shriveled fruits of the 'Van Eseltine' crabapple outside my study window. There was a huge gray rush of movement, as a hawk swooped down, grabbed one of the songbirds in his talons, and then swooshed up as swiftly as he had come.

Tuesday, May 12

Our weather here made the national news last night and again this morning. Today is the thirteenth rainy day in a row. (There was even some rain last Thursday, which on the whole was nice.) We have broken the record set in 1894 of eleven consecutive days of the stuff. Radar on the weather channel right now shows the rare sight of rain clouds scudding along from east to west instead of west to east. A low pressure system sits off shore, drenching us almost without surcease. I just went out for lunch at a new restaurant adjacent to the bay. There were whitecaps, something we seldom see. Birds could barely fly against the wind, and I almost couldn't walk against it either. In the dining room, every time someone opened the door to the outside any paper place mats not anchored down with ketchup bottles or sugar bowls flew from tables. All over town streets were heavily littered with debris. (Where there were sycamores it looked like a hurricane had just passed through.)

It rained like fury all last night, and there was high wind. I woke up every hour from midnight on. It's still raining cats and dogs, and the trees are whipping around fiercely. I'm keeping an anxious eye on our hollow maple.

The sodden, soggy weather and absence of sunshine are starting to wear on my nerves. Here we've had a taste of the sort of gray, depressing weather friends in the Pacific Northwest complain about in winter. Bleak thoughts press their way in, but one good thing about the rain is that the large hostas have never been bigger. 'Sum and Substance' and *H. sieboldiana* 'Elegans' are absolutely immense. So is the slug population . . .

And speaking of 'Sum and Substance', did that turn out to be the one Martha brought you last month? If not, I can bring it down. Hella flies to Nashville Saturday to see her mother and attend the fortieth reunion of her nursing class at Vanderbilt. I drive to Durham the following Wednesday. A week after that (the 27th) Hella flies to Raleigh/Durham for five or six days before we come back to New Jersey together. Since this time I'm driving down instead of flying, I have room to bring plants along. Let me know about the hosta and anything else you might fancy from here.

Affectionately,
Allen

Wednesday, May 13, 1998

Dear Allen,

Shortly after my last letter to you my father died, and with him went the last remnants of my childhood. I watched him die slowly, from the brain first, and with each change I felt a terrible pain. I remember wondering what it would be like to live without my parents. Somehow even though I seldom had a conversation with him during the past few years, I felt he was there for me to talk to. And, unrealistically, I believed he understood. I honestly believe he heard more than he responded to. His eyes remained expressive even on the afternoon of my last visit to him.

He taught me more about gardening than anyone else. He loved the soil, and I remember his taking the neighborhood baseball field, our front yard, and turning it into loam. I also remember suffering the hatred of the children who thought it theirs when he plowed and planted it with crowder peas. Not only had we taken away their playground, we had not planted a lawn. After two years of crowders, he planted the best lawn on the street. One year Mother decided we would eliminate the wild onions from it. No, she didn't poison them, but dug out each and every one. He planted clover to keep the soil healthy and always told us he asked for seeds of the clover with the highest percentage of leaves in groups of four. I had a marvelous four-leaf clover collection. I pressed them in every book I read. He grew the best vegetables in the world, and Mother knew just how to cook them. We ate tiny butterbeans, the freshest corn on the cob, tiny "English" peas, okra, tomatoes that were warm from the sun and perfectly ripe. He also grew peanuts, and one of our fall rituals was a supper of boiled peanuts. We had black-eyed peas from the freezer on New Year's Day and believed each pea devoured represented good luck for the year. Until I left home at twenty-two, I had never tasted a commercially frozen vegetable.

He was stern and stubborn, but I will always remain grateful to him for giving me my values. He didn't use pesticides or herbicides but rotated his crops, growing crimson clover or buckwheat on the "resting" areas. He knew trees and shrubs and had an excellent sense of design. He understood the need for restraint in planting. He was a fine scholar and believed the life of the mind as important as the life of the body. He worked on his intellectual interests in the morning, gardened in the afternoon, and read again in the evening. It was he who cared for me when I was ill, cooked lunch for me when we were home together, and always went to the chamber concerts with me. He had a wonderful sense of humor that masked his basically sentimental nature.

Love,
Nancy

Friday, June 5, 1998

Dear Allen,

Almost a month has passed since I last wrote and much has happened, including your visit and Hella's. We have gone from spring to summer. Early in May the air was crisp and cool in the morning but warm by afternoon. Now it is warm when I get up at 6:00 A.M. and walk slowly down to the gate to get the paper. The air is no longer crisp but heavy and humid. Much of the moisture has gone from the soil. Trees take it up, so many of my favorite plants are going below ground to rest until fall or spring. The grass remains green but the earth feels hard, not springy as it was for the past six or seven months.

The dianthus walk was good this year. It remained in flower and fragrant through the entire month of May. We kept after it continuously, cutting away the old bloom stalks of each plant as it finished blooming so the border never looked ragged and unkempt. As always the garden changed from a fragrant delight of spice pinks to smelling of *Arum dioscoridis* and Chinese chestnut flowers. But that, too, has passed. Now it smells of summer—freshly mown lawns and *Magnolia grandiflora*.

The roses came and went. I believe they were more beautiful than ever this spring because my staff tied them up to the arches and onto the lath house better than ever before. They intertwined clematises with them. 'Mermaid' will continue to bloom against the west side of the garage. I know of no better rose for healthy foliage and beauty of form. Large, single, pale yellow flowers crowned with a circle of gold stamens will appear all summer. Well, now that I think of it, 'Dortmund' is a good competitor. It, too, is disease free, and has a beautiful single flower, this time in red, followed by the best hips on the property.

We are busy cutting back the garden now. Much to my amazement, as I think I mentioned in an earlier letter, I have concluded that *Helleborus foetidus* is a weed here. I don't believe in dogmatically excluding exotic plants from this continent, but I do know that this one needs watching. I remove cartloads each day from the border in the main garden as well as the woods. One reason for worry is that it appears now quite a distance from my original planting sites. Another is that it grows so thickly that nothing else can compete with it.

We continue our vigilance against the deer and rabbits. Last night after supper I saw a mother deer and her two fawns—I've named them Do, Re, and Mi—plus Peter and Molly cottontail, so I went out with my pepper spray. It is a little cooler now with about .15 inch of rain a day, just enough to wash off the spray. Perhaps it is time to invest in Tabasco sauce stock!

Mr. Huskins finished clearing off and laying gravel for our new shopping mall. We set our shallow cold frames in a grid pattern and for the first time in years have arranged the stock in a logical pattern. This means our visitors who arrive in new white tennis shoes may be able to leave in new white tennis shoes.

The month was interrupted in the middle by my trip to the West Coast. I went to Seattle to speak to the Northwest Horticultural Alliance and arrived a couple of days before my talk in hopes of re-setting my biological clock before I had to speak. I was surprised by how cold it was. I was not surprised by the beautiful gardens I saw. I finally gave up my dream of gardening in the Pacific Northwest when Craufurd and I moved to Montrose, but I find myself long-ing for those cool nights and days now that we are in the midst of summer. I visited Heronswood and, when invited to lunch, de-clined in order to spend every minute in the garden. What treasures Dan Hinkley has! And the garden is beautifully groomed. I felt no envy, though, as I watched Dan cope with each crisis, each group of visitors. I wondered whether he still gets on hands and knees in the garden accompanied only by bird songs. Linda Cochran's garden on Bainbridge Island near Seattle was beautiful too, planted with masses of color placed with an understanding of design and the needs of each plant. The most unusual place I visited on the island was the sculpture garden of George Little and David Lewis. It was unworldly. I wanted to go around and around it, for although it was relatively small, each bit of sculpture was placed carefully near a plant companion and each enhanced the other. To see it from one angle made me want to see it from another. I believe I liked best the columns with gentle drops of water. Wells-Medina nursery, in sub-urban Seattle, was a special treat. Although the nursery produces almost none of its plants—maybe none—Mr. Wells really cares about his stock. I have never seen a better-run, cleaner nursery. I saw no sick or hungry plants. I saw no weeds. And I saw many excited, sophisticated gardeners carrying away cartloads of plant treasures.

The visit to Portland was equally exciting but much shorter. There I saw one of the best gardens I have ever seen anywhere. The tranquility and beauty of the late Jane Platt's property will remain with me forever. She began with trees, then added shrubs and underplanted them with the best perennials. The trees were beautifully placed and she brought in marvelous rocks for walls and a rock garden. I wanted to stay there forever, but instead I returned home thinking my garden looked messy.

I went to a superb bookstore, Powell's, where I was delighted to see *The Inviting Garden* prominently displayed. It is one of your best books—the one I have been waiting for. You know better than anyone how to express what some of us may feel but can't find words for. What you have written makes it plain to all that gardening involves our souls, not just our bodies. Thank you, Allen, for giving up so much time in your garden to write it down for us.

Much love and more soon!
Nancy

Thursday, June 11, 1998

Dear Allen,

This was a most painful day. I knew this time was coming as I watched the enormous white oak in the circle garden die. Several years ago it lost a number of large branches in a storm and after that was never the same. Last summer the top was thrifty with only a few small leaves. As spring approached this year I saw no swelling buds and no leaves developed.

I had to face it with every visitor who came to the garden. Many people asked whether the tree was dead and most wanted to know why. I also want to know why. I want to know why any plant in my garden dies. First of all, I want to know whether it was my fault and then whether I might have prevented it. I refused to build a proper brick walk into the circle garden because I was afraid of damaging the roots of this oak. We planted shallowly, digging each hole carefully. White oaks are good neighbors, for their roots are neither invasive nor shallow.

This is the third white oak to die since we moved here in 1977, and another one died the year before we saw Montrose. I remember a discouraging visit from a botanist shortly after we came to Hillsborough. He predicted that all the white oaks would die within twenty years. How I wish he were wrong! I grieved over the slow death of our tree, but today was terrible in every way. The tree removers arrived early this morning with an enormous crane, a bucket truck, one large dump truck, and several pickup trucks. We also had, by chance, Mr. Huskins, who had just finished making the paths through the new garden and still had his Bob Cat here. One young man climbed to the top of the tree to tie ropes from it to the crane. They cut large branches and ground up the small limb wood. They carried the chippings to our leaf pile, and we will spread it on paths through the woods garden. We cut the medium-sized logs into firewood lengths, and Mr. Huskins carried the biggest pieces, which were truly enormous, to rest beside the remains of the *Magnolia acuminata* whose death you described so eloquently six years ago in the *New York Times*. We had hoped to salvage the bole for lumber, but it was too heavy for the crane.

Today all that is left is a trunk with a small *Hydrangea anomala* subsp. *petiolaris* up about ten feet. The shade-loving plants now have full sun, but tonight they also have a covering of sawdust. I won't move anything until I see which plants suffer. I will still have to answer the question, "What happened to the tree?" And each time it will be painful. The lawns nearby have deep ruts to remind me of the men and their heavy machines.

I can't think of a more wonderful tree than that oak, so I hope this will be a good year for acorns from the remaining oak in the rock garden. I won't grub out all of the young seedlings as they appear in late fall and next spring but will leave one to replace this magnificent tree, knowing that I will not enjoy its shade. I hope it will be as straight and beautiful as the one we grieve over tonight.

With love,
Nancy

Monday, June 15, 1998

Dear Nancy,

You have written me three times since my last letter to you. Before me are yours of the 5th and the 11th. I'll start with the latter and with the great white oak that just came down.

About ancient and venerable trees I'll tell you something I'd never whisper in public, for fear of being mistaken for some New Age enthusiast. When a tree like yours goes to earth, I turn Druid. I think you are also of that persuasion. I don't believe that plants are sentient, but consider the things your oak might testify to if it were a conscious being. It must have been at least a sapling when Cornwallis and his Redcoats camped in Hillsborough.

It's odd that a couple of months ago I was writing you about my maple tree and that now you write about your oak. But there's a difference. Your oak is dead, while my maple is terminally ill but still in leaf, following major surgery. It happened in mid-May, before I drove down to Carolina, so I never wrote you about it. The foreman of Big Pine's crew called one afternoon. They happened to be in the vicinity and could do the job right then if I wished. It took only a couple of hours. They first removed the top half of the big trunk that endangered our deck and greenhouse. It was a graceful operation to see. One of the men climbed high into the tree, chain saw in hand and lashed to another trunk with a rope. As he got ready to cut each big piece of trunk, he tied it with a rope fastened overhead, one end trailing down to the ground, where it was handled by two other workers. Kind of a pulley affair. When the log was cut, it would swing down almost gently to earth. The crew also thinned out the tops of the other three trunks. The men did a fine job. The deck is sunnier in late afternoon than before, but there's still a tree to see. It may live another five or six years.

Some months ago we parted company on winter, and now it seems that we are also of different minds about summer. It isn't my favorite season. Autumn earns that honor, as the one season in which we far outstrip the Brits in gardening possibilities. Summer runs a close second, however, probably in part for reasons of climate and geography. The Jersey Shore can be horribly hot and humid in July and August, but never for more than a couple of days at a time. Down your way, the summer air can sometimes be so still that trees can go hours without moving a leaf, but here there's almost always a breeze. (You touched on this topic earlier this year, as it pertained to our differing experiences of winter.) I can generally work in our summer garden in perfect comfort even at midday except on rare days of scorching temperatures, and then the deck is a cool and leafy retreat. It seldom stays hot after sundown, and we've never really felt the need of air-conditioning. But, come to think of it, I never much minded summer when I was growing up in Texas, either. It was scorching hot, but it was also the season of peaches, watermelon, and no school.

Some other differences between us likely figure in our divergent opinions about summer. We garden on entirely different scales, considering that you have—what, five acres of gardens out of sixty acres of real estate?—and that I have considerably less than an acre to tend. We both have help, of course. You now have a couple of people, plus Mr. Huskins (about whom you must tell me more one of these days). Here, Hella and I have the occasional student helper. But the work of maintenance that must go on at Montrose is virtually unceasing from late winter to the end of autumn. Here, from time to time there's something that almost approaches leisure. Our property is only 100 by 155 feet, including the house and the decks, but I do not long for anything larger.

We have come to similar conclusions about the invasiveness of *Helleborus foetidus*. I started about ten years ago with just one plant, probably from Montrose. In time I had fifteen or twenty, then sixty or seventy, all blooming and all dropping their seeds everywhere. I swear that at the end of the mild winter just past every last seed produced the previous year germinated. In March, Hella cut off almost every stalk before this year's crop of seeds could ripen, and I have just pulled up all the seedlings I could find. I haven't yet had a similar problem with *H. orientalis* (or, if you prefer, *H.* × *hybridus*), but I know the potential for trouble is there: in Hannah Withers's garden in Charlotte, Lenten roses sprout between every brick in her walkways.

You missed a real treat at Heronswood by not taking up Dan Hinkley's invitation to lunch. His culinary talents match his horticultural ones, but I can understand your desire to give over your whole visit to the garden. We've been to Heronswood twice. It's one of the best nurseries in the entire country, likewise a top-notch and inspiring garden. And we've also visited Wells-Medina a couple of times, although what I mainly remember is that it was selling gallon containers of our eastern pokeweed (labeled *Phytolacca americana*, with no common name) for $9.95. We also spent some time in Portland browsing in Powell's amazing offering of gardening books. We did not, however, make it to Jane Platt's garden, although she was still alive years ago when we attended the Perennial Plant Association meeting in Portland.

Still awaiting planting next to our deck are all the plant goodies from my two weeks in North Carolina. Here's the inventory of acquisitions. From Montrose: *Anthriscus sylvestris* 'Ravenswing' and *Cryptotaenia japonica* f. *atropurpurea* (whose names testify to their splendidly dark foliage); *Allium senescens*; *Brunnera macrophylla* 'Lang-trees'; *Campanula glomerata* 'Joan Elliott', *Dicentra eximia* 'Boothman's

Variety', and *Erysimum* 'Bowles Mauve' (all three champions of prolonged bloom); *Phlomis longifolia*; and *Salvia nipponica* 'Fuji Snow'.
From Big Bloomers Farm in Sanford: *Cuphea llavea* 'Georgia Scarlet';
diascia 'Blackthorne Apricot'; *Hibiscus acetosella* (red shield); *Gaura
lindheimeri* 'Siskiyou Pink'; *Lonicera japonica* (I bet that scares you, but
the cultivar is 'Aureoreticulata', a lovely variegated form that doesn't
carry on enough photosynthesis to be troublesome, or so I hope); a
small-leafed begonia that was labeled "lobelia," which can't be right;
a variegated saxifrage (bronze blotches on a chartreuse ground), labeled *Saxifraga umbrosa*, but more likely a cultivar of *S. stolonifera*; a
single gardenia, 'Kleim's Hardy' (or Klein's, as I see it both ways),
touted as being winterproof, but I had it before, lost it, and plan to
overwinter it with protection; hybrid penstemons 'Ruby' and 'Purple Passion'; several plants of dahlia 'Bishop of Llandaff', which I
saw in your garden last August and loved for its smoky dark foliage
and smoldering red flowers. From Home Depot just outside
Chapel Hill, a pot of agapanthus in full bloom that cost $9.93. (It
was labeled 'Peter Pan', but that can't be. Peter is a blue-flowered
dwarf; some of the several plants in my pot were white, others blue,
and their flowers sat atop five-foot stems. Incidentally, Home
Depot often has unusual plants at rock-bottom prices, even though
what will turn up there is impossible to predict.)

There were a lot of other things, too. I've listed only what I can
remember off the top of my head. We picked up five oval galvanized tubs from that hardware store near the inn in Hillsborough.
Hella filled them with the smaller plants acquired on our visit.
They all fit on the back seat of the car, and the larger ones went on
the floor. The flower heads of the agapanthus nodded and waved
in the rear view mirror, and all the way home we relished the delicious perfume of the gardenia, which was in full bloom. And our
plant-scavenging didn't end in North Carolina, either. There's a
very nice nursery on U.S. 13 a few miles west of Chincoteague—
called Thomas's, I think. There I got a gorgeous bugbane with incredibly dark leaves, *Cimicifuga ramosa* (or is it *racemosa*?) 'Hillside
Black Beauty' and *Tupistra chinensis*, about which I know nothing except that it looks interesting.

Tuesday, June 16

Now summer has really begun, even though we've not had a single
really hot day. The greenhouse is empty and tidied up. All the hanging baskets and other containers on the deck and elsewhere in the

garden have reached a certain fullness of either flower or foliage or both. (This morning, second and third cups of coffee in hand, I deadheaded all of the petunias.) All of the treasures from Montrose and other places are planted. If someone were to tell me I had to get rid of all but one of these, the choice would be easy—*Allium sene-scens!*—or, more accurately according to your label, *Allium senescens* subsp. *senescens*. I saw and admired it a whole lot at the end of last summer, but I didn't really know what I was looking at until I saw it again now, in full bloom as spring was ending and summer creeping in. Most alliums bloom briefly, their foliage often going dormant and getting ratty before their peak of flowering. This one obviously holds its own for months and months. In the circle garden above the dianthus walk it washes around in waves of lavender-pink, with fresh-looking blue-gray foliage, too. I came back with three little pots of it. Yesterday I divided them, getting fifteen plants, which I potted up until they establish themselves. Some have seeds forming. You said, I think, that they can also be raised from seed. When? How?

It just occurs to me that in the last paragraph an important principle of gardening popped up or announced itself very casually. "I didn't know what I was looking at until . . ." There are many ways of finishing sentences that lead off that way. "I didn't know what I was looking at [in my own garden] until I had visited garden X, Y, or Z." In your last letter you said that after you came back from Jane Platt's garden, your garden "looked messy." (I can't agree, of course.) Looking at other people's gardens, however, does enable one to see things in our own that we have missed. You came here once, years ago. Thinking of all the panoramic vistas and sweeps of color you lived with at Montrose, I was a bit fearful that you would find nothing here even worth mentioning, but almost as soon as you got out of your car you exclaimed, "Allen, it's wonderful. Everywhere you look there's garden!" That was true, I think, but I'd never recognized the everywhere-garden aspect of this old homeplace. You enunciated at the level of principle something we were striving for fairly unconsciously. Your remark hit me like an epiphany, a vision that has guided me ever since. I sometimes hear people saying that they've "been to Montrose." Perhaps, but how many times? How many times are necessary to understand what's going on there? I have no idea how many times I've been there. Somewhere between fifty and one hundred, anyway. On my first visit there was plenty of garden to see, but of course only a fraction of what there is today. I can remember a lot from that first visit—the cardiocrinums behind the billowing hedge of box next to the meadow, the oxypetalums at the corner of the pump house, the pots of cyclamen down in the woods. With every visit there was more to see. I never know what it will be each time I drive through those gates and start up the hill.

Something always stands out. On this visit, some individual plants caught my eye, like *Digitalis thapsi*. I loved the silky look of the flowers, also the way they hung on their stalks, on stems that swooped down slightly, then out, much like the flowers of a blue, tropical thunbergia now blooming in one of my hanging baskets. Some parts of the garden also linger in the mind, after a visit. This time it's the yellow and blue garden. This is the closest thing at Montrose to a true cottage garden, because of the great depth and profuse planting of the two borders. But the design of the space is formal—two rectangular borders that face one another symetrically, the central molasses pot that serves as a focal point, the axis that lines up with the urn in the aster garden. Never before have I fully realized how perfectly geometrical are all of the gardens that combine to make up Montrose. I wonder: did you have this geometry in mind from the beginning, or was it something more intuitive, not something you planned and did, but something that laid hold of you and asked to realize itself, to come into being?

Back to the blue and yellow garden. Late May must be its absolute height, yes? The virtual hedges of brilliant gold and yellow achilleas are magnificent, especially with yellow verbascums steepling up through them. Love-in-a-mist is really splendid at this time, when out of their lacy ruffs both whirligig flowers and armored-looking seedpod puffs are in evidence. Larkspur? They remind me that I have forgotten larkspur far too long, and that no garden is fully a garden without them. Then, of course, what makes the blue and yellow garden finally a triumph is that it is not dogmatically restricted to those two colors. Red and yellow kniphofias and other wanderers into other parts of the spectrum are allowed to put in their word.

The Inviting Garden was reviewed yesterday in the *Philadelphia Inquirer*. It was a good review, though not, of course, as magnificent and generous as Michael Pollan's in the *New York Times* two weeks ago.

Love,
Allen

Friday, June 19, 1998

Dear Nancy,

Yesterday I called to give you the jist of it, but think I babbled idiotically. Here's the story.

Hella usually has NPR on all day long, but yesterday she drove up to Wall to take some belated birthday presents to Jennifer, Paul and Debbie's youngest. Just before 1:00 P.M. I drove up to our little shopping center to return a videotape, listening en route to Terry Gross's "Fresh Air," the segment in which Maureen Corrigan reviews a book or two. It would be a magnificent understatement to say my ears perked up when I heard my name mentioned as Corrigan started saying utterly delightful things about *The Inviting Garden.* She called it "gorgeous" and said that Cynthia Woodyard's photos were "luscious." I can't remember all that she said, but I'm getting a tape of the segment through the college from NPR, though it will take a week or two. This follows on the news yesterday that Holt has sold 5,500 copies in a month, has only 500 left in the warehouse, and has gone back for a second printing.

Hella didn't hear the review. My next-door neighbor Ed Plantan usually listens to "Fresh Air" while working in his basement shop, but yesterday he decided to mow his lawn instead. My agent didn't hear it, nor my brothers, nor Martha, nor you. The husband of someone who used to work with Hella did call from Pennsylvania with congratulations. I alerted Cynthia in Oregon. She managed to catch "Fresh Air" that evening when it was broadcast on the West Coast. She called this morning and confirmed my "gorgeous" and her "luscious."

We had a little unpleasantness this morning. A dove has built a nest up in the kiwi-vine-covered rafters of the pergola above the deck. This morning while Hella was reading the paper and having coffee, the singlet dove chick fell to the floor of the deck. Its mother or maybe father flew down and started feeding it. It tried to fly but only fluttered. Then its mother (or father) flew away, and the chick hopped off the deck to the lawn. There were cats around, so Hella shooed the baby bird into the greenhouse. I went upstairs to work at the computer, looked out a minute later and saw the semiferal gray tabby that haunts the neighborhood stalking through the kiwi vines on the pergola toward the dove's nest. I shouted and the cat scurried to the ground and turned tail. Then the chick's parent returned and sat on a rafter. I picked up the baby bird and deposited it gently on the deck, then retreated to the greenhouse to see what would happen. After a while the mother or whatever flew down to the deck and fed its offspring, then suddenly flew off in obvious alarm. There was a blur of something ginger rushing up the steps of the deck—the yellow tabby, even wilder than the gray one, that often prowls on our premises. I flew out of the greenhouse, shouting curses and frightening the cat off into the bushes. Then I turned around to see if the little bird was okay, my legs spread apart. Before I could even realize what was happening, the ginger cat swooshed through my legs and without a pause caught the bird in its mouth and vanished into the shrubbery. Hella was really shaken. She wants the peaceable kingdom to be realized on this earth, wants animals of different kinds to live in harmony, wants carnivores and omnivores to switch to vegetarianism.

I just wish these two tabbies would leave baby doves alone and get on with the task I have assigned them, ridding us of the chipmunks that have tunneled everywhere in the garden.

Next week we fly to Martha's Vineyard for the opening of the Polly Hill Arboretum. I'm giving the keynote address, "Gardening Over Time." It deals with why we need institutions to preserve some worthwhile achievements of individual persons.

Love,
Allen

Friday, June 19, 1998

Dear Allen,

All day yesterday I thought of your call and what wonderful news you had. I cannot imagine listening to the radio and all of a sudden hearing your name, followed by praise for your enchanting book. I am not a bit surprised that it is already time for a second printing. I am truly happy for you. Politicians and other notorious persons must be accustomed to hearing their names whenever they turn on radios or television, but it seldom happens to really nice people who have done really worthwhile things.

The calendar may dispute this, but believe me summer is here. It arrived in mid-May while I was in the Pacific Northwest. You had a taste of it when you were here in late May. The weather forecast is for heat—every day the high will be in the mid-90s. We have about a 20 percent chance of a thundershower each day, but that doesn't mean a 100 percent chance in five days. It most likely means we will not get a drop. It is terribly dry here. The established garden looks fine, but as you know, we are planting the final third of the sunny kitchen garden area, so the newly planted areas must be watered. We use the cheapest little plastic rings and low pressure. We move the rings every fifteen minutes or so and that way can water deeply about once a week.

I can't escape the death of the oak. We spread the chippings on the woodland paths, and that acrid smell permeates the garden. I thought this morning as I was washing dishes that the last time a major tree died in the garden my mother died. This time the tree and my father died within a few weeks of each other. I saw my parents suffer shortly before they died, but the trees gave fewer indications that they were in trouble. Two years before the end the oak had fewer and smaller leaves. It dropped enormous branches in minor storms. Perhaps if I had been more perceptive I would have grieved during its dying process as I did with my parents.

We have reached the cutting-back period in the summer garden. Many plants have delivered their brief show of flowers, and we are left for the remainder of the summer with foliage. The longer I garden, the less I focus on flowers. We sawed out the tough, woody stems of yuccas that bloomed and find many pups ready to grow. *Penstemon digitalis* 'Husker's Red' has grown new rosettes of bronze leaves.

I will continue this letter another time but want to get my piece on cardiocrinums off to you for the next issue of *Homeground*.

Love to you and Hella,
Nancy

Summer

Sunday, June 21, 1998

Dear Allen,

Now it is officially summer, and I already wonder how much longer I can stand it. I get up early and wish that the night's low could be the day's high. There's a min/max thermometer in my bedroom, so I have a reminder of what I survived the day before and a suggestion of how it will feel when I open the front door.

High heat and still, muggy air aren't the only unpleasant features of our summer here. There are also abundant insect enemies. We have mosquitoes, deer flies, gnats, and ticks, so before I go into the garden to work, I cover myself with insect repellent—sticky insect repellent. I have tried many herbal remedies but never found anything to work unless it contains DEET. I also put flowers of sulphur about my ankles and at the top of my shoes. Did you have chiggers in Texas? Well, we have them in North Carolina, and I dare not go into the woods without this deterrent. I never feel clean again until night, when I can finally wash everything off. I know this must make my climate seem miserable to those who haven't lived in it. I don't get used to it, but I can stand it, partly because I am living in the future. Yesterday I found *Cyclamen hederifolium* blooming in the woods, and *Scilla autumnalis* has bloomed almost all month. I know summer will end, and I believe the plants and I will survive.

Monday, June 22

More about summer. You say you can't stand air-conditioning. It is the only way I can bear living in this climate, but I miss waking up to the sounds of the birds. I hear them in the early morning when I step outside, but during the heat of the day, which lasts until after dark, they are silent. Last night it was 90° when I went in at 6:00, so I heard no songs; the silence was oppressive. Occasionally I hear the frantic chirping of birds defending their young from snakes, cats, or other birds. I sympathize with Hella's grief over the young dove. I remember when Craufurd and I dragged out a hose and tried to drive a black snake out of a bird's nest with water under pressure. It didn't work. I get angry with weather forecasters who declare that we are lucky to have a rain-free weekend when we haven't had a decent rain all month. Our rains this month have added up to less than one inch, and we have thus far had thirteen days with temperatures above 90°. The forecast is for higher temperatures and decreasing chances of rain. But despite the heat and lack of rainfall, I can hardly wait to get into the garden each morning. There is always something new and exciting to see. Right now it's lilies I grew from seed obtained many years ago from the Lily Society. I think the cross was made in Russia, and one of the parents was *Lilium regale*. These lilies have large white flowers tinged with pink and dark purple on the outside of each widely flared petal (tepal?). The blossoms appear on stalks eight feet high and have incredibly beautiful yellow throats. Speaking of tepal, have you noticed that the word is just "petal" with the "p" and "t" transposed? I realize it avoids the problem of distinguishing sepals from petals but am not comfortable with it.

More insect enemies: Japanese beetles are back, so I haven't seen a perfect flower on *Abelmoschus manihot*, and I won't see another perfect rose for a month or so. We don't have anything like the huge infestation of beetles we had when we moved here twenty-one years ago. The school next door put out milky spore, and I believe we have profited from it. I will not spray with Sevin or anything like that, so I just wait them out.

Your letter of June 15 was great. Thank you for your thoughts about the tree. I miss it terribly and though I hesitated to predict the fate of the enormous number of plants that depended on it for their comfort, I can see some that are suffering.

In your observations comparing your garden and mine — and also your summers and mine — you are on the mark about two items. First, the gardens at Montrose are so extensive that there's no such thing as leisure, certainly not in summer. Second, helping hands are absolutely essential.

We are trying to control close to twenty acres. Only part of this is intensely gardened, but Craufurd mows the fields nearly as often as he does the lawns near the house. In the summer, our focus changes. I get to the woods only on good days. The sunny gardens need constant maintenance, so we weed and plant there as long as we can stand it in the morning. I worry about our staying out in the heat, so in the afternoon our work shifts to shadier locations or we retreat to the old kitchen (now the potting room), where with a fan on and the east-west breeze through the doors and windows, we pot plants or stick cuttings while listening to classical music. (These are peaceful moments.)

I couldn't maintain this garden alone, so I am happy with the support and help I get from my staff, and also, even more importantly, from Craufurd. He keeps everything on track. He is an excellent critic, and though we have intense discussions about new projects, I always listen to him and more often than not agree with him. In some matters our interests diverge. He doesn't want to know the common or scientific names of plants, much less cultivar names. I don't think he could tolerate one of the tours I give visitors. But he does want the paths to be free from obstructions and the gardens to be beautifully maintained.

You asked about the geometry of the gardens. That was here when we came. I believe the Grahams laid out the kitchen garden in squares, about 60 by 60 feet. Raised grass paths connected and separated one from another. I have honored that layout, changing only the new section (roughly one-third of the total). The paths here are also straight, but they are extensions of existing paths. The broad path through the blue and yellow garden now leads through the old aster border and the new garden to the fence edge. And the narrow path, interrupted only by the lath house, extends from the barnyard, through the new garden to a tall urn. It's a recent acquisition, high Victorian, and we call it the Albert Memorial.

I appreciate your enthusiasm for the blue and yellow garden as you saw it last month. I like its restraint. It is an incredibly hot part of the garden because it is the lowest section, but it looks the coolest. When we designed it, we vowed not to give in to plants whose flowers contained red pigment. We quickly changed our minds. In the first place, our original design, using only true blue and true yellow, was impossible, because there are even fewer true blue flowers than true yellow ones. In the second place, the color scheme was a little dull.

You asked me to tell you more about Mr. Huskins not long ago. He lives north of Hillsborough and spent much of his life building highways for the Nello Teer Company. I believe his greatest challenge and accomplishment was building the West Virginia Turnpike. Now that he has retired, he comes from time to time with his Bob Cat to help us with projects that we can't manage alone. Craufurd and I would need several years to haul away the refuse from the dump in the woods.

My childhood summers were similar to yours. Air-conditioning didn't exist, so we played in the mud or walked barefooted through the rivers that ran in the curbsides after rains. We had swings, the best with knots at the bottom, on which we stood. We made ice cream, cooled watermelons in the spring at the back of our property, and slept with our windows open and the fan on. I played the piano until I heard doors slamming and people mumbling about being driven crazy by the noise. I loved playing the piano. It was my escape and my way to express those emotions that I could never put into words.

Enough for now. It is 8:30 and already hot, and I must get into the garden at least for a little while.

Love,
Nancy

Tuesday, June 23, 1998

Dear Nancy,

Thanks for your letter of last Friday, also the piece for *Homeground* on your cardiocrinums. The first paragraph, about the anticipation, hope, disappointment, and fulfillment in the lives of gardeners is a good frame for the rest of the piece. I know readers will enjoy it, also the drawing Martha made of your "gigantic lilies" last month. No reader, however, will have as much pleasure as I have. As you wrote, its flowering in May 1985 coincided with my first visit—the first of many—to Montrose in 1985, as it just coincided with my latest visit last month. I edited the piece lightly. I didn't touch a word of yours but pruned the quotation from Gertrude Jekyll a bit.

It was boiling hot here last Saturday, but since then foggy mornings and overcast afternoons have kept the temperature in the comfortable 80s. Everything is growing like crazy, especially the hundreds (no exaggeration whatsoever!) of plants in containers. Lantanas are very strange, perfectly enormous shrubs already. The two weeks of daily, often heavy, rain the first part of May leached away all of the growth retardant.

Wednesday, June 24, 1998

Lots of mail today! Joanne Ferguson sent a seven-page, single-spaced account of her day in Chapel Hill last week as an extra in Robin Williams's new movie about Patch Adams. She and hundreds of other people were in a scene taking place in 1975 at Adams's graduation from med school. Joanne is in the audience, right up front. She gets to see Robin Williams moon the onlookers several times. Your good letter also came, so I had ten pages of dense stuff to edify and occupy me. I put everything in a big envelope and read

Linwood

it all over lunch at a nearby deli, en route to do errands to get ready for Martha's Vineyard. Among other things, I had to go by the optometrist and get two pairs of glasses I had slept on bent back into shape.

Now to your letter . . .

You asked did we "have chiggers in Texas"? In Texas, we had everything nasty you could think of! Scorpions, occasionally a centipede, and, farther west than Dallas, vinegarroons (large, ugly whip scorpions that let loose a harsh vinegarlike smell when they're riled); nineteen kinds of stinging wasps; red ants that stung hard and then left knots in lymph nodes in armpits; stinging nettle and bull nettle; copperheads, rattlers, and cottonmouth moccasins; black widow spiders, probably brown recluses, though no one knew about them. (In my mother's family there was a legendary Aunt Pearl, who was bitten in the rump by a black widow while sitting on the privy. She "swole up bigger than a barn by that afternoon and never got back to the thin little self she had been up till she was bit.") Fire ants came along much later. Besides all these varmints, we had regular dust storms and plagues of grasshoppers and crickets from time to time. Texas weather is a story all to itself, but, yes, we had chiggers. Mother also had me dust my body with sulphur every morning, but I still had chigger bites, even after swallowing sulphur tablets, which have disgusting side effects.

We also had sticker burs.

Romantic nature poetry never impressed me very much. Nature, in Texas, wasn't very friendly and certainly not maternal.

I am told that there are also chiggers in New Jersey. They're more likely to live in trees than in lawns, however, and they are particularly partial to certain plants, like the so-called sweet fern, which isn't a fern at all but a shrub, *Comptonia peregrina*. There's a lot of it in the nearby Pine Barrens. It loves poor, dry soil. The leaves have an astringent, spicy scent if crushed, and on hot, still summer days no crushing is needed. The scent reminds me, oddly, of honey and Mentholatum.

I do not want to leave you with the impression that Texas is paradise lost, New Jersey paradise found (although the latter is infinitely better than its reputation with those who have driven its Turnpike and decided that anyone who gardens here must do so in the shadow of an oil refinery tank). Southern New Jersey has some flying beasts, a succession of flies in summer. Strawberry flies (little triangular horrors, so named because they appear as strawberries ripen) come first, followed by greenheads, big flies with jade eyes. Greenheads bite fiercely and hard, usually on the back of an exposed leg, often leaving a little rivulet of blood. Our mosquitoes are also world-class.

Tepals? Never touch them! I leave it to botanists to worry about whether or not something is a petal or a sepal. For gardeners, I think they can all be called petals, as can the ray flowers of a daisy. We have to borrow a lot of terminology from botanists, but then I suspect that "petal" is in the public domain, that the word was used in English before modern botany got going. With dogwoods, poinsettias, and some other things, I alternate between speaking of their bracts and of their petals. For gardeners it's not essential to know whether something is a true petal or a modified leaf instead. When teaching horticulture, I do explain about the disk flowers and the ray flowers of daisies, but I don't get pedantic over it. By the way, my best times teaching horticulture were when the college let me team teach with my botanist friend, Sandy Bierbrauer. We sometimes argued with one another to show that gardening and botany both have their languages, with some overlap but also differences. We had to stop team teaching (too expensive, said our deans). We each still teach horticulture, I more often than she, and we drop in occasionally on each other's classes to continue our little disagreements.

I just remembered something. We didn't have Japanese beetles in Texas. We did have them, lots of them, in Virginia, in the first garden Hella and I made. They were very abundant here when we moved from upstate New York. I haven't seen one in years. We also had lots of gypsy moths. They've disappeared—or at least retreated for a while.

Must close and pack. Back Monday afternoon.

Best,
Allen

P.S. A friend of Martha's told her she had problems germinating *Zinnia peruviana*. I said I had plenty of seed that germinated well and would send them to her friend. Then I realized that the zinnias that had come up okay were *Z. angustifolia*. With *Z. peruviana*—seeds from Montrose, kept in fridge over winter—I got about .01 percent germination. Hmm.

Friday, June 26, 1998

Dear Allen,

We are off to England for a week.

I forgot one thing I wanted to include in my answer to your letter of the 15th. Allen, I will never forget my first visit to your garden. I knew you didn't really want me to come but I, being also a Capricorn, had made up my mind to see it. After all I had read your columns in the *Wall Street Journal* and many magazines, plus your first gardening book. You wrote about your experiences, your successes and failures, and your love of all the good things about gardening. I read that and felt we had a common approach to plants, gardens, and nature. I had to see the soil you were digging, feel the wind and smell the air. I remember not being able to see all of your garden at a glance. I wondered what lay around each corner and beyond each shrub. Didn't it take us a couple of hours to see the whole thing and talk about every single plant? I wanted to see it every week for a year to know what surprises lay beneath your soil and how the light changed with the seasons. And I remember coming back to Montrose and thinking my garden needed work!

Today the temperature reached 96°, and I couldn't work past noon. I went down to see the newly planted urn and noticed that there were none of the bees that normally swarm all over the flowers of *Hypericum frondosum*. It hasn't happened yet, but soon the cicadas will begin their racket. I don't mind it, but it is a summer sound. The tree frogs have already begun to sing, mostly in the early morning or evening. The lightning bugs are back. I love to see them when I go out late at night to bring in the last of our cats.

I look forward to hearing about your trip. I hope it was cool. I'm sure Polly Hill's garden is one of the best.

Love to Hella, too,
Nancy

Thursday, July 2, 1998

Dear Nancy,

Congratulations on being able to get away on short notice to England for a week!

I have much to write you, starting of course with Polly Hill and her arboretum. I'm sending along a half-hour videotape based on footage CBS shot for an episode about Polly that Sunday Morning aired a year or two ago.

You must know the rudiments of her story, how she inherited the old sheep farm of sixty plus acres her parents bought on Martha's Vineyard in the 1920s. When she assumed responsibility for the property, she felt strongly that the woody plants being grown on the island were extremely uninteresting. She made it her business, at age fifty, to improve this state of affairs. She took courses in plant-related subjects at Longwood and the University of Delaware and began planting her personal arboretum—from seed, not cuttings or somewhat established plants. It was her idea that seed-grown populations would have sufficient genetic variation that while some plants might not get through the Vineyard's winters, others might. Her idea was correct, and the evidence is everywhere visible on her farm, where cultivars of *Camellia* and *Magnolia grandiflora* and *M. macrophylla* thrive and blossom well beyond their supposed range of winter-hardiness. Polly grew many different kinds of woody plants, but specialized in rhododendrons (including azaleas), hollies, magnolias, Asian dogwoods, and stewartias.

She introduced over eighty cultivars, although she is best known for her North Tisbury azaleas, mostly named for members of her family—'Joseph Hill', 'Jeff Hill', 'Susannah', and so on. These are small-leafed, rather evergreen, late-blooming, mostly low and spreading plants. They are also the first azaleas I've really cottoned to for their beauty and toughness.

The farm is beautiful, in its New England way—stone walls, weathered, unpainted buildings, meadows and woodlands. It all nestles into the rural landscape around the village of West Tisbury.

Polly is 91. Her husband Julian (one of the inventors of nylon, I think) died a couple of years ago. Her grown children are not interested in preserving the property intact, nor able to if they wanted to. The farm is a precious resource if looked at in one way, but real estate developers see it as sixty acres just waiting to be divided into five-acre residential plots for $2M+ mini-mansionettes or faux-chateaux. You and Craufurd understand the issues better than almost anyone. You have your own sixty acres and your own desire that Montrose remain intact after your own years of caring for it.

The Polly Hill story has a happy ending, even a deus ex machina, in the form of Dr. David Smith. He trained as a physician, but has never practiced, nor had to, thanks to his developing a vaccine against infantile meningitis right after med school. He lives on the Vineyard and devotes much of his energy to Good Works of Rescue, including getting a lot of undeveloped island land into the hands of various conservation groups, such as the Nature Conservancy. David Smith purchased Polly's land and outbuildings and established a foundation to preserve the arboretum.

The official opening of the Polly Hill Arboretum was Saturday, June 27. I was the keynote speaker.

I thought I was to be one speaker among many, and thus planned to speak ex tempore only about twenty minutes. Then when we got to the Vineyard and I saw the program, I discovered I was the sole speaker. I ended up talking for twenty minutes, then reading part of the chapter on becoming a gardener from *The Inviting Garden*. The audience was large and terrifying, as it contained representatives from umpteen other American arboreta. The talk seemed to go over well. Polly said she loved it, and that was the important thing.

We were treated royally during our stay, and put up in a hotel in Edgartown overlooking the harbor and Chappaquidick across the way. Like most people who visit Martha's Vineyard, we decided we'd love to live there—or summer there. There's not a single traffic light on the island, and people drive with consideration for others. The brutal fact is that we can't afford to live there, so we'll be content with the occasional visit, hoping that Polly will be around for many more years to come. One of the great thrills of life is to be chauffeured by her, lickety-split, around her farm on her electric golf cart!

On another matter, yesterday I got a phone call from a television producer in New York who had read *The Inviting Garden* after hearing Maureen Corrigan's review on NPR's "Fresh Air." For the Odyssey channel, he hopes to develop a series on gardening that would emphasize its spiritual dimensions. He'd like possibly to come here to talk about this project. It's an interesting idea. In my Methodist childhood and youth, I heard a lot of talk about stewardship, but didn't see that it was practiced very much. Gardeners, however, practice it all the time. Our gardens are not our possessions. Instead, we are entrusted with a bit of land and a span of time in which to improve it in order to pass it on to the next generation.

You report no bees on your hypericum. I fear that's a very bad thing, and of wider import than a mere Hillsborough phenomenon. Ed Plantan mentioned about a month ago not having seen a single honeybee, not even on the clover in his lawn. I have kept watch here, and not seen any either, nor could I find any at Polly Hill's last weekend. Plenty of bumblebees everywhere, but no honeybees.

And, on a less ominous note in re bees, my friend Ed Brightly, the super carpenter who built my greenhouse and much else that's good on these premises, pets bumblebees. Just rubs their backs, an attention they seem to enjoy. I think that I'd get stung if I tried it. They would smell my anxiety.

Love,
Allen

Friday, July 10, 1998

Dear Allen,

What a delight to find the tape of "Polly Hill and Her Arboretum" plus a good letter from you when we returned home from England yesterday. Weather shock is what I felt. I stepped off the plane at Raleigh-Durham Airport—oops, Raleigh-Durham International Airport—and wondered why no one had opened a window to let in fresh, cool air. We had perfect weather in England, never even reaching 70° and with a cool breeze. I was comfortable in a sweater and jacket the entire time, and we had only about four drops of rain. Unfortunately we had only four drops of rain here, too, and temperatures hovering around 90° the whole time. The garden looks wilted and tired already, and I constantly think of how much longer summer will be with us.

Craufurd and I went to get a break from the heat and to see several people closely related to members of the Bloomsbury Group. I had no plans to visit nurseries, so on the first day there we bought *The Good Garden Guide 1998*. We expected it to be similar to *The Good Food Guide*, a valuable source of information about restaurants. The garden reference guide gives two stars to its best gardens, so I found one near London for our only unplanned day. We took a boat on the Thames to Chiswick and quickly walked to Chiswick House. It is a strange but grand house built in the eighteenth century by Lord Burlington to house his extraordinary art collection. William Kent designed the gardens to complement the house. The guide book describes them as "full of splendid vistas, avenues and changes of contour" and says of the grounds that they were "planned as a microcosm of garden art." It continues: "Drawings of the time show the degree of perfection the English lawn had reached even in the early eighteenth century. The Victorian garden with parterres is now filled with technicolour bedding plants in front of the handsome conservatory."

I was curious and expected something quite overwhelming and splendid. The grounds are now a public park, and we saw many people and dogs playing games of various sorts on the lawns. There was litter everywhere. We had great difficulty finding the Victorian garden. The house and grounds were close to the river. We walked to them quickly, but I couldn't see a conservatory or garden of any kind. We finally saw a sign for the Information Center, and followed handmade arrows to what looked like an abandoned nursery.

There were empty cold frames, greenhouses with broken glass, and no evidence of a gardener. Finally we came upon a trailerlike building and found inside a woman sitting in a room heated to about 80°. We asked for directions to the garden, and she said it had been too wet to plant but that what they had was in front of the conservatory. There were red geraniums alternating with dusty miller, a few begonias, and I can't remember what else. The garden was planted in a stiff, formal way and was about twice the size of our purple and orange border. Someone had vandalized the beautiful conservatory, leaving many broken panes. I felt sad about it, for I believe it must have been at one time a spectacular garden.

That was the only disappointment in the trip. Our friend, Tony Bradshaw, planned the rest of it. We had a lovely visit to Charleston, the house where Vanessa Bell and Duncan Grant lived, painted, and gardened. The splendid garden is small, slightly overgrown, and filled with color. The design is formal, with straight paths, but the plantings are delightfully ebullient. Against the wall we saw cherry trees still bearing fruit and raspberry canes laden with fruit. There were touches of whimsy, such as the partial torso with a hydrangea growing in the top. There were no flamingos or anything approaching the current fashion for whimsy in this country. Is this the time to state that I think flamingos are tacky? I mean, really tacky! If one wants underwear pink in the garden, there are always hibiscus and cannas. I must report that Craufurd's first reaction to my little water feature was that it was the same as putting a flamingo in the garden. For a while we called it the Flamingo Pool, but he has since changed his mind.

We went to Oxford to see Robert Reedman, who has one of the few complete collections of the hand-printed books of the Hogarth Press. He seemed happy to show and tell, and we were delighted to look and listen. He had a lovely, tiny garden with most plants in pots but with wonderful artifacts lying around. We wandered in several of the college gardens during the afternoon. The beds are immaculate and filled with perfectly grown plants, not a spent flower to be seen. Roses bloomed with their full, intense coloring, the way they will for us only when our nights cool off in fall. They were trained against ancient walls in the garden or against the buildings. The British have mastered gardening as an art for their climate. Americans invariably fail when they try to copy it. We don't have ancient walls. We don't have cool nights in summer. Nor do we, especially in North Carolina, have that northern light that I have seen only in northern New England and Canada. But I do believe we are making progress. Many of us have accepted our restrictions and are working within them to express our taste in form, texture, and color, with plants that like what we have.

We went to Cambridge a few days later to visit Dadie Rylands in his rooms. He is delightful, ninety-six, but with a sharp mind. He entertained us in his lovely sitting room and told us of the luncheon party when he entertained Virginia Woolf, who had come to Cambridge to give a lecture. He showed us the table where they dined, told us that Leonard Woolf, Julian Bell, and Morgan Foster were also there, and pointed out where Virginia sat. She wrote a description of the feast in *A Room of One's Own*. We saw room decorations by Carrington and a lovely painting by Duncan Grant.

Several days after that we visited Frances Partridge, who is now ninety-eight and also very bright. She remembered visits from my father and later my father and mother. She even remembered the other people who stayed at Ham Spray House when he was there and that my father's favorite book was *King Lear*. Paintings by Duncan Grant and Carrington hung on the walls, and a charming mosaic by Boris Anrep covered the fireplace opening.

We brought home a tea set designed by Duncan Grant. We also brought a drawing by him of Roger Fry, a faceless painting of Helen Anrep in the garden at Charleston, and four paintings of Adam and Eve. The Adam and Eve series is most exciting. The first one shows Adam just after God created him and set him on earth. The second has Eve coming from his rib. The third is a tree with a snake that has a human head, Adam about to bite into the apple, and Eve encouraging him to do so. The fourth shows an angel or God (not sure which) driving them out of the garden. We are especially interested in the way members of the Bloomsbury Group interpreted this story. It often appears in their paintings and writings.

We went to galleries and saw an excellent Chagall exhibition with a superb tape and headset to explain it. Now I understand a little better the floating people and animals.

I came home to the most delightful discovery. I left a list of work about two pages long, and my staff had done everything on the list except "make it rain." They edged all the beds, cut back plants that had finished blooming, and planted more coleus. They finished spreading the chips through the metasequoia garden and made a little path through the lath house. I should go away more often now that I have such dependable people! The kitties were happy to see us and have forgiven us completely.

But to your good letters—

I never imagined that Texas could be paradise, but I believe I might think it was if I lived and gardened there. I hear, incidentally, that Texas now has Japanese beetles.

I don't know why your Montrose seeds of *Zinnia peruviana* gave such poor germination. I remember once hearing Klaus Jellito, the German seed wholesaler, say facetiously that it was always the fault of the producer, so mea culpa. We can't get good germination from *Ceratotheca triloba* this year. I hate to be without it. It is like having foxgloves bloom all summer.

I am still on London time and have been up since 4:30, so now that it is 8:30 I feel ready for lunch. I will stop here and continue in a day or so.

Love,
Nancy

Monday, July 13, 1998

Dear Allen,

This is but a continuation of my last letter now that I am back on North Carolina time. I have readjusted to my garden and can enjoy the few areas that look pretty good and many flowers and leaves that still look happy despite this desertlike summer.

Polly Hill must be amazing. She certainly didn't waste her life. The older I get, the more important I believe trees are. Perhaps it is that I have seen some of our oldest and most beautiful ones die in the twenty-one years we have lived at Montrose. They provide us with so much and demand so little—careful planting in an appropriate site, attention for their first few years, and that's about it. We receive blessed shade, and beauty of form, leaf, bark, and sometimes flower. They give us the necessary leaves to make the mulch for the rest of the garden. We don't have to cut them down in the fall, or divide or reset them after three years. Most grow happily without extra water or fertilizer.

David Smith also sounds like a dream come true. I assume he has put conservation easements on the property. Will the arboretum be open to the public regularly, or just by appointment? I am especially interested because of our concerns for the future of Montrose. We have no models to help guide us. On Wednesday of this week we will meet with the staff of the Triangle Land Conservancy to discuss setting up some sort of arrangement. Eventually we will probably give them conservation easements for most of the land. We worry about the rest of it. I would love any advice.

You are absolutely right that we are the stewards of the land. I happen to believe we have an obligation to leave it in at least as good a condition as we found it. My father never left any rental property without better soil than we found when we moved onto it. That is why I feel so hostile to most developers. As for gardens themselves, that is the most difficult stewardship of all. Gardens must consist of living things, and as with all living things, they change imperceptibly day by day, noticeably from year to year, but dramatically from decade to decade.

I must correct the misunderstanding about our honeybees. We have bees, but they vanish during the heat of the day. They nest in hollows in our junipers. Shavings from these trees—mistakenly called cedar shavings—are a well-known miticide, so I believe that is how ours have survived. You are right that the general disappearance of honeybees is a distressing ecological omen.

I thought of you and Michael Pollan's perceptive review of *The Inviting Garden* when I saw Philip Sidney's portrait in London, so here's a postcard of him to put up on your mirror to remind you that Pollan compared your defense of gardening to Sidney's defense of poetry. I also suspect that you would like seeds of *Digitalis thapsi* so those collected today are enclosed.

Craufurd and I are stunned by the disappearance and probable murder of Irene Silverman. She was our landlady in Manhattan in the 1970s, long before we met you or found Montrose. We rented an apartment on the ground floor of 20 East 65th Street. It was a grand house, and we loved the apartment. It was quiet and centrally located, and the Silvermans were very nice to us. I believe Mrs. Silverman liked Craufurd at first because of his Canadian accent. I especially remember a delightful evening with them that began and ended with champagne but also included Godiva chocolates. Craufurd was with the Ford Foundation at the time. He was unwilling to give up a tenured professorship, and I was unwilling to give up a garden, so we compromised with this apartment. I spent one winter in it with him and during the remainder of the nearly ten years he was there he commuted every week. He was home just long enough to do the mowing in the summer. I had one weekend a month in New York, which was great — just long enough to see the exhibits and plays and hear the music we both enjoy.

Last Saturday I conducted a tour through the garden. My guests were friends who had last visited here in September. It was a disaster. My friend kept saying, "But this isn't the same garden at all. Why doesn't it look the way it did in September a year ago?" I tried to explain that the image of the garden last September is obviously frozen in her memory, and that gardens look different at different seasons. I'm not sure I ever got through to her. It is a major problem with nongardeners. They don't understand that plants just don't perform at their peak all year long. Perhaps you may remember my telling you of the visitor who was disappointed at not finding roses in February.

Love,
Nancy

Sunday, July 12, 1998

Dear Nancy,

We were visited last Wednesday first by terror, then by delight.

The terror came shortly after I picked Hella up from work in Ocean City. A storm was rapidly approaching from the mainland. We could see black clouds boiling furiously over the Linwood area and lightning flashing every minute, it seemed. The storm caught us halfway across the bridge coming home, pouring down so hard that I really couldn't see more than five feet in front of the car. Somehow I managed to make it to the end of the bridge and then pull over. Then the wind started, in bursts at least seventy miles per hour, maybe more. The car rocked from side to side. I was very frightened, I think justifiably. There surely must have been a funnel cloud right above us. The wind abated, the storm moved across the marshes toward Atlantic City, and we came on home. Watching the storm surge across the bay, I saw no funnel, but clearly there was a huge amount of energy in the cloud system.

The delight came later in the evening. The night-blooming cereus in our bedroom produced four blossoms. It would clearly win any contest for the most gorgeous flower on the ugliest plant.

The plant is all elbows and knees, the gangliest and gawkiest thing I know. But the flowers! Huge, pristine white, silky, absolute pure beauty in every detail, down to the pistil, which looks like a sea anemone. I brought the plant downstairs to the living room (a perilous trip, considering how top heavy the thing is). At 8:30, just as the flowers started to shake slightly and begin opening, we invited Ed Plantan over to have a drink and enjoy the spectacle. Here are some snapshots of the three of us, all looking kind of silly.

Do you have one of these plants? If not, let me know. They root easily from leaf cuttings, and in about ten years you'll have blooms.

Today is an anniversary of sorts. Six months ago, toward midnight, I smoked my last Carlton 100—or cigarette of any kind. So did Hella.

July 15, 1998

Your good letter of the 10th arrived yesterday. Welcome back—and I loved reading about Chiswick and Charleston, but for very different reasons.

I want to see your new Bloomsbury artifacts, especially Duncan Grant's Adam and Eve quartet of paintings.

Welcome back to the hot world, where eastern Florida is still ablaze. I read in today's paper that Dallas to date this year has already had twenty-nine days of temperatures in excess of 100°, including the last nine in succession. The summer 1980 record there—sixty-nine such days—may be broken this year. The drought is the worst since Dust Bowl days. Yes, I do like southern New Jersey!

It is high summer now. The shortening of the days has not yet become perceptible. From morning on, there's the buzzing sizzle of cicadas up in the trees somewhere. Daturas and brugmansias have started blooming. Yesterday we had our first huge white flower on *Datura inoxia*. Its gray-green leaves smell funny—musty, like a basement in need of airing out—but the flowers have a delicate perfume, although nowhere near as deep, sensuous, and intoxicating as brugmansias. I have a new datura, new last year, anyway, that's just produced its first flower of the season. *D. metel* 'Cornucopia' doesn't flower prolifically; four or five blossoms per plant seems to be it. But the flowers are spectacularly beautiful. Each double, trumpet-shaped flower emerges from a substantial charcoal gray calyx. The flowers are greenish gray at their bases, then change to a deep, rich purple. Their interiors are pale lilac, but because of the intense doubling—and also because of the odd little upturned protuberances on each of the fused petals (characteristic of daturas and brugmansias alike)—the effect is bicolor; bicolored petticoats, I'd say. I saved seed last year but didn't expect much. For one thing, these flowers are so intensely double that it's hard to see how pollinators can reach their private parts. But the seeds were fertile—all germinated. Then, I suspected I'd get mostly singles, and only few if any doubles, but the offspring all came true. I like other things about the plant. The leaves look like those of eggplants, and come to think of it, the purple of the flowers' exteriors is eggplant purple, as are the stems. The flowers, besides being ruffled inside, are very fluted on the outside, like a Corinthian column. The flowers are so heavy that they hang at half-mast, somewhere between the perky uprightness of *D. inoxia* and the languid droop of the brugmansias. (I hear that some towns in Florida ban both genera. Kids experiment with their hallucinogenic properties and their production of altered states of consciousness, one of these altered states being death.)

I know you are growing some brugmansias, but not which ones. I have 'Jamaica Yellow' and *Brugmansia versicolor*. 'Jamaica Yellow' is more prodigious in bloom, the record being twenty-seven at one time. *B. versicolor* opens creamy, then changes to a lovely soft pink within a few minutes. Next morning the flowers are salmon orange. I want more, now that I have a greenhouse (although here they can also be overwintered in an unheated garage). I hear good things about 'Betty Marshall' (white), 'Ecuador Pink', and especially 'Charles Grimaldi' (large orange flowers).

Back to your letter, the part about gardening, the Brits, and us. I say it over and over in my horticulture class, in talks here and there, and in stuff I write. I've probably said it already, maybe repeatedly, in letters to you, but it's a sermon that needs to be preached and preached repeatedly. There is only one rule in gardening, really, and I'll put it in caps for emphasis. YOU HAVE TO GARDEN WHERE YOU ARE, NOT SOMEWHERE ELSE. I'll repeat it again, for effect. YOU HAVE TO GARDEN WHERE YOU ARE, NOT SOMEWHERE ELSE. That seems obvious and elementary, but it isn't to a whole lot of people. I'd be a rich guy if I had a dollar for every American now alive who's ever said, "I want an English garden." "But you can't have one!" I want to shout, unless, perhaps, I'm talking to someone who lives and gardens in Victoria, B.C., where the climate is almost (not exactly) like England's. When my mother died some Aprils ago, my brothers John and Robert took Hella and me to see the Dallas Arboretum. I was appalled, for someone had planted hundreds and hundreds of tall delphiniums, all doomed to perish within a week or two, as soon as the Texas heat and humidity began to crank up. The tale here, surely, is that someone with more money than sense visited Sissinghurst, went into raptures over delphiniums, came home wanting Dallas County to be Kent, and shelled out some cash for planting delphiniums. There wasn't a single perennial salvia in sight, despite the fact that many are native southwesterners that flourish and bloom for months in the worst summer weather that Texas can serve up. You don't have an English garden. I don't. Wave Hill isn't an English garden, and neither is the Conservatory Garden in Central Park.

Friday, July 17

Another good letter from you! I'll finish mine now and fax it to you c/o Craufurd's office.

To answer your question, the Polly Hill Arboretum is public, open all year from dawn to dusk. The state conservation people were involved with some kinds of easements. There were legal requirements in going public—ramps for handicapped access, public johns, a visitor's center. Enclosed is a brochure with some details and a little history of how the arboretum came to be.

I'm glad you have honeybees, but we don't. Not a one.

Thanks for the postcard portrait of Philip Sidney, also the seeds of *Digitalis thapsi*.

Love,
Allen

Friday, July 24, 1998

Dear Allen,

The heat and drought continue. It is painful to walk into the metasequoia garden and see cardiocrinums with leaves hanging limp, the sheen now vanished. I walk to the circle garden and cringe when I see veronicas with normally green leaves looking dessicated and gray and helianthemums with leaves burnt to a crisp.

Craufurd and I worry about the three large deciduous trees in the main garden, so we are watering them. The death of the two large white oaks and that magnificent ash behind the house would change the garden in terrible ways, so we leave hoses dripping slowly. It takes about a week to water each one thoroughly.

Trillium seeds ripened last week, so I had the fascinating challenge of reading the woods to try to find indications of vestigial moisture in this dreadful drought. It was fun. I carried down a bucketful of seeds and looked for that horrid annual grass, *Microstegium vimineum*, as I now know its scientific name to be. Sure enough, everywhere I saw it I found soil moist enough to dig, and in went the seeds—along with my hopes and visions of masses of trilliums naturalized throughout the woods.

I see signs of fall now. I realize that July is the correct season for *Lycoris squamigera* to bloom, but nevertheless I think of all lycoris as fall-blooming bulbs. We have masses near the boxwood border, north of the vegetable garden fence, and through the woods. I don't understand what stimulates their blooming or what gives us a good display from them. Certainly they don't seem to need a wet summer! Other lycoris hybrids from China bloom in their pots. I don't have enough to dare plant them outside but will do so before summer is over. Meanwhile, the cyclamen year continues. *Cc. graecum* and *hederifolium* look fresh and happy blooming in the driest places, but *C. purpurascens* needs more moisture.

We have a few plants that actually look happy. The most exciting one is a new one. (Is the new plant always the most exciting?) I believe it is *Scutellaria baicalensis*. It is in full sun, has had no water from me, and has bloomed for about six weeks without drooping. Blue, tubular flowers are slightly hairy, and the leaves are healthy and bright green. It is decumbent, sprawling into the path, and now that I know it I want more. Petunias, hibiscus, salvias, agastaches, and lantanas also look like nothing is wrong. They love the heat, and tolerate the drought beautifully.

The brochure you sent on the Polly Hill Arboretum is delightful. Polly Hill must be a remarkable person. And certainly we are all grateful to her family, friends, and the various institutions that make possible the continuation of such a garden. But she is the one to whom we owe the greatest thanks. She had the vision. She had the patience. And she had the love absolutely necessary to persist in doing it. It is the best legacy one can leave, and we are all the recipients. Incidentally, Craufurd and I finally got around to watching that video about her. We loved it! I liked especially the parts without the piano in the background so I could hear the birds.

Love,
Nancy

Monday, July 27, 1998

Dear Nancy,

First, I want to tell you that when it is hot here, I feel it. Other people's heat, however, is just an abstraction. Ditto for drought. I am sorry when I hear that Texas has had twenty, thirty, or forty straight days of temperatures over 100° and that the corn and soybean crops have dried to dust, and of course I wish you rain and cooler weather. Gardeners are generous souls, you know: we love to share plants. But if the Master (Mistress?) of the Universe were to come to me and offer a deal whereby I could trade weather with people — give Texas twenty of my 80° days and take in return twenty of its scorchers, or offer you three rainy days and forgo them myself — I wouldn't do it. Please remember that you probably would not gladly give us your winters (in colder years than 1998) and take ours.

Last week was h-o-t. I had jury duty in Atlantic City (but wasn't called to serve). By 9:00 in the morning Monday when I got to the courthouse, it was over 90°. Tuesday was worse. Wednesday was horrible. It got to 100° on our kiwi-shaded deck. The heat index was 115° at the airport. I'm no stranger to heat, but there's something new now. I find it hard to breathe when the temperature gets over 90°. It probably has something to do with last January's surgery. Thursday was Hella's birthday, and we were pleased to be invited for dinner at Michael and Christine's, for several reasons of course, but one was that they have air-conditioning. When we got home it was hard to sleep; the attic had now gotten so hot that it made our bedroom uncomfortable. But then, about midnight, a cold front roared through. The ferocious lightning and thunder went on for almost an hour, and we got over an inch of rain. Next morning when we got up, the sky was clear and blue, not hazy, and the temperature had dropped into the mid-60s. Since then, days haven't gotten above 80°. This morning I woke up at 5:30, so chilly that I put on a sweat suit for the first time since mid-May.

Summer is only slightly over a month old now, but our local garden centers have already put out Halloween stuff! I made the rounds of these places Saturday, looking for a few plants to replace some flagging bedding lobelias, 'Purple Wave' petunias and also *Petunia integrifolia*, but the few things still on sale looked worse than the ones I wanted to replace. I decided to root some cuttings instead, borrowing an idea I had observed at your place last May. You had filled an aluminum foil pound-cake pan with a mixture of half perlite and half coarse sand, punched drainage holes in the bottom, set everything in a larger pan half full of water, and then stuck cuttings. I don't know whether the cake pan was then left in the water or hauled up and drained, but I decided to try the idea and keep the pan in water to see what happened. I stuck impatiens, holy basil, several kinds of coleus, and also plectranthus. That was Saturday afternoon. The holy basil has rooted already!

The days are shortening noticeably now. Once I had put on warm clothes and grabbed a cup of coffee from the kitchen, I went out to the deck. It was light, but the sun had just barely come up. Sipping coffee, I studied all the containers on the deck, making mental notes about what to do and what not to do next year. Get rid of all the orange lantanas but keep those that are predominantly red, also the pink and cream ones. Keep the grassy things—the true grasses like hakonechloa and *Pennisetum setaceum* 'Rubrum', also the sweet flags and phormiums. (Phormium 'Maori Sunset' is truly marvelous with the highly variegated bronzy red hypoestes coming up through it!) Avoid marguerites altogether! The bedding plant industry praised to high heaven one called 'Summer Pink', but the praise is undeserved. Blooms got smaller and smaller and fewer and fewer until now there's just a great mass of foliage. Its ferny texture nicely contrasts with bolder leaves of plants like *Begonia grandis*, but there's too much of it. Only one of our hanging baskets seems to work now—single white impatiens, slightly trailing, combined with a small-leafed English ivy variegated with dark green and white. Next year I'll repeat this planting in several baskets. This combination looks very cool and elegant, especially together with a very tall meadow rue that has volunteered in the little bed beneath the deck. When I say "very tall," I mean that it stretches itself all the way up to the hanging baskets suspended from the front rafter of the deck.

Our mainstays, of course, are coleus and plectranthus. Did you see the article on coleus in the fall issue of *Pacific Horticulture*? I was happy from the photographs to be able to identify 'Big Red' (burgundy foliage deckled green), 'Coppertone' (mature leaves cerise, new growth pale lime), and 'Purple Emperor' (really big plant, huge scalloped leaves of deep black-purple). I've grown all of these for several years but with no names, although 'Coppertone' came to me as 'Alabama'. I want some others that are shown in the article's pictures: 'El Brighto', 'Max Levering', and 'India Frills'. The article and

I agree on one point—the best coleus of them all is 'Inky Fingers'. This article also reminds us that coleus isn't *Coleus* any more, that "taxonomists have recently transferred *C. blumei* to the tongue-twisting *Solenostemon scutellarioides.*" I'm not sure that this is a valid complaint against these taxonomists. Checking in reference books shows that the genus name *Solenostemon* comes from Linnaeus himself. The nineteenth-century English botanist George Bentham came up later with *Coleus blumei*. Linnaeus has priority, hence the change. (I think this explains the change. I'm not certain, but the ways of taxonomists are sometimes stranger than those of God.) Further checking shows that Bentham's *C. aromaticus* and earlier the *C. amboinicus* of the Portuguese or maybe Brazilian João de Loureiro have been banished from the now-nonexistent genus *Coleus* but have not accompanied *C. blumei* in becoming *S. scutellarioides*. *C. aromaticus* and *amboinicus* are both now classified as *Plectranthus amboinicus*. I don't suppose any of this botanical pedantry matters very much except that both coleus and plectranthus are such superb tropical plants for temperate-zone summers.

I've grown *Plectranthus amboinicus* (both the pure green and the green and white variegated kind) for years, also *P. argentatus* (the best gray-leafed plant I know). I wrote you earlier about discovering the yellow and green 'Athens Gem' this spring. It is just a super plant. You should see it here with hakonechloa, coleus 'Inky Fingers', and the iridescent, rainbow-colored but mostly purple Persian shield or *Strobilanthes dyerianus*. A sensational combination! (Will send pictures . . .)

Obviously, the containers on our deck rely very heavily on foliage plants, but first-time visitors in the several weeks ahead will hardly notice at first because of the floral spectacle that just started where the older deck meets the newer deck. Many years ago, before either deck was built, I started some dwarf crape myrtles from seed I got from Park's, which called them "crape myrtlettes." There are three—a strong-growing watermelon red, a pale pink, and a lavender. When the old deck was built, these lagerstroemias were by the steps. When Ed Brightly enlarged the deck. they were blooming, so he suggested just leaving a hole for them right in the deck. It was a stroke of pure genius. The flood of summer color at the end of July is breathtaking!

To return to a theme from earlier in the year, the theme of repetition, this morning as I surveyed the curving back border from the deck, something was clear: the left half was somehow more satisfying than the right. Why? The left side repeats patches of chartreuse at intervals — *Liriope muscari* 'PeeDee Ingot' and a little hosta of unknown identity. The right side is all greens.

And before I forget, a question. I have always thought that once hellebores were planted they had to stay planted, that dividing them or even transplanting them was impossible. But last summer when I was at Montrose you told me that was nonsense, that you regularly divide and transplant them, thus getting drifts of one kind. I think you said August was the time. I have four truly fantastic hybrid hellebores — a black-purple, a paler purple, a pink, and a greenish-white — all from Fairweather Gardens. Their parentage mixes strains from Elizabeth Strangman in England and one of the German breeders. These are planted by the lower deck, where we can see them through the French doors off the living room, but they are far too close together. Any advice on how to divide and transplant will be both appreciated and followed.

Cheers,
Allen

Tuesday, July 28, 1998

Dear Allen,

We had a glorious day yesterday. It was overcast, and the high was only 78°. We even had a slow rain during the afternoon. The rain was so gentle I stayed out in it the entire time. I planted *Zephyranthes* sp. 'Labuffarosea' and *Z. morrisclintii*, thinking how appropriate it was to plant rain lilies in the rain. As I bent over to work, my hair was so wet that the rain drops ran into my ears. I thought of that song, "I Get Tears in My Ears When I Lie on My Back and Cry Over You." I can't remember the tune, but I won't ever forget the words. At the end of the afternoon I went hopefully to check the rain gauge, but it contained less than one tenth of an inch.

Weather forecasters! They're bemoaning the possibility that we might get showers on the weekend while I grind my teeth and hope that we do.

You mentioned that we were but a month into summer. I like to think that we are two months along. By September 1 the days will be shorter, and the light will come at an angle. Then, there will come that first clear day telling me that autumn is here at last. This long-awaited day always arrives before September 21.

How splendid that you are still planting! I won't let up until the ground freezes in January, but most of my visitors are amazed that I continue to plant now. I, too, stuck a flat full of *Petunia integrifolia* cuttings just last week. We debate whether it is better or worse to leave the cuttings in a flat in a basin of water. I'm not certain. One year we had great luck rooting tiny bits of tiny forms of dianthus and *Phlox subulata* by sticking them in sand in an unglazed flower pot. That pot was set into a larger pot with about a half inch of sand filling the space between the two pots. I put the larger pot in water. The moisture absorbed through the walls of the pots was just enough to keep the cuttings moist but not saturated.

I am a little envious of your success with *Phormium* 'Maori Sunset'. Mine mugged out in our humid heat. And how I wish I could see your containers! The one planted with white impatiens and the variegated ivy must be enough to keep you cool even on the hottest day.

I agree with you that coleus and plectranthus are the mainstays for summer color. By the way, I am happy you don't call the former *Solenostemon*. I fear we are coming to that, but I am resisting. I am comfortable with *Plectranthus* and think *P. argentatus* is without any question the best gray-leafed plant. What else can survive the drought without a whimper? What else has lovely, softly purple tinges to its stems? I would hate to be without it. (Actually, *Centaurea cineraria* 'Colchester White' is also pretty good, especially in containers where it gets a daily drenching.) But back to plectranthus, specifically *P. amboinicus*. We have it in sun and shade, and it is successful either place. Do you grow *P. forsteri* 'Marginatus'? I have two different plants so labeled. The one I believe to be correct has brilliant white markings and the imposter has slightly creamy ones tinged with apricot.

It is a zoo around here. On Sunday afternoon about 2:30 I looked down the path to the pond and saw three foxes. One was adult, the others young ones about eight inches long. They looked like hybrids, neither gray nor red. They had gray bodies and red ears and tails. I walked to within about ten feet of them and then noticed that just beyond them were Do and Re, who, I'm afraid, have now become a couple. Re has small but noticeable antlers and both are extremely healthy thanks to the exotic diet they enjoy in my garden. The woodchuck who lives beneath the smoke house sat and chewed his dinner of plantain until I was within five feet of him.

No, I haven't seen the article on coleus in *Pacific Horticulture*, but I have some of the coleus you mentioned. I, too, like 'Inky Fingers', but this summer's winner is 'Black Duckfoot'. I'll share it with you if you don't already have it

You asked about hellebores. Yes, indeed, Allen, you can divide *Helleborus × hybridus,* and fall is the perfect time to do it. Wait until September and dig the entire clump. Look at the base of each leaf stalk and if you see a growth bud there, take your sharpest knife and cut right through the base, taking care to get a bit of root with each division. Replant the divisions immediately, and don't expect much display this winter or next spring. We seldom kill a plant divided at this time. I have also done it in the spring but that is trickier because the small divisions have to get through the summer before they have a chance to settle in well.

Love,
Nancy

Wednesday, July 29, 1998

Dear Nancy,

Your news that *Lycoris squamigera* is blooming now reminds me that this is one of those plants I always mean to acquire and grow but, so far, have never got around to ordering. I like these bulbs of high to late summer. In *Gardening for Love*, Elizabeth Lawrence reported that she had gathered a number of folk names for the plant from the farm women who advertised in the various market bulletins of the South. One was "surprise lily," which is apt considering how quickly and unexpectedly these flowers blow their trumpets up out of the earth at this time of year. Another name was "pink amaryllis Hallie," which represented a survival of an older but discarded botanical name, *Amaryllis hallii.* Another name, I think, is "naked ladies," although that name is shared with the colchicums that are true bulbs (well, corms) of autumn. At any rate, I don't grow this lycoris, though I may one day, but the one I really would like to grow I can't grow. It's *Lycoris radiata*, the red spider lilies of my boyhood, which isn't winter-hardy this far north. It was also a surprise "lily," although actually a member of the Amaryllidaceae, not the Liliaceae. Did you know that the genus *Lycoris* got its name from a mistress of Marc Anthony? (That's not a piece of information I've carried around for very long, as I just learned it when I looked up these plants in *The New RHS Dictionary of Gardening* to be sure I was right about their family membership.) Red spider lilies were much planted in rural Texas, usually in large circles. Since the flowers on each spike are also arranged in a circle, the plant always reminded me of carousels, not of spiders, although the stamens and pistil of each blossom were somewhat spidery in the way they stuck outward and upward beyond the petals.

I just checked the dry shade beneath our old Virginia juniper, but there's no sign yet of *Cyclamen hederifolium*. You are ahead of us.

I have been pondering why I turn first to garden centers when at this time of year I need new plants to replace those annuals that have exhausted themselves in blooming. The convenience of these places has made many of us gardeners lazy, and also forgetful that in late June we should make provision for the long growing season that still lies ahead at the end of July. In my old, battered copy of *The Standard Cyclopedia of Horticulture*, Liberty Hyde Bailey writes that at the end of June we should make sowings of sweet alyssum, candytuft, marigolds, petunias, zinnias, and other annuals. He goes on to observe that "the tendency to sow everything for early bloom deprives the garden of much freshness and interest in autumn." His words still hold true, except that few of us sow anything any more, due to our reliance on those garden centers for some plants we could perfectly well grow ourselves. You, of course, still hold to the old ways in your long season of planting, now, and even unto January.

I did, incidentally, grow tomatoes from seed this spring, in the new greenhouse. I never got around to ordering seed of those heirloom strains, 'Mortgage Lifter' and 'German Johnson', but from Shepherd's I got seed of 'Carmello'. I also cheated by buying in May from a roadside nursery a plant of 'Big Boy' or maybe 'Beefsteak' that already had little fruits on it. I thought it would give me a real early start on tomato season, but I got maybe five tomatoes before 'Carmello' started to bear. My crop is nothing to brag about, for we don't have enough sun, but you should see the plant I gave Ed next door. It is simply huge, branching off in several directions and reaching, thus far, to over ten feet. He has it trained on a really remarkable trellis made of twine, wire. and pieces of old metal fencing. Yesterday I counted over forty tomatoes in various stages of ripeness. Ed will get two or three bushels before the first frost of autumn touches his vines. 'Carmello' is just about the best tomato I've found. The good-sized fruits are pleasantly acidic and are very meaty and firm.

Your remarks about plectranthus now have set me to wondering—and to scrutinizing pictures of various species in T. H. Everett's *Illustrated Encyclopedia of Horticulture*. I have tentatively come to the opinion that what I have isn't a variegated form of *P. amboinicus* at all, but *P. forsteri* 'Marginatus'—and the one you describe as an imposter, the one with slightly creamy, apricot-tinged leaf edges? The surest thing about this whole genus is that it's very mixed up in the nursery trade. And, by the way, I'm rooting 'Athens Gem' for you, as it's really superb.

I'm confused about your deer. Didn't you write me earlier this year that Do was the mother, Re and Mi her fawns? Now you write that Re is growing antlers and that he and Do are a couple, which I take to mean that sex is either going on or about to go on between them. Clearly there is incest involved here, but I'm not sure whether it's of the mother/son flavor or the brother/sister persuasion. And has something happened to Mi?

Now it's Thursday morning, and I'm off shortly for Philadelphia to see two doctors. The first is Keith Calligaro, the surgeon who operated on one of my carotid arteries in November, and the second is Susan Gregory (our fellow Duke alum), the pulmonary specialist who attended me during my long bout with pneumonia. In retrospect, it's clear that these good people saved my life. I haven't written you much if anything about Calligaro, but the endarterectomy he performed last November did correct a severe, life-threatening condition. Even more importantly, he had to decide whether to perform that particular procedure or make do with angioplasty instead. If he had made the latter choice, there would have been no chest x-ray. In that case, the spot on my lung would not have been discovered until later, possibly much later, with very weighty consequences. As for Susan Gregory, if she hadn't clapped me back in the hospital as soon as I walked into her office late last February, I'm pretty sure that pneumonia would have gotten me within a couple of days. Apart from her saving my life, I like her very much. She is quite attractive and very personable.

And ending on another somber reflection, my friend Lucy Marzolino discovered that there was a spot on one of her lungs about the same time I did. We both had surgery, same surgeon too, about three weeks apart last winter. Another friend, the owner of a fine local bookstore, was similarly diagnosed last fall, but her case wasn't an early-stage matter. I went to her funeral last Sunday.

Fondly,
Allen

Thursday, July 30, 1998

Dear Allen,

Such a box of treasures arrived from you this morning. Thank you for that wonderful book on the Bloomsbury Group and Charleston. We were there for a private tour in July, and I can assure you the book does it justice. The Charleston Trust has done a lovely job maintaining the ambience of the place. Vases containing fresh flowers, looking casually arranged but probably done with great skill and care, decorated each room and kept the house from appearing to be a museum dedicated to a noteworthy time recently past.

The summer issue of *Homeground* is a delight. I enjoyed reading more about Polly Hill and our newest arboretum. But I was shocked by the wonderful photograph you took of Montrose from the circle garden when you were here in May. That was the last time we had any real moisture in the soil.

You haven't told me about your greenhouse recently. Is it empty? hot? Mine is beginning to fill up with freshly potted cyclamen now. I believe most species grow better if repotted annually. Besides, it is a wonderful excuse to be in the potting room in the cooling breeze of a fan and, on a really good day, to listen at the same time to Bach or Mozart on public radio.

I knew it would happen. I've never yet gotten through a summer in North Carolina without it. I stepped right on top of a yellow jackets' nest. Dare I ask you whether you knew yellow jackets in Texas? I ran about a quarter of the way into the field with those dreadful creatures in pursuit. I got four nasty stings that prevented me from weeding the garden around the big greenhouse as I had planned because it hurt to kneel on my swollen leg.

I decline respectfully your kind offer of a bit of your night-blooming cereus. I had one when we lived in Durham. I loved it in all its awkwardness, but guess when it bloomed, the only time it did bloom. The month we were in Australia. I had a *Lilium catesbaei* bloom that same time. It didn't bloom again, either. I kept the lily, but I finally left the cactus outside for the winter.

I expected my brugmansias to bloom earlier than yours, but no, they have barely produced one flush of flowers. I believe they need some tropical downpours. I do have a good collection of them but barely know their names. I have one labeled "opens yellow, turns pink" (could this be *B. versicolor?*) and another just called "yellow." We also grow 'Charles Grimaldi', but it's not in flower yet. Brugmansias are almost hardy enough for us. Four survived last winter, but, as I have said before, last winter hardly counts.

Congratulations on your anniversary. I hope you will have many, many more smoke-free years. I will await with a little anxiety your reports from the physicians.

Love,
Nancy

Friday, July 31, 1998

Dear Nancy,

Yesterday's trip to Philadelphia was full of good medical news. Dr. Calligaro found that my left carotid artery (operated on twice) is free of scar tissue. Dr. Gregory hardly recognized me when I walked into her office. ("You look like you've never been sick a day in your life.") She gave me a clean bill of health.

Best,
Allen

Sunday, August 2, 1998

Dear Allen,

Something here is different. The air is clear, the sky blue, and the nights for the rest of the week will have lows in the 60s. There is also something the same. No rain, not even a glimmer of hope except from the tropical storms in the Atlantic. Having lived recently through Hurricane Fran, I want the drought to end—but not in that way.

You must try *Lycoris squamigera*. I'll send you bulbs just after the foliage dies in spring. I think it might just be hardy enough for you, partly because it sends up foliage in spring rather than in fall. I dug some for a friend shortly after we moved to Montrose and received a note expressing thanks and surprise at finding a box of "naked ladies" on the back porch. Perhaps you remember that I sold divisions of our clumps when I had the nursery. I don't know how hardy it is, but a customer advised me that the bulbs mustn't dry out. I remember digging them on the morning we shipped them.

The bulbs of fall are every bit as exciting as those of spring— and for many of the same reasons. Some precede the season. I have both *Scilla autumnalis* and *Leucojum autumnale* in flower beneath the *Cedrus deodara* in front of the house.

As for *Lycoris radiata*, I can imagine what it means to you, for I, too, remember it in all of the old gardens of my childhood. I have long sought the early form, which blooms in August and which I used to have in my old garden on Cranford Road in Durham. Finally, about two years ago, I went back there and got permission to dig a few bulbs. This turns out to be *L. radiata* var. *pumila*. The main difference between the two, in addition to the fact that they bloom a month apart, is that *L. radiata* var. *pumila* is fertile while *L. radiata* is sterile. We plant masses of *Coleus pumilus* where we know both species of spider lilies will spring up this month and next. When the tomato red spider lilies burst into bloom amid the dark burgundy foliage of the coleus, it's a dramatic sight.

Why, I wonder, aren't your *Cyclamen hederifolium* blooming yet? I have puzzled about the variation in this plant's blooming season for years. The Cyclamen Society often publishes notes from gardeners reporting their flowers in July and declaring this to be incredibly early. I almost always find one flower before the end of May. I have one theory, not tested of course. North Carolina is hot before the end of May, and we usually have a spell of cool weather after that. The heat followed by cooling may fool a few tubers into thinking that fall is approaching.

You have every right to be confused about my deer. I am too. I believe that Do, Re, and Mi are a fatherless family, and that Do is the mother of the other two. I no longer believe that Do and Re have an incestuous relationship, although I suspect that Do went off on a fling with a handsome buck for a weekend. The three are back together now, and I have seen the big buck with his own herd of about seven. Reynard, the little fox, is remarkably tame. I haven't seen the kits again, but Craufurd met her on the road to the pond yesterday. Last night when I went to turn off the water on the oak tree near the rock garden, I saw her near the house. She followed me, not chasing me but walking facing me, in the direction I went. If I stopped, she stopped. We went to the greenhouse, and when I turned and went to the house, she stood watching.

Craufurd and I are trying to eliminate one of the last vestiges of Montrose Nursery. In the area below the big greenhouse we kept some nursery stock in pots set in mulch. Now, years later, it is a jungle. Craufurd compares it to the Amazon, but I think of the Amazon as dripping with moisture. It ain't that! Blackberries, grasses of all sorts, and small, medium, and even large trees have invaded the area. Craufurd can't mow it down because some of the pots beneath all of that contain plants worth saving. Besides, if he mows the pots, the plastic will be there forever. I see this work as a giant treasure hunt. Plants certainly have a powerful will to live. Yesterday I found two pink-flowering *Clematis integrifolia*, two *Clematis viticella*, about two dozen 'Golden Sword' yuccas, and some unknown irises, probably white forms of *Iris pseudacorus*. We pull out, sort, and empty the pots to wash and reuse, and I keep dashing up the hill with rescued plants to repot or plant. At the end of each session, Craufurd and I stand back and assess our progress. We are just over one-third of the way through it and hope to complete it by the end of next week. It reminds me of the way the two of us used to work together clearing the land for our first garden. Somehow during the past ten years or so, with my having a staff to direct or a business to run, he and I haven't been able to work together on many gardening projects. We notice with the passage of time differences in our energy level and the ease with which we get up or go down onto our knees, but the joy is still there.

I am happier than you can imagine to hear such a wonderful report from your doctors. You certainly found the best doctors for your case, and I am glad you found them when you did. The frightening part is that all along the way you had to choose one solution or another, and every time by some stroke of good luck you made the right decision. Any wrong choice might have deprived me of a dear friend. I'm not ready for that!

Love,
Nancy

Monday, August 3, 1998

Dear Nancy,

Did we have yellow jackets in Texas? It's an interesting question—linguistically, to begin with. Some of my earliest memories have to do with yellow jackets, but for me those words denoted rather large, yellow and black paper wasps that built irregularly shaped, gray, flattened nests, sometimes under the eaves of houses, sometimes in shrubbery. These were narrow-waisted critters whose dispositions were gentler than those of hornets or a larger, dull red wasp we also had. But both of these were more inclined to sting than mud wasps or dirt daubers, which were pretty, blue, iridescent creatures. When I moved to New Jersey, I became aware that other people didn't use the words "yellow jacket" the same way I did. Here and pretty much throughout the rest of the country this term denotes the smaller, blunt-bodied, yellow and black abominations that start to become evident about this time of year. These (but I need not tell you so) are ground wasps. At first glance they may be mistaken for honeybees, except for their jittery and erratic flight pattern as they dart forward and backward.

As for using "yellow jacket" to refer to a different wasp altogether from those found here and also in Hillsborough, I don't know whether that was a regional colloquialism common in my part of Texas or whether the family members from whom I learned our mother tongue were simply mistaken in their grasp of entomology. And I don't see any reason why there could not have been species of true yellow jackets—species in the genus *Vespula*—in Texas. They seem to be present everywhere else in the country, including Alaska, and certainly Texas had its full share of life-forms that sting or bite. I do not, however, remember ever seeing any, and I do remember eating lots of watermelon in late summer and early fall without having to retreat indoors to avoid these wicked bugs, which love both fruit and meat.

I've never been stung by a yellow jacket, but it's pure luck. Michael was badly stung when we first moved here. I have a friend who was hospitalized after she drank from a can of Coca-Cola where yellow jackets were already imbibing. Hella was stung about forty times summer before last when she stepped on a nest in the back of a flower bed. Characteristically, she carefully came inside and showered, not wanting to go to the hospital with dirty hands and feet if she went into shock.

I hate these beasts. From mid-August until the onset of really cool weather in late September they make it impossible for us to take our meals out on the deck. I also dislike the way they gang up and chase anyone who disturbs their nest as summer wears on and their numbers reach a certain critical mass.

I have a new toy—a tricycle! Last year I gave Hella a bicycle for her birthday. I also gave myself one for her birthday. It wasn't that I wanted one. I just thought that (1) I could stand the exercise, and (2) Hella would like company when she rode. I took precisely one ride, last summer, four blocks down to the town park and four blocks back. It's not true that people never forget how to ride bicycles. I had forgotten. I couldn't keep my balance, and I kept slowing down until the bike finally started to wobble and careen.

Hella often rides, although she also gets up at the crack of dawn and takes walks. Meanwhile, I have been eyeing a number of men and women, older than I, who have trikes and use them on the attractive bike path that runs all through Linwood. Saturday morning I went out and bought my own trike.

"You bought what?" Hella asked, when I hauled it out of the van I borrowed from Ed Plantan. She sounded like I'd just come home with a wheelchair! But she quickly got used to the idea and even approved when I triked down to Michael and Christine's and back yesterday and when I went to the post office this morning.

It's interesting to go on small, local errands this way instead of by car. I see more, closer at hand. Yesterday and today on the bike path I passed by thousands of white clover plants. There really weren't any honeybees to be seen, not even one. I thought about *Silent Spring*. Today's *Philadelphia Inquirer* reports huge losses of honeybees from tracheal and varroa mites and from hive beetles in both Pennsylvania and New Jersey, also in the New England states. Besides the South African tracheal mites and varroa mites, honeybees are also being decimated by hive beetles from South Africa. They lay eggs in honeycomb cells. They also defecate in honey, bringing the bees to abandon their hives in disgust.

The *Inquirer* also informs us that armadillos are headed our way from Texas. There's no reason that they can't live this far north. They just haven't made it yet.

You asked about the greenhouse. It's empty except for the tricycle and a few cuttings I rooted. It doesn't get as hot as I had feared. There are two fans, and the cross-ventilation between the door and a window is good. There's also summer shade from our old swamp maple and one of its seedlings, which has become a sizable tree since we moved here.

It got down to 58° last night and won't go above 75° today. The sky is clear, cloudless, and free of haze. The only clouds yesterday were cirrus. The late afternoon light is getting golden and slanted. Most of August still lies ahead, but there's a hint of fall in the air.

Love,
Allen

Friday, August 7, 1998

Dear Allen,

It sounds to me as if you have exactly the same yellow jackets in Linwood as we have in Hillsborough. What a miracle that Hella didn't go into shock after forty stings. I also hate them. Around here people call them ground bees, but they are meaner than any bee. After I realized that I had stepped on their nest and then run into the field, I looked down to see them bent double on my shirt trying to sting me to death. We sprayed into their nest—this one had two entrances. The next day when we went to see whether the poison had worked, I noticed only a few confused wasps flying around the area looking for their nest mates. The day after that I found that some creature had come and torn up the nest. I believe possums or raccoons must eat the larvae.

Somehow I can't imagine you on a tricycle, but I can picture you on that wobbly bicycle. Bike or trike, it's a wonderful idea. No wind can compare to that you feel on a two- or three-wheeled conveyance. I bought a bike about twenty-two years ago when we had the gas shortage throughout the country. I loved it but had a little trouble changing gears. The difficulty was as great as the first time I tried playing two against three on the piano or when I tried to pat my head and rub my stomach simultaneously. The bicycle now resides in the top of the barn.

Our cool, clear weather (58° at night and lower to mid 80s during the day) lasted for nearly a week. Today we return to humidity but not to extreme heat. We still haven't had any rain. There is no question that the August light is different. Plants know it, too. I have more lycoris blooming now, although they are in pots. *Lycoris haywardii* and several hybrids that have *L. chinensis* as one parent bloom in the cold frame.

Craufurd continues to water the large ash behind the house, and I water one of the few surviving large white oaks at the end of the day. After we finish watering the stock plants and the newly planted garden, I use what water remains in the well.

I had a most unpleasant tour last weekend—only two people, a couple from South Carolina who declared themselves very interested in gardening. The entire conversation was confrontational. The woman first said pointedly that it was obvious that I didn't just stick to natives. I said I didn't but that I believe gardeners who grow exotics have a responsibility to be sensitive to any aggressive tendency of these imports. I also mentioned that many so-called natives did not occur spontaneously. Many plants came to this country years ago. A West Coast native has as little or as much business living in an East Coast garden as does a Japanese native. I pointed out the ripened seeds on arums beneath the metasequoias, and she argued that jack-in-the-pulpit was an arisaema. "Yes," I said, "both are aroids." From there we proceeded to the circle garden, where I pointed out that we were not watering the beds and borders but were watering deeply the large trees. "I've never heard of such a thing!" she declared. "I would never dream of watering a tree!" I responded that one can buy a perennial for about $5 or $6 and within a year have a good display, whereas it takes over a hundred years to grow a tree. I also pointed out the loss of habitat for all those plants that grew in the shade of the tree that died this spring.

More on watering. Besides trees and plants in containers and new plantings that need time and extra care to become established, I don't irrigate my garden and never have. When we moved here, I accepted my personal challenge to make a garden that does not require artificial irrigation. I like to believe that much of Montrose will live after I die. If the garden I make depends on me or some other human to intervene with water, it is not viable. I try to find the right plant for the site—the plant that can survive and make the fewest possible demands on me. If I had a well nearby producing thousands of gallons a minute, I still would not water.

We have a full moon now, and I enjoyed walking through the main sunny gardens tonight. *Lilium formosanum* is at its peak. The tall stalks are strong enough to support flowers that open out at right angles and perfume the night air in splendid ways. I have the nicest staff I have ever had but enjoy having the garden to myself or just with Craufurd. We even sat on the fern bench near the new vegetable garden and tried to imagine how it will look after a rain and after another year's growth.

The yearbook of the RHS Lily Society arrived this week. It includes an interesting article by Sylvia Liane Laws, "Growing *Cardiocrinum giganteum* on a Welsh Mountain." She followed Gertrude Jekyll's advice and dug a pit four feet deep, filled it with mulch, grit, compost, and loam, then set the bulbs with their crowns barely covered. After a four-year wait, her bulbs flowered on stalks twelve feet high, and they bore twenty-two flowers. I am going to try that!

Thank you for sending your photographs. It was almost like having a little tour of your container garden. The only problem is that they lacked the narrative. That plectranthus growing near *Canna* 'Pretoria' and *Pennisetum setaceum* 'Rubrum'—is it your 'Athens Gem' or your something else? I can see why you like those crape myrtlettes. That is a luscious shade of cerise! The galvanized containers from the Hillsborough hardware store Hella picked up back in May make excellent planters. What a good eye she has. The photograph looking up onto the deck makes it look like you live in a jungle—a wonderful jungle. How I wish I could cross the street and have a visit with you both.

Love,
Nancy

Tuesday, August 11, 1998

Dear Nancy,

The drought here was broken last night slightly after dark, with the welcome sound of rain splashing on our wooden deck. It rained steadily all night, not stopping until about 8:00 this morning. We got at least an inch, maybe more. Thunderstorms are forecast for late afternoon, but it's clear and bright now. Last night's rain seemed autumnal. There's another sign of a season changing. Crickets have started adding their chirping to the continual din of our cicadas.

Now, I hope soon to find in our mailbox a letter from you saying that your drought has ended, too.

About those visitors who observed that you were still growing exotics, I would have found it hard to remain polite. It's silly to think in terms of native plants versus exotic ones. Some natives are

Linwood

wonderful of course, and some exotic plants are pestilential, but the idea of excluding anything non-native defies understanding. About any plant there are only two real questions. First is it worthy in some way—for, say, beauty or utility? Second, does it have any bad habits that will make us regret planting it?

Besides, if we think in geological time, the native/exotic distinction becomes meaningless, thanks to a great many genera from different parts of the world stemming from common ancestors that grew before the continents began breaking apart. Good examples are hollies, stewartias, and rhododendrons, just for starters. We should also keep in mind that if we're going to have dogwoods in the future, they won't be our eastern dogwood but hybrids between it and the Chinese species *Cornus kousa*, which carries genes making them resistant to blight. It is probably useless, however, to argue with those who espouse a policy of "natives only, no exotics allowed." We are dealing here with something akin to religious dogmatics. It isn't horticultural patriotism, but horticultural xenophobia.

Enough.

Another sign of the approach of fall—Hella and I are starting to think what to do next year, a sure sign that we've reached the point when little can be done about this year's garden. We have turned our attention to a part of the garden I may not have mentioned lately, the shady half of the front garden, what I call bamboo land, because, unless we are vigilant, in time it (and our entire property) will be nothing but a grove of yellow-groove bamboo. It looks good from the deck. A path of round stepping stones leads into this area, just past a handsome bird feeder about ten feet tall. Beyond that there are redbuds, some hostas, and a few ferns, but then the whole thing just peters out. A few flowering perennials, like *Campanula persicifolia* and *Penstemon hallii*, are out of place. We've been thinking what to do about it and decided that we've really got the start of a little shady woodland garden there and now should follow through. I got out the Heronswood catalog and checked off some items — several cultivars of *Pulmonaria*, likewise *Epimedium*. (Virginia bluebells and celandine poppies already have a beachhead in the space.) Yesterday Hella and I drove way out in the country to a little nursery Ed Plantan told us about. For a nominal price we picked up a dozen ferns in gallon containers, substantial, very well-grown plants. Eight are *Dryopteris erythrosora*, the autumn fern, which I already grow in some quantity and value highly for its evergreen, perky fronds that don't go half-mast in winter, also for its coppery new growth in spring. We also bought some tassel ferns and two shaggy shield ferns. Both are new to me, and both are gorgeous, especially the tassel fern.

I have a new appreciation of your reasons for not irrigating your garden. I had assumed, wrongly, that it was a matter of not having a well adequate to the task, but now I see it was a deliberate choice. I can't follow suit. On our sandy soil, it's either water or don't garden.

As regards your questions about the plectranthus on our deck, yes, it's 'Athens Gem'. You'll get a plant from me very soon.

Love,
Allen

P.S. I have one flower on a white *Cyclamen hederifolium*.

Tuesday, August 18, 1998

Dear Allen,

What a lovely letter you sent on August 11. Thank you for your wishes for an end to our drought. We had a good rain of about 1.25 inches a week ago on a Saturday morning. The forecasters bemoaned the fact that golfers would be inconvenienced and those who work during the week be unable to have their cookouts on the weekend. Craufurd and I went early to the farmers' market where we heard only rejoicing. Once again we were "threatened" with a rainy weekend this past weekend, but we received barely a third of an inch.

I couldn't respond to your letter immediately because I was involved with the memorial for my father. I had no service for him when he died but decided instead to gather the closest members of his family for a celebration of his life. I chose the Sunday nearest to what would have been his ninety-fourth birthday. His brother, sister, and a nephew came from Tennessee; two of his favorite nieces came from Vermont and Georgia; and one of my brother's sons came from Raleigh. Neither my brother nor my sister came, the latter because she had recently broken her arm. We began by telling of our earliest memories. Mine was of his coming to the back door with a basketful of vegetables. I can remember how proud he was. At his memorial, we told funny stories and a few sad ones, and we felt closer to him and to each other than we had in years. We ended by drinking a champagne toast to him. I gave each person a copy of a set of sonnets found among his papers. We decided not to visit the gravesite, declaring that he was closer to us here than in any municipal cemetery. It was a beautiful occasion, and I believe he would have loved it. Perhaps you will understand that I haven't yet read his sonnets. I will read them early one Sunday morning. I had not wanted to have any service but am glad I did.

Many major events in life need boundaries. Even though my father lost his mind before his body, I felt I could confide in him. I am certain your grave illnesses of this past winter altered you and your life. One boundary that has thus far only a beginning is gardening. How did you get into it? Or perhaps I should ask, who led you to it?

Yes, you are right. August is different because it heralds fall. The light has changed even though the heat remains. I think I saw my first chickweed seedling yesterday and the first colchicum, *C. kotschyi*, opened on the weekend. *Cyclamen graecum, Scilla autumnalis,* and *Leucojum autumnale* make a carpet beneath our deodar cedar. I can finally see them at a distance.

It is the beginning. Even the boxwoods have their autumnal dressing. Spiders have spun their horizontal webs, and each morning they glisten with dew. School days have begun. Each morning, starting last Monday, I hear the buses arriving at the elementary school next door and down the hill. We have survived the worst of summer, no matter how many more uncomfortable days we have ahead of us.

I am fascinated by your questions for measuring up the plants for your garden. Beauty is indeed in the eye of the beholder, but the standards for beauty vary with the season. I would delight in the tiny flowers of spring even if they bloomed in competition with the gaudy, showy flowers of summer and fall. But they matter to me most because of their time of bloom. As for where a plant comes from, I prefer to remember from whose garden it came or from which nursery. I want to know where it is native primarily as a guide for me to know where to plant it or as an indication of hardiness (both winter-hardiness and summer-hardiness, the ability to take our long, hot, humid summers). If it grows in places with cool, moist summers, then I tend to skip it. If it comes from Japan, I will probably try it. I realize that Japan has a variety of climates, but I have more luck with Japanese species and forms of our own native genera than with any other group of exotics.

You noted that you might not have been polite to my unpleasant guest of several weeks ago. What I didn't report to you was my first reaction to her accusation that I grew exotics. I responded that in any radical evangelical movement there was generally much to suspect and perhaps a little to admire.

You recently mentioned using the old Bailey cyclopedia. I have read several articles praising it. I have also found in bookstores in Chapel Hill two sets of the three-volume edition. Do you think I should get one of them?

Love,
Nancy

Wednesday, August 26, 1998

Dear Allen,

I am tired of summer now even though the sunny gardens have just begun to peak. The asters and goldenrods are fat with unopened buds, some so far along that I can detect their color. I know you think goldenrods are wonderful, and I agree with you. I love the way some hold their bloom stalks horizontally. Much of my fall garden is purple, and yellow is just what it needs. Have you grown

Solidago caesia? It is a lovely, wispy thing that loves shade. It doesn't spread aggressively. Each stalk bends to one side in a gentle arc, and the flowers are a clear yellow, not a harsh yellow. Best of all, it doesn't mind drought.

The loveliest aspect of the garden now is the silent movement and color provided by the butterflies that flutter and float from plant to plant. I have seen a few monarchs, but most are swallowtails. Hackberry butterflies are my favorites. They often perch on my shoulders and stay there as I walk through the garden. Hummingbirds are active now and dart from one plant to another. They do aerial dances in pairs accompanied by shrill cries. The albino hawk shrieks, and I can sense the terror in the smaller birds nearer ground. I hear meadowlarks and indigo buntings at the edge of the field near the woods. Goldfinches sing as they fly away after eating the seeds of *Agastache nepetoides*. Although this is our least attractive agastache, goldfinches are reason enough to grow it. On cool mornings we hear warblers in the tops of our pecan trees. It won't be long before the white-throated sparrow returns. And I was right, chickweed has germinated where I watered under the large white oak.

Lycoris radiata var. *pumila* blooms now in the woods. I have this spider lily on the path below most of my cyclamen, where the heat seldom builds up, the soil remains slightly moist, and I can work soothed by the sound of birds or of squirrels running through the woods. I seldom hear a human sound down there.

I am in the midst of one of my pleasant summer chores. I spend several hours every day repotting my bulbs. Some, such as the autumn-flowering *Narcissus serotinus* from North Africa and the various species and cultivars of nerines from South Africa that bloom at the same time, are tender. Others can take at least a bit of frost. Besides nerines, I grow many bulbs from the Cape—species of *Habranthus*, *Ixia*, *Tritonia*, *Watsonia*, and so on. Many come from areas where winters are wet and summers dry, but some come from South African microclimates where summers are moist. To succeed with any of these lovely bulbs it is absolutely essential to provide the same conditions that prevailed in their native habitats. When I repot them, I take each pot, invert it onto a tray, and then scratch through the soil in search of bulbs. It is like finding buried treasure. I can usually find a radio station with good music to accompany my work. On Saturdays it gives me an excuse to hear Click and Clack on National Public Radio and during the week *All Things Considered* late in the day. It also gives me an excuse to be in a fairly cool place with a fan moving the air. Every year I improve my technique; this year I am planting the bulbs and corms higher in their pots to provide good drainage.

Perhaps you remember that day in May when you and Martha came by and she gave me two large black bags of her father's dental tools. They are wonderful gardening tools! I believe I have used every single one at least once, and several many times. I can probe into the pots without disturbing roots. I can tease delicate seedlings apart without damage. I prick out weeds with the tweezers. An enterprising garden supply company could easily produce and sell sets to gardeners, but I'm afraid these are now like the grocery stores we have hereabouts. If one has it, they all have it, and if one doesn't, none does.

Tomorrow Craufurd will have the first of two cataracts removed. These are the very fast growing ones, a direct result of prednisone taken when he had lymphoma. He had a choice of surgeons, one who will do it with a topical anesthetic or another one who will give him a more complete one. His physician recommended the latter. She wants to have absolute control over his eye. I must go with him and remain during the entire procedure. Since we will have yet another 90+° day, I hope to enjoy my time in the air-conditioned waiting room. My pleasure depends in part on how much space and silence I can have! It is torture to have to endure talk shows blaring over television sets.

Love,
Nancy

Friday, August 28, 1998

Dear Nancy,

It has been over two weeks since I last wrote you, and now I must lead off with that perennial concern, the weather. One morning last week we checked the min/max thermometer and discovered it had gotten down to 46°. I thought fall had come for sure, and rather early. But from Sunday through Wednesday of this week, afternoon temperatures were 95°, with steam-bath humidity. And of course we've had an anxious eye out for the track Bonnie might take. Paul and his family were in Orlando all week. Our first relief came when the hurricane turned away from Florida. Then once it came ashore in North Carolina, I followed its course on my computer and was pleased that at least it spared our friends in the Piedmont. Here we started seeing its influence Wednesday. The surf was high and boisterous, the sky a swirl of elegantly patterned, low-hanging gray clouds. Yesterday we had over an inch of rain in ten minutes at midday, and then it rained steadily all night. In all, we had about five inches. There was some chance we might have been brushed by the hurricane late today, but now it seems about to pass us well off shore. Hurricanes have some significance in my family. My Lacy grandmother was orphaned in September 1900 by the Galveston hurricane, in those days when hurricanes just arrived with no advance warning. You surely remember Hazel hitting Durham just before Homecoming weekend in 1954 (or was it '55?). I drove right through it to get from West Campus to East at about two o'clock, for Dean Roberta Florence Brinkley's Milton course. Just as I reached the building, the wind ripped most of the Boston ivy from the wall, so I walked in festooned with a drapery of vegetation, looking, I should imagine, a little like Alcibiades dropping in on Socrates' drinking party, except that I was sober.

Since we moved here we have been brushed by a couple of hurricanes, but not seriously. There is, however, absolutely no reason that we could not experience a Hugo or an Andrew or a Camille.

Hurricanes have changed their meaning now that we name them and know that they are perhaps coming our way. Our adrenalin rises as we carry out chores of preparation. Tuesday I made sure our cars had enough gas, and I went by the bank to get extra cash (in case of evacuation). I went to the hardware store for candles and batteries and to the service station to get an extra tank of propane so we could cook on our outdoor grill if we lost electricity. When I went to the grocery store for drinking water and cans of tuna fish, the place was crowded with other people on similar errands. The possibly incipient storm made a community of us all by giving us a common concern. Then I waited and waited, saying to everyone, "I hope we don't get it." When it was clear that we would not in fact get it, I said, "Thank heaven that it's gone out to sea." But the fact is that, as always, I felt oddly . . . well, let down, somehow. That's irrational, I know.

Spiders are increasingly evident here, as at Montrose. Some I don't like. I think there's a nest of very small ones somewhere in the house. About two weeks ago they—or maybe just it—bit me in the upper thigh, leaving a perfect row of six little fang marks that itched like crazy. Other spiders have taken up residence under the greenhouse benches. Their webs are very messy and unorganized, like those of black widows. I have heard that, despite appearances, the spiders that make these aesthetically unappealing webs are more highly evolved than those that spin out such thrilling orbs as autumn comes on.

We had one of these thrilling orbs last week. Taking out the trash one night, I walked into a web on the deck, attached on one side to a wayward stem of the kiwi vine and on the other side to a blade of purple pennisetum in a container. Next morning there was no evidence of the web, but that evening I noticed that a rather small garden spider—dull brown, not the large and spectacular gold and black sort—was perched on the stem of the kiwi vine, spinning out into empty space a single strand that finally found and stuck to a blade of pennisetum. I sat down to watch something I'd never seen before, a spider building her web. She spun out more lines, framing the architecture of the web, and when those were done, turned her attention to the center of the web, working her way from the outside toward the middle. Her labor was only half done when suddenly the greenhouse floodlights, which are switched on by motion nearby, came on. A mother raccoon and two nearly grown cubs rounded the corner of the greenhouse. At this moment, to see what was keeping me outside so long, Hella opened the door from the utility room to the deck, and the raccoons shuffled back wherever they had come from. When I came inside, the spider was still at work, but the next morning her web had disappeared.

We haven't seen that spider since, but others, of some other species, work unseen every night to spin their horizontal webs, like those on your box hedges, on our little lawn. Their webs are not architecturally ambitious, but in very early morning the dewdrops they have captured sparkle like crystals. Our acreage is much smaller than yours and we have no foxes (nor, praise be, deer), but we do have our fauna.

Hella and I have been working on the front garden. A sidewalk from street to front door bisects it. There's shade (and advancing bamboo) to the south. That's our woodland garden. We haven't yet got round to planting the ferns we bought or to ordering pulmonarias and other appropriate plants from Heronswood. We have, however, made a start on the north, and sunny, side, our so-called cottage garden, which is actually a jungle of invasive stuff, some tall (plume poppy, tartar aster), some short (fragaria 'Pink

Panda'). Last spring I tried planting some things we use heavily in the back and deck gardens, coleus for instance, but they were swamped by more established and more muscular vegetation. I want to keep a few tall plants, particularly those that are so splendid in autumn, such as *Aster tataricus*, New England asters 'Hella Lacy', 'Purple Dome', and 'Andenken an Alma Pötschke', *Helianthus angustifolius*, and *Salvia leucantha*. I will cut down on their numbers but position them where they can be easily seen from the front door as we come downstairs. Otherwise I want to cut back the height of everything else that we grow here. I saw a picture in *Pacific Horticulture* of a garden in Munich that struck me as a perfect model. There were lots of clumps of little grasses, particularly dwarf and miniature forms of pennisetum, scattered here and there, mixed with other low perennials. Saturday we went on a buying expedition, coming back with pennisetums 'Hameln' and 'Little Bunny', miscanthus 'Adagio', fescue 'Elijah Blue', 'Bowles Golden' carex, *Imperata cylindrica* 'Red Baron', and a variegated sweet flag, several plants of each. We also got several perennials, including sedum 'Vera Jameson', artemisia 'Powis Castle', and Russian sage. Sunday we worked together, planting a good-sized section next to the sidewalk where I had killed with glyphosphate a thick mat of *Vinca minor*. The sprinkling system doesn't quite reach this part of the front garden, but you will have discerned already that all of these plants tolerate drought. We planted everything somewhat loosely, with space between each clump. My idea is to load the space with huge numbers of spring bulbs. Late in the spring we'll fill in with tender foliage plants, especially purples, grays, and silvers, and chartreuses.

In re Liberty Hyde Bailey's *Standard Cyclopedia of Horticulture*, yes, get it; it's worth having. Years ago Elisabeth Woodburn gave me volume I with the cover ripped off and volume II intact, but no volume III. I would love to have all three volumes, so that I can find out what Bailey has to say about plants that come after *Ozothamnus* in the alphabet. Next time you are in Chapel Hill would you find out a price for a complete set for me? Or tell Martha where they are sold so she can check for me?

You wrote about boundaries and you asked me what started me on the gardening life. I have something to say about both topics, but I will stop for now and put this letter in the mail.

Cheers,
Allen

Monday, August 31, 1998

Dear Nancy,

You wrote of your father's death as a "boundary," speculated that my recent appointments with the scalpel might also be boundaries of some sort, and then asked how my passion for plants and gardens began. Some of the existential philosophers talk about "boundary situations." These are moments in which some unusually significant event—a wedding, the birth of a child, the death of a parent—divides the course of someone's life into a "before" and an "after." And yes, my recent medical adventures were that sort of thing. Dr. Johnson was right. The thought of death (and I did think of it!) does concentrate one's attention in a very powerful way.

Now, another boundary is about to be reached. Tomorrow I go out to the college for the usual meetings at the start of the academic year, but I won't be at the lectern when classes begin. I won't be teaching my two classes in philosophy and my one horticulture class. Next spring I'll teach two horticulture classes, and no philosophy. I'll be teaching only a third of my usual load, for full pay. I may teach next year, but only one semester for one semester's pay. If so, that will be my last classroom experience, but the likelier thing is that I will just call it quits at the end of the present academic year. Either way, I have accepted the college's offer to buy me off with early retirement.

Were I nineteen again and facing a decision about a profession to follow, I'm not sure I would choose an academic career again, but when I did choose it, it was the right choice, even if academe isn't quite the fraud my dear brother Johnny thinks it is. ("Allen, let me get this straight. You work only from early September to early May. You don't work half of Thanksgiving week, you get three weeks off from mid-December into January, and a week off in March or April. You teach only on Tuesdays and Thursdays. The state of New Jersey pays you enough that both you and Hella drive a Volvo. Every six or seven years you don't have to teach at all, but they still pay you. *Does anyone know about this?*") I do, of course, admit to Johnny that teaching has been a fine way of life for me—that for one thing it has given me sufficient leisure to be able to write, and write prolifically, about things I love.

For thirty-seven years, slightly over half my life, the classroom has been the center of my professional life. This past academic year I taught only a few weeks before the first medical crisis came along.

This coming year will mark a step-down or perhaps a diminuendo in my involvement with students. Teaching and its obligations have been the framework for everything else—meaning, for example, that if I wanted to take off three weeks in October to go to Italy I couldn't do so unless I were on sabbatical. I will probably miss the classroom from time to time, but not the obligation to be there on a regular and fixed schedule. And I will miss the horticulture course more than introduction to philosophy. I'm looking forward to retirement, but it will change things, alter certain balances between work and leisure. But when I mention retirement, Michael says, "Retirement, Dad? How will you be able to tell you've retired?" (His work demands his presence morning till night, five days a week, at a bare minimum.)

As to your other question, about how I got started with gardening, it happened in Irving, Texas, during the war (you know which war), when I was in the third grade, and there were two passions, not one. The first started when my mother brought into our house a record album that wasn't the Andrews Sisters singing "Three Little Fishes," Jesse Crawford playing "When Day is Done" on a theater organ, or Bing Crosby crooning "Stardust." It was the Robert Shaw Chorale performing Bach's Magnificat in D. From that first rhythmic surge and the first bright trumpet-statement of the theme, I was hooked, hooked on this musical work, hooked on Bach, on Robert Shaw, on choral music, on classical music. Soon, as a boy alto, I was a member of the choir at First Methodist Church, Dallas. The passion for music has continued unabated ever since, though I regret that I have long been only a listener, that where I live, unless I've missed something, there are no choirs worth belonging to—or listening to. (Okay, I'm a choral snob!)

My passion for gardening I credit first of all to a fourth grade teacher named Mrs. Harkey, a breeder of bearded iris. In the same year I discovered Bach, I helped her on Saturdays at her little nursery just outside Irving. She showed me how to brush pollen from one iris onto the pistil of another, how to tag the flower with a label recording the cross, and how to wait—to wait first to see if the cross had taken, if a seed pod formed and swelled and ripened, and then to wait two years to see the result. The result usually was nothing very much, but it might instead be a flower of enormous beauty—something that human effort had brought into being. Mrs. Harkey taught me the wonder of gardening.

At about the same time, maybe a little later, there was a radio show called "The Old Dirt Dobber." If my recollection is correct, it came on on Saturday mornings, right after "Let's Pretend" and right before my mother drove me over to work at Mrs. Harkey's. The dobber was a crusty fellow who talked about his garden—what to do when and why, I think. He taught me that gardening could be the subject of pleasant and civilized discourse.

I don't remember the name of the third person who figured in my horticultural initiation, but I called her "Ma'am." She managed Nicholson's Seed Store, in Highland Park, a suburb of Dallas. My first paying job, when I was in the eighth grade, was at Nicholson's. The shop closed many years ago, but I still remember it vividly. It was narrow and dark, and smelled of lemon oil. (My first chore before the store opened was to polish a long wooden counter near the cash register.) Lemon oil wasn't exactly the only aroma there, as from the warehouse area behind the shop itself some stronger pungencies emanated—the odors of cottonseed meal and bonemeal, also various animal manures in paper sacks.

Ma'am had blue hair and impressive posture and dignity and, I suspect, a fine corset lady, as such folks were then known. My job, Saturdays only, involved sales, unpacking merchandise, and carrying customers' orders out to their cars. Before she would allow me to work, Ma'am had me memorize the names of all the plants Nicholson's sold, so if a customer asked for something I would know whether we had it or not. She initiated me into at least a dawning awareness that there was a considerable body of knowledge out there somewhere that I needed to get a grip on if I was to garden as I should. She also invited me to peruse the nursery catalogs, gardening magazines, and reference books in her little office cubbyhole. I accepted her invitation, using my lunch hour to browse. Ma'am taught me that plants had names and that I'd better learn them and learn them right.

Later, I supplemented my horticultural instruction in Ma'am's little office library by browsing in the only gardening book in my parents' "library" (which was little more than lots of copies of various *Reader's Digest Condensed Books*). The book was *10,000 Garden Questions Answered by 20 Experts*. Michael and Christine found a copy of this book at a garage sale and gave it to me last Christmas. It runs to 1,390 pages, of which 177 are devoted to "Plant Troubles and Their Control." A paean of praise for DDT, chlordane, and scores of other miraculous chemicals, the book makes horrifying reading today.

In bloom now for the first time here is seven sons' flower, *Hepta-codium miconioides*, which I planted in 1994. You must also grow this Chinese plant, introduced not long ago by the Arnold Arboretum. I love the sweet, vanillalike fragrance of its small white flowers. The scent carries far on the air. When I walked downstairs this morning, their intense perfume filled the dining room, even though the tree is about fifteen feet from the window.

Regards,
Allen

Monday, September 7, 1998

Dear Allen,

Craufurd's operation seemed to go smoothly. I was concerned but tried not to show it. I let him answer all the questions about his diet, his allergies or lack thereof, and his activities before we arrived that morning. I did pretty well until the nurse asked if he had a living will. "A living will!" I exclaimed. "Of course not. I want him back!"

Bailey's *The Standard Cyclopedia of Horticulture* (all three volumes) will leave the Avid Reader Bookstore for Linwood on Tuesday morning. Yesterday Craufurd and I purchased one for you and the other for me. Perhaps we will find more solutions to our puzzles there. I have one other useful encyclopedia, valued mostly because it has pictures. The pictures aren't glossy, nor are they in color, but they are beautifully drawn, indicating the feature that distinguishes each plant from all others. It is *An Illustrated Flora of the Northern United States, Canada, and the British Possessions* by Nathaniel Lord Britton and Addison Brown from the New York Botanical Garden. Also a three-volume work, my copy was published in 1943. I recommend it highly. Last week we were curious about the difference between boltonias and asters and found a key in Gray's *Manual of Botany* declaring the primary difference to be the presence or absence of a pappus. That sent us scurrying to the dictionary to find out what a pappus is and where we might find it, but we discovered where to look only after studying the drawing in Britton and Brown. I believe most thinking gardeners bring with them an insatiable curiosity about plants. It is often a much greater challenge to find the answers. I know I will never lose the excitement that accompanies each answer.

Montrose

You mentioned Hurricane Hazel in your next-to-last letter. We were both there within a mile of each other but might as well have been on opposite sides of the globe. How could I forget that storm? It was one of the highlights of my college days. I was a freshman. (There were no freshpersons in those days.) I was walking to the dope shop—and in case one of your grandchildren should get hold of this letter, I hasten to explain that long ago in the South "dope" was another name for Coca-Cola, which at one time did contain an extract of coca leaves. I'm afraid that nowadays there are many dope shops of entirely different character, but in 1954 the two dope shops at Duke were places to buy school supplies, to get a cherry coke, a big double scoop of ice cream, or, if you were really sophisticated, black coffee made early that morning. No drugs stronger than aspirin were sold there. If you were lucky, you might find mail in your box in a tiny little post office near the rear of the building. But, back to Hazel, someone shouted in alarm that a hurricane was headed straight toward us and no one was supposed to be outside a building.

I returned to the dorm and stood watching with a feeling of excitement and wonder as the enormous oaks I had known all my life blew over, bringing with them roots and all the earth that used to anchor them. It was beautiful. It never frightened me. I knew I was in a well-built brick building and that nothing could harm me. I was ignorant and innocent.

I never feared hurricanes until Fran came through two years ago. Of course, I had seen the damage that Hugo had done, not only in Charleston but also in Charlotte. That gave me a new respect for such storms. But I never really understood what a hurricane means until I felt, heard, and saw Fran immobilize this area. I got up over and over during that long night to look out and try to remember the skyline as it was before I went to bed. I needed to know which trees remained. I remember how long we were without power. I remember not being able to get food, gas, or light. I also remember that they didn't cancel classes at Duke.

I never walk through our woods without noticing the enormous uprooted trees still lying where they fell. I was happy we didn't get Bonnie, even though I felt desperate for rain.

I am glad you haven't had a hurricane hit your garden there. Weather really matters to me. Not just my weather—I worry about weather in gardens I know around the country. So I watch the storms move up the coast toward you and wonder how they will behave.

The spiders of fall continue to decorate our boxwoods. Inside the house they have tied every chair to the nearest wall and connected the legs to their railings. They link the treads of the staircase. They eliminate right angles where the wall meets the ceiling, draping each corner with swags of nearly invisible threads. It is only after they have been there for a month or so and gathered dust that I see them—usually when I am showing the house to friends or visitors!

How splendid that you could watch a spider constructing her dining room. I like spiders, better outside than in, but I am afraid of black widows. I remember one day when the staff sat behind the house having lunch during packing season for Montrose Nursery. We saw a black widow in her web over the trap door to the basement. What to do? Martha came to the rescue. First we poked the web and saw the spider drop to the terrace, and then Martha bravely stepped on her. It was such a simple solution.

The deer population at Montrose has a new set of twins. As Craufurd and I washed dishes last night, we saw a buck and a doe lead their wobbly-legged twins to the large oak tree near the barn. I can't imagine what they found to eat there, for we haven't yet planted that area. I believe they were on their way to the delicacies in the purple and orange border. When I approached, all four stopped and stared at me, holding their large ears toward me to catch any sound. I followed them down to the woods, where they vanished. They never ran and probably watched me long after I lost sight of them.

How I wish you were here to see the colchicums. This is the year to divide them, and I did so last week, just before we finally got a wonderful soaking rain. I now have hundreds. I think of Elizabeth Lawrence's friend Mr. Krippendorf when I divide these corms, for he said he might have 50,000 if only he hadn't waited so long to begin making his divisions. Colchicums are obliging—they bloom and thus reveal their location before they make roots. It is a simple matter to dig or pull up the corms. They keep right on blooming, later grow roots, and finally in the spring grow foliage for the next fall's bloom.

Love to you and Hella,
Nancy

Wednesday, September 9, 1998

Dear Nancy,

Thanks for your call. I look forward to your next letter and to finally having all three volumes of the Bailey *Cyclopedia*. But Hella and I were both very concerned about Craufurd's reaction to cataract surgery and hope you managed to get him to the doctor as soon as possible. Why do these medical emergencies seem to love flaring up on weekends, especially holiday weekends?

The turning has come. Yesterday was ferociously hot and extremely humid, one of those days when nudism has huge appeal. The high was 92°, but it felt much warmer. A cold front came through in late afternoon, with huge black clouds boiling up furiously, obviously filled with dangerous energy. The system was clipping along at about fifty miles per hour, with gusts up to seventy. We had a few drops of rain, a few distant bursts of lightning followed by prolonged, rolling growls of thunder, but by that time the brunt of the storm was further north. It stayed hot and humid until midnight, when another thunderstorm hit us. Lightning was flashing all around for about thirty minutes, with enough rain and wind that we had to close windows. We awakened this morning early to one of those perfect days of early fall, the air fresh and clear and cool enough for long sleeves and a cotton sweater. Now, shortly after noon, the sky is azure, with only a few small puffs of clouds in sight.

The autumnal flora has been here for a couple of weeks already. Sweet autumn clematis is evident everywhere, especially where it has naturalized itself along the verges of our salt marshes. It is also growing up a plant of *Heptacodium miconioides*. (The other day I caught the intense vanilla scent of the clematis, and I mistakenly attributed it to the heptacodium. People praise its perfume, but to my nose it is no more fragrant than a piece of paper). Joe-pye weed is near its peak, in what little vacant land remains in Linwood. Under one of our Virginia junipers, white and pink *Cyclamen hederifolium* are in their second week of flower. These, now huge tubers giving us over fifty flowers apiece, date from the first year of Montrose Nursery. Others, only now showing buds and on much smaller plants, are silver- or pewter-leafed forms from the nursery's last year. We have these at the easternmost edge of the deck. There, the decking is at ground level, where it's much easier to admire the flowers up close—and later their leaves—than under the juniper. Oh yes, patrinias are also at their height of bloom.

Classes started today at the college. It's odd not to be there, for reasons other than medical ones. I'll get used to it. But I don't think I'll get used to something else at the college. I made an appearance last week at various meetings. In my prolonged absence a system of voice mail has been installed. Faculty members are supposed to check it regularly. I just left a message, "Sorry, but I'm on leave. Check back with me next semester." When I go back in January I may just forget to change the message!

Tomorrow I have a talk at Shipbottom on Long Beach Island, thirty miles up the Garden State Parkway. It's to a men's garden club. I don't do garden clubs anymore. Usually. I'm sure that there are some very good ones and that by refusing all invitations I'm missing meeting some delightful people. But I decided years ago, "Never again." I learned my lessons from talks when: (a) no one listened; (b) it was noon and there was no way to darken a room to show slides; or (c) much of the audience was half-crocked on white wine or martinis. I did accept this invitation, however. The fellow who called me last week sounded both congenial and desperate. Maybe someone had stood him up. Maybe he had just procrastinated about getting a speaker. My topic for a half-hour talk is foliage plants for deck and patio. I've got slides of strobilanthes, castor beans, colocasias, plus some very sexy coleus. I'm also taking a couple of buckets filled with cuttings.

I may or may not hear further from the Odyssey people, but I will be filming for a TV series next month. I'm not at all clear on details, since I talked only briefly last Friday with a woman in New York who called here. Her company will fly Hella and me to Orlando the end of next month. At the Disney Institute I'll do three brief segments (under ten minutes each) on inviting gardens for a show whose name I didn't quite catch. You can probably guess already what I'll do. The senses, the mind, and the spirit, each one gets a nod.

Thursday, September 10

Yesterday was that talk in Shipbottom. I was the youngest guy there by far. The room was so dim that it didn't have to be darkened further for showing slides. It was also so dark that the plants I brought could have been almost anything. The lectern where I was to speak was halfway across the room from the projector. The remote cord was yards and yards away, so someone in the audience agreed to operate the projector according to my cues. I got up to speak, but no one had turned on the PA system. A waitress was called to fix it. As soon as I started talking, a man sitting in a chair right at my feet fell to the floor unconscious. Other club members lifted him back in his chair, still, it seemed to me, unconscious. I asked if he was okay. I was told that he was probably okay, that he often did this, and that I shouldn't be surprised if he did it again before the end of my talk. I cued the slides, but the fellow with the remote control couldn't see well enough to tell if a slide was in focus or not, so he kept sliding the focus-control button back and forth. The meeting ended. I took the basket of cuttings outside so people could see what they looked like and go home and start them in water if they liked. When I went back in the dining room to retrieve my belongings, I discovered that the copy of *The Inviting Garden* the president asked me to bring so he could show it around was nowhere in sight. Someone liked it well enough to swipe it.

I agreed to do this talk for nothing, by the way. I think I'll go back to my old policy when invited to do garden clubs: tell them that my fee is $5,000 plus expenses.

More on spiders. Michael dislikes them intensely. I don't know why. The greenhouse and shed are full of them now. I haven't seen any black widows, though some webs are suggestive enough of them or of brown recluses that this weekend I'll seal both buildings from drafts as best I can and then fumigate.

Saturday, September 12

Took the train to Philadelphia yesterday—another medical check-up there, this time with Dr. Kaiser. Everything looks fine, he said. x-rays show both lungs free of even the slightest suggestion of trouble. This is one more testimony to how very lucky I have been.

The Bailey *Cyclopedia* just came, nicely wrapped in cellophane, plastic film, and Chapel Hill newspapers. There was a receipt inside one volume for $156 for books and shipping. Check enclosed. Let me know if that's not the right amount.

The second-busiest time of the gardening year has begun, with all the chores of fall. They are of course more leisurely than those of spring, but just as necessary. Hella is bringing inside scores and scores of houseplants—checking them for hitchhiking insects, removing unsightly foliage, repotting them as needed. I am about to deal seriously with the greenhouse. I have to decide which plants belong there, with no experience to guide me on questions like how to handle the coleus plants from which I need to propagate new stuff for 1999.

We have Japanese anemones now—my favorite, the lovely white 'Honorine Jobert', also a deep rose semidouble whose name I don't know. No colchicums here yet, nor autumn crocus. I only have three. *Crocus sativus* strikes me as slightly ratty, with weak-necked flowers and fairly untidy sexual parts. I love *C. goulimyi*, though. The prim little flowers look like bluish-pink lollipops, and they stay in bloom a long time. Best of all, they self-seed everywhere. I'm also fairly keen on *C. speciosus* and some of its cultivars.

Cheers,
Allen

Sunday, September 13, 1998

Dear Allen,

The first two weeks in September brought me all the happiness I could ever want. Tropical storm Earl left just over three inches of rain, and early the following week we had eight tenths of an inch. It was glorious. The rains were mostly soft and gentle, occasionally heavy but only occasionally, so the ground soaked up the water and the plants drew it up through their roots. We all perked up. The lawns still have large brown areas but the grasses whose roots survived are now green above ground. Best of all, everything looks freshly washed. The sharp edges of the deepest cracks in the earth have softened. Of course I want more rain, but now we have heat, with no hope of rain until possibly late in the week.

We spent one morning last weekend in the emergency room of Duke Hospital, where two residents argued over all the conditions that might have given Craufurd the new problems with his eyes. They were red, swollen, itching, and sealed shut every morning. I was present for the examination, and I listened closely. As you well know, there are many similarities between medical Latin and botanical Latin, and I thus understood about 90 percent of what they were saying. But there was one word I didn't understand, and so I asked what it meant. The incipient doctors looked at me with scorn and replied, "That was just doctor talk; you wouldn't understand it!" I protested but was ignored. These young residents missed the diagnosis altogether, proclaiming that Craufurd had an allergic reaction to something. Two days later (still the Labor Day weekend) Craufurd called again, hoping in vain to reach a real doctor but this time finding a more knowledgeable resident who gave the correct diagnosis—viral conjunctivitis in both eyes. Finally on Tuesday his surgeon confirmed it. Craufurd is slowly getting better. He has to wear sun glasses all the time. No one seemed to think that strange until he gave his evening course on Bloomsbury and had to feel his way along the corridor to his classroom.

We went to a retirement dinner last night for one of Craufurd's colleagues. Having attended some painful occasions in the past, neither of us really wanted to go, but it was pleasant. The department honored the guest of honor instead of roasting him. Several people commented that Craufurd was next in line. Some even asked if he was still teaching. These are the times we realize that we look our age. These are also times when we think of the next stage of our lives. I often think neither of us will ever retire. We are lucky. Just as you enjoy teaching horticulture with a delicate overlay of philosophy, Craufurd enjoys teaching his interdisciplinary course on Bloomsbury, which he overlays with economics. I think you both share your enthusiasm for your subjects and thus inspire your students to learn. These are the courses students never forget. I love giving the seminars on gardening here. I enjoy sharing my excitement at discovering a new technique for germinating a seed or stimulating a plant to produce more plantlets. I love discovering the correct names for plants and determining what makes them members of one family rather than another. I think a garden or maybe a garden center makes a classroom far superior to one with walls. We don't need slides of each plant or part of a garden at its peak when we have the reality of many plants at various stages. We don't need music when we have the sounds of the birds.

This is not to say I don't share your love of Bach. He, better than all others, expresses the inexpressible. I tuned the harpsichord last week and worked yet again to master bits of the Goldberg Variations. I know I won't succeed. I could never play it as I hear it.

Mrs. Harkey must have been wonderful. My Mrs. Harkey was my second grade teacher, Mrs. Pridgen. She showed us how to plant a sweet potato by sticking it with toothpicks and setting it on top of a jar nearly filled with water. The base of the potato barely touched the water. She then placed the jar in a dark closet behind the blackboard. We brought it out after about a week and saw roots that lengthened day by day. We later put it into sunlight and saw leaves appear above the tuber. It was a miracle beyond any other I had experienced or imagined. As I knew Mrs. Pridgen better and my fear changed to admiration and finally affection, I came to know her garden. The soil was deep and rich behind her small house. She dug holes and put into them all of her organic kitchen waste the entire time she lived there. She planted her compost throughout the garden; she had no "proper" pile to be watered and turned. We entered her house from the side door, never the front door, and along her side walkway she had rows of jars covering rose clippings from friends' gardens. They always rooted. She taught me how to spell *hippopotamus* but I don't think she mentioned *Ipomoea* as the proper name for sweet potato. I have a few treasured roses rooted from plants in her garden, and, yes, I rooted them as she did under jars in the shade.

Love to you and Hella,
Nancy

Thursday, September 17, 1998

Dear Nancy,

Last Saturday Hella and I went to Egg Harbor City to the fall festival and membership meeting of the Herb and Botanical Alliance. This used to be Hilltop Herb Farm, owned by my friend Lucy Marzolino and her daughter Anita Beckwith. I've mentioned them before; in December Lucy had the same surgery and same surgeon that I had in January. They transformed Hilltop into a nonprofit organization with a growing roster of members and an ambitious program of community gardening and other good works.

I'm on the board of the Alliance, and must pass on one item from our meeting for your amusement. Another board member works for our county extension agent. Not long ago, someone called to ask why her tomato plants bore no fruit. The lady said, "I just can't understand it. Why I've done everything I'm supposed to do—stake the plants, fertilize and water them, and deadhead all the flowers." This story led to a lively discussion of horticultural basics and not assuming knowledge where there may not be any.

You wrote that you have tuned your harpsichord and are working on bits of the Goldberg Variations. I'd like to hear you play sometime. For the past thirty years almost all my experience of music has come from concerts (very rarely) and recordings. There was a time before that, however, when in addition to listening to recordings I was part of a circle of people who actually made music themselves. During almost a decade as a choirboy at First Methodist Church in Dallas, I sang all four parts of all (no cuts!) the choruses in the *Messiah*. (I started as a boy alto, briefly moved up a notch to soprano just before testosterone kicked in, tried tenor for a short time, and then settled in as a baritone.) One of my close friends was a fine organist. My first two fairly serious girl friends in high school days were pianists. The first I associate still with Mendelssohn's "Rondo Capriccioso," the second with Chopin's "Ballade in G Minor" (or was it G Major?). No one that I knew, however, played the Goldberg Variations. But I do remember the excitement that I felt when Glenn Gould's recording of them came out in the mid-1950s. It would be good to hear a friend play them one of these days. And, by the way, speaking of the Goldberg Variations and Gould, I have just discovered an amazing musician, someone everyone else seems to know about. He's Keith Jarrett, and he plays piano, harpsichord, and soprano saxophone. In this country he's known primarily for piano performances of popular classics and for jazz. In Europe, however, he's known for his piano and harpsichord performances of Bach, Mozart, and Handel. There are a lot of recordings, but they're not available here. I searched them out on the Internet, however, and ordered several from Germany—some Handel suites and the Goldberg Variations and the Well-Tempered Clavier. I got them within a couple of weeks, and Jarrett is really a stunning performer. And, unlike Glenn Gould, he doesn't hum along as he plays!

So, considering that your garden doesn't leave you much leisure to work at that gorgeous harpsichord of yours, I shouldn't tempt you to take on another interest, but I do wonder sometime if you'll ever start using the Internet. (I have a dandy new iMac.) There's a lot of excellent horticultural stuff available online, for example the Paul Christian Rare Plants nursery in Wales. It has a huge catalog of mostly bulbs. I'm enclosing printouts of just a fraction of their offerings: eight species of *Habranthus*, seventeen species of *Zephyranthes*, twenty-three species or cultivars of autumn-flowering *Crocus*, and twenty-five kinds of *Colchicum*. I imagine that you'll be particularly interested in Christian's extensive list of *Galanthus*, many of which I know you grow, including *G. reginae-olgae*. I'm fascinated by his offerings of *Muscari*, particularly *M. macrocarpum*, described as having "golden-yellow, tremendously fragrant flowers in April." The perfume of this grape hyacinth is said to resemble that of gardenias. Christian does ship to North America, but the prices are a bit steep. *Muscari macrocarpum* is £4.50 for just one bulb, and some of the galanthus (*Gg. allenii, platyphyllus*, and that *reginae-olgae* you grow) rise to £7.50 each.

After a touch of cool, fall-like weather we're back to summer. Yesterday it reached 95°, with intense humidity and not a trace of our usual breeze. We haven't had rain for about ten days. Everything looks tired, dusty, and drought-stricken. Our hostas are particularly dreadful looking. Some, such as 'Sum and Substance' and *H. sieboldiana* 'Elegans', are virtually immune to slug damage, but the majority by this time of year are chewed ragged. Yesterday I cut the worst of them right to the ground. I'd almost wish for a good hard freeze, except that I know most of the delights of autumn still lie ahead. *Solidago rugosa* 'Fireworks', a magnificent plant, is not at peak bloom yet, and the first magenta-pink bud of *Colchicum speciosum* is just poking its way through a solid carpet of *Ophiopogon japonicus*.

Best,
Allen

Sunday, September 20, 1998

Dear Allen,

Thank you for sending the article about *Homeground, Hortus,* and similar periodicals from the Philadelphia *Inquirer.* The pictures of you are excellent. I don't remember seeing the surface of your desk when I visited you in Linwood. Has the new iMac done that? I especially like the photograph of you in the garden. Now I know how your trellis looks. I like Betsey Hensell's description of your writing but think "personal" and "elegant" more appropriate than "simple." You use simple words to express profound ideas. Perhaps that is what she meant. I hope you have had a good response to the article in the form of new subscriptions.

This seemingly endless summer continues. We have just survived another week with temperatures in the upper 80s and 90s and without any rain. At last I can see in the long-range forecast for the coming week temperatures in the 70s, but I am getting worried about Hurricane Georges. We have two days of gardening seminars on Friday, the 25th, and Saturday, the 26th. I need good weather!

The days are much shorter now, though I notice it more in the morning than the evening. It is definitely harder to get up. I am looking forward to a return to standard time and will find that adjustment easier than the spring switch to daylight saving time. Cyclamen cover the slope in the woods where I cautioned you not to step on your first visit to Montrose. At last I have a vision fulfilled—a real groundcover of flowers! I have had the leaves for years but not enough flowers. Several groups visited the garden this week, and I took those who seemed really interested down to that woody slope. The slanting light illuminated the flowers from below where we stood. People gasped—and I was thrilled. One person said she was breathless over such beauty. I don't have time to go alone and stand and stare, so I am grateful when a group of appreciative visitors gives me an excuse to marvel at what is there. The variations of color and form in the blossoms are wondrous. Every now and then I kneel to take in the fragrance of those I know to have scent. In moments such as these, I give silent thanks to the ants of Montrose. Our aims are divergent, but we converge on the results of their activity. I have planted thousands of cyclamen here, but the ants have gone further. They helped spread them into the path, across the path, down the hill onto the next terrace, and finally up into the field above.

Arum pictum blooms now beneath the metasequoias near the

house and below the cyclamen in the woods. Last fall I saw my first flower, after waiting seven years from sowing the seeds. There is confusion over the name, for many people think *Arum italicum* 'Pictum' is the same thing. *A. i.* 'Pictum', by the way, is now *Arum italicum* subsp. *italicum* 'Marmoratum'. Can you imagine walking through the garden and pointing out a plant and using that name? But back to the blooming arum. First I saw a bulge in the mulch and then a spear pushing up through the soil. The flower has a nearly black spadix and purple-maroon spathe. Thus far I haven't detected a typically malodorous scent but it is probably there. The small, shiny leaves unfold just as the flower reaches maturity and are shield-shaped with gray-white veins and a purple margin. I remember from last year that the shine disappears from the leaves and the veins become more subtly marked. That purple edge, however, remains until summer. I wish you could see it.

Near these arums, sternbergias are just pushing up, showing their fresh, light green shoots. They pierce the soil like snowdrops, with a spear containing flowers that seem covered with pale green silk edged with darker green. The covering peels back to reveal flowers of brilliant but pure yellow without a hint of red. I grow sternbergias in sun and shade and find they do equally well in both places, probably because those in shade have sun all winter when their foliage needs it. They bloom throughout the metasequoia garden, in the paisley border nearby, and in a bed at the edge of the woods. I divided some yesterday and began a new planting in front of the house where the large white oak once stood. I am glad I brought over those three bulbs of *Sternbergia lutea* from my Durham garden twenty-one years ago when we moved to Montrose. They are protected in the wild now and rightly so. This is another of those easily propagated bulbs that dealers wouldn't take the time to produce. They preferred sending cheap labor into the fields of Turkey to dig the bulbs, thereby removing and nearly exterminating the much rarer, tender *S. candida*.

September 22, 1998

Finally—the last day of summer! I keep wondering how your garden looks and also how much daylight you have. I realize that your days in summer grow longer than mine and your days in winter are shorter, but surely somewhere between those seasons we have one day that is the same length in Linwood and Hillsborough. I planned to report the times of sunrise as stated in our paper but the paper was not down by the gate. I'll look tomorrow. One reason I am curious is that you report *Anemone* 'Honorine Jobert' in bloom, and my plants don't have the slightest bit of white showing through their tightly closed buds.

Back to your lovely letter of September 9: sweet autumn clematis has been over here for weeks. I will cut the plants all the way down when we finish our seminars. I don't want more seedlings! It is one of those splendid plants I couldn't be without that needs watching lest it smother less vigorous neighbors. I was intrigued by your comment in an earlier letter about the intense fragrance of *Heptacodium miconioides*, an observation that you later corrected. I can detect a little, subtle fragrance here, but only at specific times of day—late morning and early afternoon. I had never noticed *any* fragrance at all until one day late last summer when we were preparing for our fall seminar. I couldn't imagine what I was smelling but finally tracked it to heptacodium. I guess it puts out its scent when its pollinators are around.

I share your frustration at giving talks. I give fewer and fewer. For one thing, I love being in the garden and know I will miss something whenever I go away. It may be only the first sight of a newly emerging bud, or it could be a ripened seed or perhaps even a new flower on a plant watched for years, but whatever it is I don't want to miss it. When I do give a talk, it's because I really do want to. I almost always enjoy the visits once I get there. I don't actually enjoy performing so much as seeing private gardens and meeting keen gardeners. Right away I know we will have much to talk about and a common approach to life. I feel the same way about tours of the garden. Yesterday we had a group of pleasant-enough people who showed no interest in the garden. I was able to show the entire front and side gardens in thirty minutes and take them through the sunny borders—now at their peak—in fifteen. I didn't even bother to mention the woods.

Let me know when you will debut on television. We don't have cable, so I hope you will record it.

I sympathize with Michael and his fear of spiders. I remember when Martha and Mary Jo Halchin helped me wrap plants. We enjoyed doing it and would often listen to books on tape, but our concentration was often broken by a shriek from Mary Jo. She could spot every minuscule spider as it let itself down from the ceiling toward the packing table.

With love and special happiness that tomorrow will be fall!
Nancy

Autumn

Friday, September 25, 1998

Dear Nancy,

Autumn—the real thing!—made its appearance right on schedule on Wednesday. Tuesday was muggy and hazy and warm, but Wednesday dawned with crystalline air, skies of deep azure, and a low of 42°. The high for the day was in the mid-50s. I wore a sweat suit all day with no discomfort. Thursday was also cool. Today is a bit more summery, but I still wore sweats until 11:00 A.M. after a morning spent planting the two orders of spring bulbs that have shown up so far.

Workmen are everywhere. A painter spent two and a half days repainting the staircase hallway. He comes back Monday to start on the living room. Jim Brightly has been here with two of his crew for two days—replacing a few posts and rails in the front and side fence, putting up curtain rods, fixing locks, and working on the greenhouse. When the greenhouse was finished last fall, there was only one bench, along one side, where, because of the curve of the roof, there wasn't much headroom. Jim and crew have now built a wide bench along the back of the house, with lots of room overhead. I had them take out a sink because it constantly clogged, wasn't really much use, and didn't justify the space it occupied. They come back Tuesday to finish a few other things, such as shelves behind the new bench.

What I'm about to say you know already, I'm sure. The greenhouse, whose sixteen by twelve foot dimensions seemed generous last winter, turns out to be too small. (Just got a greenhouse and greenhouse supply catalog in yesterday's mail and looked in disbelief at the six by eight foot models!) Only a fraction of the sizable tropical and subtropical plants in containers on the deck and throughout the garden will fit in our greenhouse. I'm allowing myself one four-foot plant of *Brugmansia* 'Jamaica Yellow' and a rooted cutting of *B. versicolor*. (I've ordered from Florida rooted cuttings of 'Charles Grimaldi', 'Betty Marshall', and a double white, with next year in mind.) There are six other containers of my two brugmansias sitting around the garden. Fortunately, tomorrow my friends Anita and Lucy will come with a truck and haul them back with them to overwinter in their warm greenhouse (and take cuttings). They're doing the same with other plants: several specimens of a cultivar of *Plumbago auriculata* with particularly deep blue flowers; a massive tibouchina; a couple of tender passifloras; a palm;

and other stuff. They'll also get cuttings of my best coleuses and plectranthuses.

Back to brugmansias: this has been a disappointing year for them here. 'Jamaica Yellow' has bloomed sporadically, *B. versicolor* hardly at all. But a rooted cutting of the yellow one that I gave Ed Plantan is now huge, multibranched, and showing twenty flowers. I don't think brugmansias will survive here over the winter in the ground, as they do at Montrose, but I mean next year to set out small plants in the ground in late spring. My hunch is that they will perform better that way than in large pots. Also, they need huge amounts of water and fertilizer. (Didn't you tell me to mulch them with an inch of Osmocote?)

September 26

I loved your piece on *Zephyranthes* and *Habranthus*. I have little experience with either. Years ago I bought several zephyranthes from Holbook Farm, but they never established themselves, probably because they were planted in medium shade. In August 1997 I noticed several in pots at Montrose but didn't give them enough attention. (I don't feel sorry over that in the least. The ongoing miracle of gardening is that no matter how many kinds of plants we come to grow and know, the supply of new ones to try is virtually inexhaustible.) Next year I want to grow several *Zephyranthes*, particularly *Zz. candida* and 'Labuffarosea' which look very fetching in that roll of film you sent, which I had developed this afternoon. I also loved the shot of *Lycoris radiata* emerging from a sea of that little spreading coleus with small burgundy leaves edged in green. What a splendid combination! I enclose a picture of a little corner of our garden, just north of the arch. At the top is a huge dome of *Solidago rugosa* 'Fireworks' and plain old asparagus below and to the left, a pennisetum to the right, spilling over a clump of sedum 'Autumn Joy', with a tiny scrap of hakon grass at the lower left corner. I like the combination, and Hella hasn't found any flaws in it.

I also enclose a package of seed from Burpee of an abutilon strain called 'Summer Sherbert'. It was hybridized in Costa Rica by my friend Claude Hope, who is now in his mid-nineties. It was Claude who gave us the virtually indispensable hybrids of *Impatiens walleriana* that grow in jillions of American front yards. When I was at his finca near Cartago in the early 1980s, he was just starting to work with abutilons. 'Summer Sherbert' is simply terrific. Coming in a wide range of clear pastel colors, it starts blooming when about six to eight inches. The large and abundant, attractively crinkled blossoms are held somewhat outward and almost upward instead of hanging down. The plants are at least half-hardy. I gave Martha a couple of plants in spring 1997, and they got through the winter on her deck without protection. I got two packs, one for each of us. I'm planting half my seed now in the hope of winter greenhouse bloom, the rest in the spring.

Take care,
Allen

Tuesday, September 29, 1998

Dear Allen,

I was delighted to receive a letter from you yesterday. It was dated September 26, and I suspect I am missing one, since you mentioned over the phone last week that a letter was on its way. The last letter from you was dated September 9th, so if you did write another letter, please retrieve it and send it. I kept looking for it at the post office last week but was always disappointed.

I, too, had autumn—the real thing!—arrive on schedule, but it turned out to be a mirage. Sunday and Monday were as bad as any day in July, and once again we broke records for high temperatures. I noted but forgot to write down the day when we had twelve hours of daylight. It was, I think, the third day of autumn. My twelve-hour day ran from 7:00 A.M. to 7:00 P.M., slightly later than yours. It makes me wonder how the powers that be determine which is the first day of fall.

Brugmansias have been disappointments here this year, too. Someone facetiously suggested giving them a one-inch mulch of Osmocote, but I haven't tried it. I think they need much more water than they received this summer, but what else? Certainly they have had all the heat they could need. I don't count on their coming through the winter every year, so we take cuttings of every single one. I won't dig them up.

Your appreciation of the combination of *Lycoris radiata* with *Coleus pumilus* proves it—your taste, sir, is impeccable! There are some events, some plantings in the garden here for this season that I always have in my mind's eye, always look forward to. When their day rolls around each year, I always think, "Now that is good." One is the colchicum garden and another that brief but spectacular show of spider lilies suddenly springing up through a carpet of burgundy coleus. The reality is even better than the picture in my mind's eye!

Thank you for your photograph of that corner of your garden. Craufurd said, "That is beautiful." I love the use of plain old asparagus. Your solidago does look like a yellow sparkler. The deer won't allow us to have all kinds of sedum so I especially like seeing yours. And thank you also for the seeds. I will plant them in the spring. I have enough to overwinter this year.

I'll stop and write you later this week about the garden. It really looks like fall!

October 1, 1998

Your missing letter arrived yesterday. It was postmarked September 18th! You sent it priority mail! I asked about this astonishing delay at the post office. The man at the post office says they don't guarantee priority mail. You pays your money and takes your chances. No wonder the USPS has such a bad name! I feel no sadness at leaving the last days of September. I will not long for the heat of summer during winter. I feel only a rejuvenation and optimism that perhaps, after a day, we will have cool, clear air. We already have the slanting light that tints the late afternoon with golden yellow. Grasses bloom now with silky plumes. At this time I wonder whether some of the larger *Miscanthus sinensis* cultivars are worth growing. *M. s.* 'Zebrinus' and *M. s.* 'Variegatus' have collapsed onto themselves and their neighbors. I prefer the neater, tighter ones such as 'Rigoletto', 'Silberfeder', and 'Gracillimus'. From where I sit in the law office writing to you, I see in the far corner of the blue and yellow garden the inflorescences of *Arundo donax* 'Variegata' that must be twelve feet high. Although I have seen it happen many times, it is hard to believe that all that growth occurs within a five-month period—and this year with very little water. Above this giant reed, *Koelreuteria bipinnata* is decorated with rosy-tinted beige seed clusters. Each pod looks like a Chinese lantern and contains pealike seeds. This is an excellent tree here, with large upright panicles of clear yellow flowers in late summer. In its corner of the blue and yellow garden it seems to stand guard between the woods and main sunny gardens. Recently one of our seminar participants said that it is terribly weedy, seeding about all throughout his garden to the extent that he could no longer enjoy its beauty. Thus far I've had only one seedling but know that I may have to be careful.

Thanks for sending me some of Paul Christian's listings of bulbs from the Internet. Catalogs are often the best and most current sources of information about plants, so even if I don't get around to ordering this year, I will in the future. Sometimes I wish I were connected to the Internet or that I had e-mail, but not often. I have spent my entire adult life trying to arrange it so that I can be in the garden almost all of every day. I don't want the temptation of looking for the treasures hidden away in this cyberspace of which you speak.

Yesterday I found the first flowers of *Crocus speciosus*, and I was both delighted and disappointed. I was delighted because it was the first evidence of a new season for another genus. I was disappointed that I missed it early in the morning, for by the time I found it late in the day, it had already collapsed from the heat. This crocus was in the rock garden surrounded by cyclamen—*Cc. hederifolium*, *cilicium*, and tiny *intaminatum*. In such company, *C. hederifolium* looks like a giant. I like the purity of the white flowering *C. cilicium* but love little *C. intaminatum*. Yesterday I knelt to see it closer and indeed could see those fine gray lines running vertically up each petal. The plant looks incredibly fragile but is tough.

Thanks for sending plectranthus 'Athens Gem' and the bulb of *Rhodophiala bifida*. I planted the latter across the circle from the rock garden, where I want to compare it with *R. advena* from Elizabeth Lawrence's garden. I want to see if they really are different enough to deserve the status of separate and distinct species. I can't make comparisons yet. My old bulbs of the oxblood lily bloomed in early September, and the fat, healthy bulb you sent has not broken dormancy yet. Next September I'll have the evidence.

Colchicums still bloom near the boxwoods. I am disappointed that some in the woods and others in the rock garden may not bloom this year, but 'Waterlily' is in full flower. It lacks the elegance of the taller hybrids, but it is aptly named and now that I have enough to form a drift I like its tousled beauty.

How extraordinary that one of your girl friends played Mendelssohn's "Rondo Capriccioso." In all honesty, I can state that I disliked that piece more than any I had to study. It seemed so insipid, so repetitive, and so undeserving of the effort I had to muster to play it moderately well.

I think that gardens are more closely related to music than to painting. You covered this point well in *The Inviting Garden*. Without a little dissonance the garden is dull. Without sound the garden is dead. That is why I add a little surprise to each color scheme, why I added the water feature, and why we don't eliminate those large grasses. The challenge comes in knowing how to manage the proportions. Perhaps I need to go back to Pythagoras.

I wish you weren't so far away, but I do look forward to your letters and think of them now on this, the last terrible, hot day of the season.

Love,
Nancy

Friday, October 2, 1998

Dear Nancy,

Late this morning your letter of September 29/October 1 rolled out of my fax machine from Craufurd's office at Duke. I'll reply in kind, and unless Craufurd leaves earlier than usual you'll get this this afternoon. That's not quite as good as e-mail, but it's certainly quicker than priority mail just turned out to be. Almost two weeks to be delivered! I figure it couldn't have taken any longer for a letter from New Jersey to reach North Carolina back in Thomas Jefferson's day.

On all my visits to Montrose during the growing season I have always admired your colony of variegated *Arundo donax*, but I've never been tempted to try it here. If I were tempted, Hella would stay my hand. At her insistence over many years I finally got rid of all our tall miscanthuses, which truly were out of scale with everything else. The worst one came to me as *Miscanthus rivularis,* but the name seems to be invalid; it's probably *M. floridulus* instead. There was a large clump by our front gate. By this time of year the silvery plumes reached seventeen feet or higher. The first stiff wind of autumn always made it bend over the fence into the busy traffic of Shore Road. Now we grow only *M. sinensis* 'Gracillimus' and 'Adagio'.

I hardly dare mention drought here to you, but the rain we got night before last—a steady rain that brought us over an inch—was very welcome. June through September set records here for lack of rainfall. Fall, I can safely say, is truly here. We live directly under the Atlantic flyway. I hardly believe my ears, but I have heard geese overhead long after dark, and the other morning I heard them again just after our sprinkling system came on and woke me at 3:30. *Aster tataricus* has started its long season of bloom, likewise *Salvia leucantha*. One other spectacular autumn perennial, *Helianthus angustifolius*, hasn't even shown buds yet, but it will be sensational this year. One clump is over ten feet high. It's right next to the front sidewalk, where it will be lit from behind just after dawn—quite a sight first thing in the morning! These are three of my favorite plants of the season, but now there's a fourth, one that came from Montrose last May—*Salvia nipponica* 'Fuji Snow'. It has just started flowering, and I love it for its pale creamy yellow flowers, its wandering ways, and its tolerance of shade. (I suppose the 'Snow' in its name refers to the white edges of its leaves.)

Let me add verbenas to brugmansias in my list of disappointments of 1998. 'Homestead Purple' sulked all summer long, I didn't mind especially, for this cultivar increasingly strikes me as coarse and brash, but 'Sissinghurst', which I value highly for its delicate foliage and elegant, soft rose flower clusters, also bloomed poorly. Among container plants that I tried this year for the first time, there were winners as well as losers. I remain very high on million bells, those little petunialike flowers allegedly in the genus *Calibrachoa*. (I suspect they're really petunias.) They're fine for hanging baskets. So are two very much improved annuals, patented cultivars of brachycome daisies and torenias. Both have bloomed nonstop since late spring. Earlier this year I was very much taken with a German-bred hybrid of *Fuchsia triphylla*, 'Gartenmeister Bonstedt', for its smoky bronzish foliage and abundant crop of tubular scarlet flowers. By season's end, however, its appeal wanes, for it is far too leggy. My favorite fuchsia, for both in-ground and container use, remains *Fuchsia magellanica* 'Señorita'. It blooms so profusely from early July right up to the first freeze that its stems arch over. Its tiny crimson and purple flowers are the essence of grace. It is bone-hardy, although it dies back to the roots. Have you grown this? If not, let me know and I will take cuttings next year. I don't think heat and humidity bother it much.

Maybe I'll grow 'Gartenmeister Bonstedt' after all. I interrupted writing this letter to bring in the garbage cans from the street, and as I started to come back inside I saw something remarkable on the deck. A male cardinal was perched on a flower cluster of one of these fuchsias in a hanging basket, feasting on its fleshy seed capsules the color of ripe Bing cherries. That was a sight not easily forgotten!

I have your photos of those spider lilies with that coleus pinned up on my bulletin board. Now, there's something I'd like you to check on your plants of that coleus. Take a quick look at their terminal leaves and let me know if you commonly find several that are untypical—shaped like clubs instead of pointed hearts and with less burgundy (just a patch) and more green. The reason I ask is that I found a couple of stems in my own plants last month that showed this alteration. I have rooted them both, and so far there's been no reversion. If this change is characteristic of the species, I don't have anything unusual on my hands. What I'm hoping, of course, is that a stable mutation has turned up here. It would be wonderful to have a new form with different leaf coloration but with the same fine spreading habit of growth.

So far, I've had precisely one crocus flower. I think that, like yours, it was *Crocus speciosus*.

I just placed the largest bulb order of my life! It's primarily for that so-called woodland garden I keep mentioning. It's really a little no-man's-land occupying the southeastern section of our property. I might be pretentious and say it was our secret garden, for it is isolated visually from anything else. A large Colorado spruce—entirely too large for our small garden—blocks it from sight from the front cottage garden. (I should have ripped the spruce up years ago when it was small, but Hella grew fond of it, so there you are.) The bamboo that we have to keep in check with a spade every spring curtains it off from sidewalk and street. Untrimmed yews just outside the living room conceal it entirely from our sight. From the deck, we see only the first stepping stones of the path into this part of our garden, and the very large, freestanding bird feeder of copper and glass.

The stepping stones circle through this area in a way that might be handsome if the planting was well done. It isn't. Over the years I have mostly ignored this space, occasionally sticking in this or that plant that somewhat qualifies under the woodland rubric—hostas, epimediums, celandine poppies, mertensias, and whenever I think of it, more ferns like those I finally planted last week. (Coming from Heronswood next week for this same part of the garden are twelve different cultivars of *Pulmonaria*. Given the promiscuity of the genus, who knows what I'll have in five years, but I wanted to get a close look at various fairly recent introductions, such as Beth Chatto's 'David Ward'.)

and patches and long black legs was spinning a web connecting *Salvia* 'Van-Houttei' to *Canna* 'Wyoming'. And, oh yes, bananas grow on the west side of the border. The largest of them (*Musa basjoo*) survived last winter, but I plan to dig at least half of it before our first freeze this year. We hope to keep bananas growing here in years to come, as substitutes for the bold foliage of our cannas, which are horribly caterpillar-ridden.

I hope you can imagine this garden. You saw it the autumn of the first year we planted it, and I wonder whether any year can equal that one. As for the lath house below the burgundy and gold border, I'm not certain you can imagine it, for you haven't seen the reflecting pool. We turn off the pump in the evening so there is no sound of water, just the shimmering reflection of sky and the woods beyond the gardens. The delicious, spicy fragrance of *Elaeagnus pungens* 'Maculata' fills the air.

I did not walk alone through the garden, for I had a young black and white cat with me. When I knelt to examine plants, he thought (rightly!) I needed someone to pet. I kept on walking, past the purple and orange border, pausing in front of my enormous plant of *Dahlia imperialis*, and hoping that this might be the year I see it bloom before we get frost.

I finally made my way to the comfortable bench of cast iron at the north end of the new gardens we've put in this year. It's the bench Craufurd and I sit on when we view the garden on moonlight nights or at twilight. I sat down alone, something I seldom do, and looked critically at the new plantings near the end of their first growing season. This part of the garden needs more of everything—more masses of large shrubbery, more creeping, delicate plants to soften the edges of the paths. But despite these deficiencies, the new garden is promising, even exciting. I could see all the way across it with an uninterrupted view of a huge new urn of cast iron at the south end of the broad walk of gray-blue gravel that harmonizes all of the strong colors used in this part of the sunny garden.

Even though the sun was about to set, from my vantage point I could clearly make out many interesting plants and combinations that pleased me.

Along the wide pathway, various grasses were at their finest. *Pennisetum setaceum* 'Rubrum' and 'Burgundy Giant' echoed the basso profundo they contributed in the purple and orange garden. Their inky-burgundy or beige flowering plumes (color depends on age) quivered in the wind above their rustling leaves. Another pennise-

When I planted the ferns just this side of the wall of bamboo—no easy task!—I happened to look up at the bird feeder and was struck by a vision of what this space might look like in spring. The feeder is really a fine piece of sculpture. The feeding chamber, which sits eight feet in the air, is attached to its pole with an ingenious arrangement of pulleys, so it can be pulled down easily for cleaning or filling. The copper has weathered to a splendid patina. Anyway, I decided that it should be the focal point of a really spectacular display of flowers all during spring. I've ordered many fritillaries, a dozen of so *Fritillaria imperialis* 'Rubra Maxima' and 200 *F. meleagris* 'Alba'. There will be hundreds of botanical tulips, several species, also hundreds of little daffodils like 'Hawera'. A hundred wood hyacinths, which I still call *Scilla hispanica* although we're now supposed to call them *Hyacinthoides hispanica*, are on their way. (Thinking of spring, just as autumn gets underway, is my way of postponing thoughts of winter. I have, incidentally, just found a kindred soul in E. A. Bowles, whose *My Garden in Autumn and Winter* [1915] was reissued last month. He disagrees with those who "read a sad note in Autumn" and like "to dwell on the fading and passing of Summer's joys." He dislikes these persons' "depressing remarks about departing swallows," for he relishes the "yet warm soil" and "cool and moist atmosphere" that make September and October conducive to "the autumn maneouvres of the garden." About winter, he is more of a Lacy than a Goodwin mind. It is an "unwelcome presence in the garden." He has a great dislike of "cold weather and its effects.")

I just called Craufurd's office. He's gone for the day, so I'll put this in regular mail, also enclosing some of Martha's sketches of our deck plantings and of various Montrose scenes (more than I feel like faxing). Oh yes, I'm also sending a copy of an article on *Microstegium vimineum* as an invasive alien plant. I found it on the website of the Virginia Native Plant Society. You wrote me earlier this year about your problems with this plant, and I thought you might be interested in its common name, Japanese stilt grass. I am delighted not to be cursed with this weed!

Love,
Allen

Sunday, October 4, 1998

Dear Nancy,

Yesterday was spent mostly in getting tender plants into the green-house. In midafternoon Lucy and Anita arrived to pick up various excess tropical things. (They were supposed to come last week but didn't because Anita broke both thumbs in a freak accident involving moving an antique icebox. She is amazed by things she never imagined not being able to do without the use of a thumb, such as eating a sandwich.)

It started raining at 3:00 this morning, and twelve hours later it is still raining. It is also very chilly—38° at dawn, only 51° now. Hella brought the heavy feather beds out today and I hope flannel sheets will follow promptly. I puttered in the greenhouse over morning coffee, but turned on the kerosene heater first, cranking it all the way to 75°. Anita and Lucy live fifteen miles farther inland, in Zone 6. They've had two frosts already. We can't be far behind. My feelings are ambiguous. I hate the thought of cold weather, but I'm ready to see impatiens and other tender plants blacken and depart. There's simply too much biomass out on the deck.

I've been pondering again those analogies between music and gardening. Maybe in a couple of weeks I can make more sense of my vague intuitions of the strong connections here.

Love,
Allen

Sunday, October 4, 1998

Dear Allen,

Last night Craufurd taught his evening seminar, so we had an un-civilized early supper. It was still bright outdoors when he left, and I took a little tour of all the gardens below the law office, starting with the purple and orange border, which should more accurately be called burgundy and gold. The fence at the entrance was rampant with vines and climbers—'Mary Wallace' rose, *Clematis terniflora* (in seed), and *Dolichos lablab*, whose upright panicles of pale purple flowers combined spectacularly with the intense orange flowers of a tall *Tithonia rotundifolia*, still bolt upright for lack of windstorms to knock it over. Chiming in and adding to the ensem-

ble were several coleus—black-leaved 'Duckfoot';
unidentified cultivar with black stems and green
cream leaves veined with red-violet; and 'Leprec
your cuttings of last May. This one is a fine addi
collection, for it is very large and bright.

I stood for a while at the entrance to this part
joying the scent of *Heliotropium arborescens*, wafting
vanilla fragrance, bringing with it all of the overt
mother's garden. We planted an old and leaky g
a large *Setaria palmifolia*, with dark purple stems
veined with red-violet. In another container, S
bears bright orange thorns along the orange vein
It is further decorated with little violet flower
fruits. Elephant ears or colocasias give this pa
tropical, perhaps Victorian, look. The plant
purple stems and leaves edged with purple. M
through outside last winter, but I won't gamble

Nonhardy, burgundy-leaved pennisetums
needed bass notes for the brilliant color sche
grow both the slender-leaved *Pennisetum setaceu*
broader 'Burgundy Giant'. The former is more
of fluffy burgundy flowers, some of which are
gundy Giant' with its wider blades veined in gr
I could never give up either one! There's more
berries with dark fruits now turning brilliar
purple or striped shoots on cannas cut back ea
plosions of furry orange tubular blossoms o
ocymifolia. *Lantana camara* 'Miss Huff's Hardy'
makes a major statement with flowers of pir
If you had told me years ago that I could li
nied it, declaring that you didn't really know
like it and even find it exciting.

The most splendid additions to the di
were eight monarch butterflies with wings
combined with jet black. Farther down the p
was in full bloom, with burgundy bracts
This salvia combines nicely with the blue-g
scarlet and yellow flowers of the *Asclepias c*
itself into the gravel pathway. Below these
have *Tradescantia pallida* 'Purple Heart'. An
floral tapestry, a splendid writing spider w

Montrose

tum here, *P. orientale* 'Tall Tails', was showing fluffy white flowers
that arched gracefully over their green bases. Here also was the most
dramatic grass I grow, the sugarcane, *Saccharum officinarum* 'Pele's
Smoke', with smoky gray leaves and lighter central veins. Horizontal bands of pink appear on them magically toward the end of
September.

As daylight faded toward evening and I began to walk back to
the house, I caught sight of two fawns and their mother in the distance. I went toward them, and they came toward me, until we were
only about fifteen feet apart. The magnificent buck joined them,
and we all stood and stared at each other, until I finally left and
broke up the party.

Monday, October 5

Have I mentioned our asters yet? Most of them look very bad this
year because of the drought, but the salvias—in almost every
color—are splendid. *Salvia leucantha* are now large shrubs, lovely already for their white flowers protruding from velvety purple calices.
S. involucrata 'Mulberry Jam' also has furry flowers, but they are a
luscious rose-purple and the plants aren't really shrubby. We have
S. greggii in white, fuchsia, and red and *S. microphylla* in many shades

from pinkish-red to dark purple-red. The Jamensis hybrids — *S.* × *jamensis* — which are natural hybrids between *S. greggii* and *S. microphylla*, add overtones of yellow to the colors of their two parents. *Salvia mexicana* in all of its forms blooms late with dark purple-blue flowers. One of these, 'Lime Green', wouldn't need to bloom at all for me to love it. The calices are brilliant chartreuse. I might also mention the blue-flowered, deliciously grape-scented *Salvia melissodora*; and furry-flowered *Salvia miniata*. The latter is my favorite red salvia, for its dark, slightly blue-green leaves and velvety, brilliant scarlet flowers. It grows equally well in sun or shade, so I may try some in the woods next year.

Love,
Nancy

Thursday, October 8, 1998

Dear Allen,

Your letters of October 2 and 4 arrived by snail mail and that was faster than priority mail. Along with the second one I received almost an inch of rain, so I am happy. I would like even more rain, for it didn't permeate the mulch, but it washed the dust away and the world looks brighter and cleaner. Before the week ends I will find more rain lilies blooming.

You mentioned growing *Miscanthus sinensis* 'Adagio'. It isn't one I grow, but sounds good if it is slow, as the name implies. All through the gardens, miscanthuses have collapsed. I want to keep a few, so will divide some clumps and compost the rest. As for *Arundo donax*, I don't want to start a family debate there but must say that even though it spreads, it does so in an orderly way. I can keep it in bounds by digging away at the edges. I must remove the clumps infringing on the boxwood circle so will have some to spare if you decide to try it.

We have started bringing in plants, beginning with those in pots on the porch. For once we did it right, repotting those that were potbound, throwing out any that didn't look healthy, and checking for unwanted critters before bringing them inside. The little greenhouse looks full, and we haven't begun on the main gardens. Wayne Hall rebuilt the floor of the pit below the law office. He used treated lumber and left spaces between each board for drainage. We will drag in some of the planted containers and fill the rest of the pit with relatively hardy plants. We completely emptied almost all the cold frames, then lined the really deep ones with bronze screening. We tried that last spring, thinking the copper in the bronze would keep slugs from devouring primulas. Now we hope that in addition to doing that, it will also keep the roots of plants in pots from growing into the gravel at the bottom of the frames. Roots don't like copper and although it won't kill them they avoid it. Some nurseries dip their containers in a copper solution just to keep the roots inside where they belong. Anyway we have cartloads of plants to deal with. Hardy perennials will go directly into the garden. The tenderest plants will go into the big greenhouse. We have more seeds to collect, more cuttings to stick. I am happy with our progress, for this is the first year we have planned ahead and not left everything until the day of the first freeze.

I got a postcard from the Horticultural Society of New York inviting me to your evening there next month. I would love to hear you read from *The Inviting Garden!* I hope it goes well and you sell many books.

I was surprised to read that your verbenas didn't perform well. You were hot and dry, and they are supposed to like that. They were excellent here in our gruesome summer, spreading far beyond their alloted space and never stopping bloom. They won't do that until we get a really hard freeze. I did have trouble with those million bells. Perhaps it was my fault for planting them in the ground instead of leaving them in containers. I put them in the "bathtub" urn, where we watered them daily, but they made only one feeble display of exquisite flowers.

Suddenly, our brugmansias are coming to life. They are magnificent, large plants, and their fragrant trumpets are worth a visit just before bedtime each night.

I like *Fuchsia* 'Gartenmeister Bonstedt'. It has bloomed all summer, was blooming in May when I brought it out of the greenhouse, and will go on blooming when I take it back inside. I don't know *F. magellanica* 'Señorita' and would love to try it. I have had so little success with the genus that I am skeptical but not ready to give up yet.

How interesting that you may have found a sport on *Coleus pumilus*. Looking for mutations is one of our most important tasks of the season. All three of us go around to all the coleuses to look for them. I haven't found a club-shaped leaf on *C. pumilus*, but have taken several shoots with a wider band of green surrounding the burgundy center of each leaf. This is not to say that I am unhappy with the plant just as it is, but, like you, I want to preserve anything unusual.

The little rain this morning tempted me to plant my new crocus and lily seedlings. The most difficult part of growing bulbs is knowing how much moisture they want when dormant. Now I take the easy way out and put them into the garden at the tender age of nine months. I would love to have so many crocuses that you couldn't walk without seeing them. I don't put them in lawns, so I won't have to caution you about stepping on them.

Hyacinthoides hispanica defeats me. When we moved here twenty-one years ago, I found masses of an enormous blue-flowered hyacinth in the woods and around the large white oak near the law office. I believed it to be the Spanish bluebell, *Endymion hispanica*. I passed it along to anyone who liked it. I also found masses of the little woods hyacinth that I now think is *Hyacinthoides non-scripta*. We have blue, pink, and white ones growing in the lawn near the large pecan trees on the west side of the house, under shrubs beyond the boxwoods, and along the fence bordering the sunny gardens. I brought more from my mother's garden, for she had collected old forms of *H. non-scripta*. I know that is the name of the bluebells that carpet the woods in England and inspire poets who see them in full bloom. I used to see them in bulb catalogs as *Scilla campanulata*. I still am embarrassed about the time I sent seeds to a seed exchange and, not believing the species name to be right, sent them as *Hyacinthoides nondescripta*.

I forgave E. A. Bowles for his thoughts of winter. His trilogy is one of the great garden-writing triumphs. His garden must have been a treasure, and his writing is infectious. I wanted to grow what he grew, so I read and reread his books, along with those of Elizabeth Lawrence, and also Christopher Lloyd's *The Well-Tempered Garden*. With my taste for Bach, how could I resist that title? Such books were my summer treats, and my best teachers. I always found something new to grow or a new hint to explain past failures.

Thank you for the information on Japanese stilt grass. I knew that it set seeds in the fall but was surprised to read that a single plant does not produce prolific amounts of seed, only "100 to 1000 seeds." Nor did I know that the seeds are viable for seven years. Oh, dear!

Last weekend we hosted a dinner to honor some of the donors

for Duke. It was a pleasant occasion. Do, Re, Mi, and the twins greeted the first arrivals. We were shocked by the second group, who announced that Montrose had the largest squirrels they had ever seen. They had never seen woodchucks before!

Surveyors marked the entire property with bright orange flags. We have found a recipient for the development rights for Montrose and hope to begin transferring them before the end of this year. Triangle Land Conservancy will accept them in perpetuity. Craufurd and I feel good about the arrangement. At least it means the property will be protected from all except botanical and horticultural development for the future. Neither of us is ill, and although we tease about incipient Alzheimer's, I don't believe we have it yet.

I care more about this land than anything I have ever owned. I want to try to protect it. Ayr Mount, the property next door, is in the hands of another trust with exactly the same goals, so together we control over three hundred acres on the edge of Hillsborough. The future of our garden, our house and its contents, and the outbuildings is still uncertain, but we hope to find a way to preserve them as well.

Love,
Nancy

Thursday, October 8, 1998

Dear Nancy,

I enjoyed your letter with the twilight tour of the purple and orange garden and so on. I took special notice of your discussion of salvias. It was Montrose that taught me that the genus *Salvia* heaped glory upon glory, that it was far more than cooking sage and those fire-engine red bedding plants that generally land next to orange marigolds at filling stations to offend the eye. The only perennial salvia I knew then was *Salvia azurea*, which had gorgeous flowers but tall stems so lax that the plant aspired to be a groundcover. You introduced me to 'Indigo Spires' and *Salvia leucantha* and got me started on another horticultural love affair. But your last letter made me forcefully aware that in 1998 I didn't keep to the vow of several years ago, to grow four or five new salvia species or cultivars until either I died or ran out of salvias, whichever came first (and there's little doubt about which will come first). I also didn't plant this year some of the tenderer sorts I would prefer never to be without: *S. discolor* (gray-green foliage, silvery on the back, flowers truly black but sparsely produced all season, a great container plant); *S. madrensis*, (so stately, so surprisingly yellow in flower, so prematurely dispatched by frost); *S. miniata*, one of my favorites as well as yours, though, oddly, I have found here that this sage from Belize does best in shade; and *S.* 'Van-Houttei'. I miss all of these this autumn, also 'Indigo Spires'. I do have, among the tender kinds, *S. leucantha*, the Mexican bush sage now coming on strong in the front cottage garden, also *S. buchananii*. This one is not very sturdy, nor does it ever produce a huge flush of bloom. But its rounded, dark green, glossy leaves are fetching, and its large, dark pink, velvety flowers appear intermittently all year. It's a good container plant that can hold its own surprisingly well against more aggressive companions. I have discovered some salvias unsuited to my garden because my growing season is not long enough. *Salvia mexicana* has never bloomed here, in any of its forms, and neither has *S. regla*, although its positively radiant foliage redeems it.

Some of the salvias we both grow have their surprises. Have you yet discovered that *S. leucantha* is as fine as Japanese honeysuckle for sipping nectar? At exactly the right time (experience will teach you when that is) gently pull the velvety flower from its calyx. Right at the base of the flower you will find a transparent drop of delicious nectar. Another salvia may or may not surprise you, depending on how you would answer the question, "Is *S.* 'Van-Houttei' a fall bloomer—that is, a plant that blooms only in the autumn?" That was always my experience of it, but then early one April Hella and I went to Charleston, South Carolina, for a week. Large plants of it were in full bloom in many of the gardens in the historic district. I speculate that initiation of bloom is triggered by near parity of day- and night-length, but only on plants of some size and maturity. The reason I have never had spring bloom here on this salvia is that at that time of year my plants are still small and immature. When does it start blooming for you? All salvias have one surprise—the scent of their foliage, which is sometimes fair, sometimes foul. There's no way to predict which it will be. You just have to sniff and find out.

There's another surprisingly fine scent that many people never discover. The fleshy, bright scarlet seeds of *Magnolia grandiflora* smell exactly like bay rum. When I crush one I'm instantly transported back to the barber shops of my boyhood. In Hannah Withers's garden in Charlotte, I once crushed a seed for Rosemary Verey, inviting her to sniff. She had no idea that it would have any scent at all, much less so distinctive and delightful a treat for the nose. And she wrote a whole book on fragrance in gardens!

We have not had a frost yet, and the colors of autumn are just starting to suggest themselves. Hackberries are getting yellower than usual, also catalpas. About a third of the needles on our white pines have turned to gold and are starting to shed. Black gums are showing crimson. Only burning bush euonymus and some sumacs are approaching anything like full color. But lots of autumn perennials are at their peak of glory now, especially in our front cottage garden. *Salvia leucantha* and *S. elegans* are both gorgeous, the former with its soft white or purple flowers embraced by their purple calyces, the latter with its soft, downy foliage tipped by torches of bright scarlet. Salvia 'Purple Majesty' is no piker, either. It's our tallest one; it earns its name entirely and over the years has proven to be absolutely winter hardy, although it might be tender in heavier soil. *Helianthus angustifolius* is absolutely spectacular. Since its flowers tend to open uniformly all up and down its height, it is a great column of pure, radiant gold. Here it has a fit companion in *Aster tataricus*. We have to look up to both plants!

Sunday, October 11, 1998

In one of the borders flanking the front walk, there's a fine, albeit accidental, combination. *Gentiana saponaria* has started its long season of bloom that will continue well into November. It is loaded with buds and closed flowers, both terminal and axillary. The stems are lax, so these teal blue, faintly striped bottle flowers have draped themselves into the bright green foliage of our winter heaths. Golden creeping jenny intermingles with everything else, and the airy, faintly lavender spikes of *Calamintha nepeta* add a frothy touch. The calamint and the gentian in this autumn ensemble both came from your nursery very early in its history.

Yesterday I was interviewed by a visiting garden writer from the New Orleans *Times-Picayune*. We had a fine time. I took her on a little tour of the snazzier part of town, a new development of $1,250,000+ monstrosities combining architectural motifs from a gaggle of periods and styles—e.g., rusticated and crenellated Tudor. We were especially delighted by a cobblestone and quarry tile driveway leading up to a water feature just below a massive stone staircase to a front door with a twelve-by-twelve-foot panel of etched glass above it. The water feature, of carved stone, had a shallow basin ten feet across at least, sitting five feet high. Rising out of it were four huge dolphins, sitting back-to-back, facing the points of the compass and dribbling water out of their mouths. The etched glass? Mermaids!

One thing was striking as we drove through more established neighborhoods here. Impatiens, wax begonias, petunias, and other common bedding plants planted in most front yards hereabouts are terrifically beautiful right now. The combination of cool nights, still-warm earth, and the ample, slow, soaking rains we've finally gotten makes all such staples of suburban civic horticulture truly wonderful to see. It can't be long until one morning they are blackened by frost, so now is the time to cast them an appreciative eye.

The Inviting Garden, I hear, is going back for another printing. Warehouse supplies are very low. Saturday I'm going to be on Felder Rushing's radio show (by telephone). It goes out to several stations all across Mississippi.

While I was writing about the dolphins and mermaids, the postal carrier arrived. It was time to eat a little snack of a lunch, just fruit and cottage cheese. (I weighed just 145 pounds last March, but, alas, I am now up to 175 and will have to buy new clothes unless I do something, quick. Not smoking—still, and no danger of starting again!—does bring on weight gain.) Anyway, I went downstairs, snacked, read your letter, opened a package with a CD of the hymns of Vaughan Williams, and now am back upstairs.

I'm glad you got rain. Now I don't feel bad for writing you about ours. It was drizzly Thursday and Friday, also today, but yesterday was simply beautiful, particularly the marshes and tidal creeks. While I was driving Jeanette Hardy (*Times-Picayune*) around, we crossed Patcong Creek several times. On its sides right where the bridge stands, there are many immense, billowy plants that look like off-white cumulus clouds. It's either the male flowers or the female seed heads of *Baccharis halimifolia*, the groundsel bush. Doesn't it grow somewhere in your sunny gardens complex? It's one of very few shrubby Compositae. (I am still of that, not the Asteraceae persuasion.) It is absurdly neglected in the nursery trade. I don't grow it, as it's big, too big for our plot, but I think it is transcendently lovely. I understand that next year Fairweather Gardens is going to introduce a very special form that a botanist found on Long Island that has scarlet pappae instead of all white ones. That should be a sight!

I don't know much about *Miscanthus sinensis* 'Adagio'. I got it in

August at the same little nursery where we bought a number of ferns. The *RHS Dictionary* describes it as "diminutive."

All right, I will keep fuchsia 'Gartenmeister Bonstedt', I hope for winter bloom in the greenhouse. As the days keep shortening, I am getting apprehensive that all the flowering plants we are bringing inside will start sulking and quit blooming. I have no experience to guide my expectations, although I know that I can get some things from Waldor Orchids just down the street that will bloom for months. I don't expect bloom till spring from any of the cuttings I've rooted, but I've cut back, root-pruned, potted up, and brought into the greenhouse mature plants of various things—red and also pink pentas; a fine heliotrope with dark, almost black, rugose leaves, and dark purple flowers that really do have that splendid baby powder smell; *Cuphea ignea*; *Calibrachoa*; and so on. Some diascias, also some new patented cultivars of *Brachycome* that were developed in Australia. They are terrific plants, blooming their heads off nonstop from late spring right up to now. Most fall into the usual mauve-blue-lavender range, but there are two yellows, one with small, the other with medium-sized, daisy flowers.

I will send you a small rooted cutting of *Fuchsia magellanica* 'Señorita'. Do you want it now, or shall I wait for spring? It might bloom in your little greenhouse, which as I recall has an eastern exposure.

There are slugs in the greenhouse, but I'm banding the legs of the benches and the bases of the large pots on the floor with copper foil as a deterrent. And I'm very interested in your use of copper to keep roots inside pots. We have two problems here. Brugmansias root into the ground through their drainage holes. They seem to be able to do this almost overnight. When they do, I can hardly lift the pot, and when I do lift it, the plants wilt from the insult to their root systems. The other problem is that our two red maples in the back garden push their roots upward into tubs and other containers, slurping up nutrients and moisture from bedding plants. Copper or maybe bronze screening sounds like a dual remedy for roots that don't know their places.

The bulbs I bought were definitely *Hyacinthoides hispanica*. It said so on the package. But now I'm wondering, could the supposed Spanish bluebells already growing here really be *Hyacinthoides non-scripta* instead? And the thought of your sending seeds to an exchange of something you called *H. nondescripta* is delicious! It seems that the gods do indeed occasionally nod. I also love those large

Linwood

Montrose squirrels of the woodchuck tribe. The title of Christopher Lloyd's *The Well-Tempered Garden* is no mere clever pun or allusion. He is as passionate about good music as he is about fine plants. I am reading with great delight *Dear Friend and Gardener*, two years of letters he exchanged with Beth Chatto. Their correspondence, which is full of musical references by both writers, ended last December, just as ours got started. The book is hard to come by here, but has been a huge success in England. There's not a single photograph in it! I intend to locate a copy for you. I'm writing a piece about it for the fall issue of *Homeground*, with marvelous photographs. Cynthia Woodyard just came back from England, on a project involving black and white photographs of a number of prominent gardeners. I have one of Lloyd and another of Chatto.

Michael will have them face each other across a two-page spread. He looks dyspepsic, and she looks like a little elf with a fine sense of humor.

In *Country Life*, Lloyd wrote one of very few reviews I've ever gotten in England, for *The Garden in Autumn*. I can't quote exactly, but here's more or less what he said. "Mr. Lacy informs us that on one day in mid-October he counted fifty-five plants in bloom. It seems that he has a small garden."

The greenhouse, empty in late August, is now about half full. I bring plants in, repotting if necessary, and taking advantage of the edges of the larger pots to tuck in ivy, coleus, and other things. I have fumigated the place twice with a fairly mild insecticide. There are bound to be a few hitchhiking pests, but I want to reduce their number as far as possible.

My new iMac has a CD player in it. I haven't used it much yet, but for the last half hour as I write you that Vaughan Williams album has filled the study with some of the best hymns ever written. "Ye Watchers and Ye Holy Ones," "For All the Saints," and all the rest—my churchly days are done, but the words and the music I grew up with at First Methodist, Dallas, still reverberate within me. An allelujah still is magic! I know most of the words of these hymns by heart, over half a century later. I have observed that the only song people of no particular religious persuasion can come up with nowadays at funerals is "Amazing Grace," and only the first verse, if even that. The notes that came with the Vaughan Williams state that even though he loved the poetry and the cadences of both the King James Bible and the Book of Common Prayer, he was an atheist from youth onward to the day of his death.

Thanks for sending Gabrielle's map of Montrose, but isn't it unorthodox, or am I wrong that the top of the map is south not north? It also looks upside down to me, because my experience of Montrose is entering its gates from St. Marys Road, then driving up that winding drive. But the map does set me right on the relations among various spaces. I had an entirely wrong notion of how the old rock garden was situated relative to the new circle garden.

Shall I make a map of 1511 Shore Road for you? It would be very simple.

What good news about the preservation of much of Montrose from the developers' hands!

Love,
Allen

Tuesday, October 13, 1998

Dear Allen,

Thank you for such a lovely, long letter. It seemed an instantaneous response to my last two, and I guess in a way it was. If it had arrived any sooner I would have thought you were with me on that twilight tour of the sunny gardens. But first I must explain about the map. Did you know the house faces north? You enter Montrose from St. Marys Road at the northwest corner of the property. Gabrielle actually drew the map the way you wanted to see it with the aster border at the top, but I made her change it so that the north is at the top of the page. The big greenhouse is on the east side of the house, the boxwood border on the west. Yes, send me a map of your garden. Even though I have seen pictures of the pool, the new greenhouse, the arch, and so on, I can't place them in the picture in my mind. Of course, no matter what you say, I will always see your garden as it was on that glorious day in November when I first saw it. I also have a second mental picture from that June day when I visited with Barry Yinger.

I enjoyed your comments on salvias. I have just purchased *Salvia discolor* for about the fifth time. I think its best use is in winter on a high shelf in the greenhouse where I can see the silvery undersides of the leaves. I would not bother with *S. madrensis* if I were you. I am expecting frost any night now, and it still hasn't bloomed for me this year. Mind you, when and if it does, we will pay homage to it for its thick stems as well as its glorious yellow flowers. I am sorry you have given up on *S. mexicana*. Perhaps with your greenhouse now you can bring it in and see it perform as it should. One of my best forms came from a friend on Long Island, and it blooms for him there. *S.* 'Van-Houttei' is a midsummer-to-fall bloomer here. It might make a show even earlier if I got around to planting it before June. I disagree with the books that suggest it is a form of *S. splendens*. It certainly has that as one parent. When our self-sown seedlings bloomed bright scarlet, I decided that the other parent had to be something else.

I have that uneasy feeling that comes every fall about this time. When will we have our first frost? Our first freeze? We have brought in many of the tender plants. We have one of everything we want to save protected in the pit, the cold frames, or one of the greenhouses. Now we will go back and fill in the gaps, digging every clump of 'Pele's Smoke' sugarcane, most of the *Pennisetum setaceum*, and more coleus. Now that the kittens are fourteen years old and we have a new radiator in the laundry room where they sleep, I want to try once again to grow plants in the room's windows. It seems such a waste of south- and east-facing light not to fill the sills with tender plants.

I realize that every garden can grow some plants that others can't. I do envy you your display of *Gentiana saponaria*. I remember the day Craufurd found it growing down by the pond. He described it as a blue azalea, and I scoffed. "But," he insisted, "it is special." So I looked, and it was special indeed. Now the deer won't allow it in the garden, and I haven't seen it at the pond for years. I have a few plants growing in inaccessible places but haven't had a good display since Belle, our golden labrador, died. I know—I should get another dog. Perhaps I will.

Please send more rain. That nine-tenths of an inch gave very little relief, and we are back where we were all summer. This is the end of the fifth month of serious drought here. I have stopped all planting, hoping the soil will remain warm for another month, by which time perhaps it will rain and I can get more bulbs divided and plants waiting in flats into the ground. But to show you how variable the weather is in these parts, a television reporter stated that the pumpkin crop in this area was ruined by so much rain. I hate to hear the weather forecasters predict that the state fair won't be marred by a rainy day. I do concede that the days are glorious, with brilliant blue skies, low humidity, and cool nights in the forties.

Yes, I do grow *Baccharis halimifolia* in the former aster border, now the color garden. It was something of a weed in my Durham garden but doesn't like this soil well enough to be anything but a delight. I would love to have one with scarlet pappae. In fact I would like a grove of them!

As regards "brachycome," please note that there is an "s" in the middle of the word, although I have never heard anyone else put it there. When I say it, people stare as if I had lost my mind. We have grown these plants from time to time in the dianthus walk for their nonstop display in summer. How exciting to think that there is a yellow one!

Let's continue the *Hyacinthoides hispanica* discussion in the spring when they bloom. I fully acknowledge the reliability of package labels. I have received some of my best unidentifiable treasures that way.

Do keep looking for *Dear Friend and Gardener* for me. I would love to read the letters of Beth Chatto and Christopher Lloyd. Oh yes, Mr. Lloyd may not have fully appreciated your account of your garden in *The Garden in Autumn*, but other English gardeners and writers have. Rosie Atkins, editor of *Gardens Illustrated*, declared you to be one of the best garden writers in America.

Many years ago when my father went to England to do research for his books on Lytton Strachey and the Strachey family, he returned with the certain conviction that Vaughan Williams was the greatest contemporary musician. That Christmas I received about a dozen records of his works. I finally confessed to my father, as I now confess to you, that I have never liked his music. It seems so wishy-washy, so sentimental, and so monotonous. It lacks the inner strength and powerful rhythms of the music of Bach.

Craufurd had his second cataract operation yesterday. Everything except the doctor was different. The first time, he was the final patient of the day; this time he was the first, and we had to be at the hospital at 6:00 in the morning. There was no talk of living wills. The worst part came when we returned home. He was in terrible pain and he remembered everything about the operation. He finally told me that there was a new anesthetist on duty. He had never dealt with cataract operations before and, if you can believe it, he asked Craufurd what he should receive—a topical or a blocker. Craufurd said he wasn't certain, but he thought a topical. When we returned today to see the surgeon, she apologized, saying that everyone had received the wrong anesthetic. It is the first time I have ever heard a physician apologize. It's terrible for any patient to advise an anesthetist, but even more terrible that the patient in this case was Craufurd, who has a very high pain threshold. I feel sorry for him but just as sorry for all the other patients who must have suffered more than he did.

Crocuses are blooming throughout the garden. I don't have the time or energy to spray them, but I do go out last thing in the evening and pepper them, sometimes with black pepper, sometimes with cayenne. It seems to work!

Love,
Nancy

Wednesday, October 14, 1998

Dear Nancy,

In a recent letter I didn't say nearly enough about the great news that your conservation easement will leave most of your land intact for the future. That is a wonderful triumph. You and Craufurd both must be feeling relief, just as Polly Hill did when David Smith came along.

When an undergraduate, I loved driving to Hillsborough from Durham, mostly to have Sunday dinner at the Colonial Inn, then drive around the village. I used to drive up the hill toward U.S. 70 on St. Marys Road, admiring the church near you. I must have gone right past the entrance to Montrose, not suspecting what was beyond, invisible from the road.

The way to Montrose from Durham isn't exactly ugly. I-40 passes through some lovely, rolling countryside, but then comes the Hillsborough exit, and I-85, Wal-Mart, and all the other developments that make this part of town something you can see everywhere in America, and never with pleasure.

Congratulations! Now, the house and gardens . . .

Thursday, October 15

Hella and I are off shortly to the doctor's office for flu shots, administered to any patient who wants or needs them, but today only, from 9:00 to 11:00 A.M. It feels like a date! We could also go for shots Friday or Saturday to one of the local grocery stores, or wait until Sunday, when the Methodist church just down the road will offer them. It's an odd kind of social occasion, no?

The name of that TV show week after next at the Disney Institute is "Way to Grow." The producer of the segments I'm on, Julie Sung, just faxed some wardrobe suggestions. Wear light-weight khakis, as the show is shot outdoors. No logos or slogans on wearing apparel. No polka dots or houndstooth patterns, and nothing black, white, or red. No long necklaces that will clatter against the microphone. And "don't wear clothing made of parachute-type material."

We fly to Orlando on Sunday, the 25th. The show is videotaped on Tuesday, and we come back Thursday. I'm really looking forward to plant-hunting at the many nurseries in the Winter Garden area—more tropicals for the greenhouse! It got down to 40° this morning, but I went out to the greenhouse as soon as coffee was ready. The heater came on during the night, so it was balmy inside. It was pleasant to shiver just a bit crossing the deck and a patch of lawn, then open the door to find summer waiting.

The light now on sunny mornings and late afternoons is fantastically beautiful. The sky is deep, deep blue, any cumulus clouds on the horizon look like heaps of feathers, the air is transparent, and everything is bathed in radiant gold. This always happens twice a year—once, for a week or ten days shortly before the spring equinox, and again now, the same span after the fall equinox. Odd corners inside the house, places where otherwise the sun never shines, are strangely illumined.

Fondly,
Allen

P.S. In regard to that plan of your garden, yes, my mental map of Montrose is totally wrong. Sorry!

Saturday, October 17, 1998

Dear Nancy,

Let us proceed to a weighty question. Does the Latin genus name of the Australian Swan River daisy have an *s* in it or not? You and I must never have uttered this word between us, or I would have heard the sibilant whistling through your lips. I would not have thought you crazy, nor, I hope, stare. I would, however, have rushed to my reference sources to check. I've never said the word or written the word with an *s*. Apparently you do. *Hortus III, The New RHS Dictionary of Gardening*, volume I of Thomas Everett's *Encyclopedia of Horticulture*, and volume I of Bailey's *Cyclopedia*—all of these references are piled on my study floor, open to the appropriate page. They testify with one voice that the genus name is *Brachycome*—ten letters, not eleven, and none of the ten is an *s*.

Ten years ago the matter might have rested there. I might have told you that you were wrong, or perhaps just dropped the whole thing, letting it pass in silence. Friendships have stumbled over lesser matters. But nowadays those of us who dwell at least partly in cyberspace have a fine tool for swift little tasks of research. I went to Google, my search engine of preference, and typed in *b-r-a-c-h-y-c-o-m-e*. Seconds later I had the names of 99 computer files in Israel, the United States, and England that use the word spelled that way. More confirmation that I was right, no? No! For I next typed it your way, the wrong way, b-r-a-c-h-y-s-c-o-m-e. I got the titles of 106 files spelling it your way.

I have only a partial hunch why there's this orthographical disparity. This genus is Australian in origin. (It's the Swan River, not the Suwanee.) Most of the files were from Australian websites, a few in England. We are, it seems, both right, but you are probably more right than I, especially since I am probably way off in accenting the first, not the second, syllable.

I did find one American file with your spelling, the catalog of the Monterey Bay Nursery in California (unfortunately, since they offer many plants I lust for, a wholesale outfit). One of its specialties is Australian flora. Enclosed is a section on these plants from its catalog. In addition to Swan River daisies, I'm growing several kinds of *Helichrysum, Pandorea, Westringia*, and, as you know, *Viola hederacea*. I do not like *Scaevola* at all! Last year I grew *Calocephalus brownii* and loved it, but I couldn't find plants anywhere this year. Bristly and skeletal, it's the single best silver-leafed plant I know. I'm also enclosing the "B" pages of the Monterey Bay online catalog, but note that if a plant name is underlined and your computer has the right stuff, clicking on the name will bring up on the screen a terrific picture in full color.

I wonder if our difference of opinion about Ralph Vaughan Williams is also easily resolved. When I was in junior high, my Uncle Al regularly took me to the Sunday concerts of the Dallas Symphony Orchestra. Antal Dorati was particularly keen on contemporary symphonic music from Central Europe—Bartók, Janáček, and so on—but he occasionally put some British stuff on the program. One piece I recall was by Delius, titled, I think, "Walk to the Paradise Gardens." It was short but dull. Nobody applauded. Dorati lifted his baton and the orchestra played the entire thing again. He occasionally programmed Ralph Vaughan Williams's "serious" music, tone poems, I think. I don't recall liking anything particularly. Vaughan Williams's hymns and hymn arrangements are another matter altogether. The melodies, many of them folk tunes, are strong and strongly singable. The best thing about his hymns, however, is that congregations that sing them may avoid some of the really slurpy stuff that's out there—"The Old Rugged Cross," "In the Garden," and other such ilk. (I do confess, however, some appreciation for "The Church in the Wildwood.")

We have never really explored how we each came—and came

early—to a passion for music—and pretty much the same kinds of music. Piano lessons failed me, or I them. Voice lessons went better. I was a decent boy alto. I had good relative—not absolute—pitch. I always had a sense of what was going on in a piece of music beyond what other altos were singing. My church choir rehearsed from 6:00 to 10:00 every Thursday night, and often from 2:00 to 5:00 on Sundays. Generally we had two services to sing Sunday mornings. I was absorbed in the music of the church, and it still is with me in some ways, even if the only times I've been in church in the last decade have been when grandkids were baptized.

Crocus goulimyi is blooming everywhere from self-seeding. Here, no pepper required! (Thank heaven for the Garden State Parkway!)

I don't expect frost this week, but trees are starting to turn. I looked out of my study window just now to see a golden flurry of pine needles raining down in a sudden breeze.

We went yesterday down near Cape May to a terrible public garden, so-called—proprietary, $5 a head. There was a pitiful little zoo of ancient breeds of chickens, in cages, with their water bottles fouled by algae. The only interesting plant was a datura, maybe *D. metel*, with black-purple stems, and hose-in-hose double flowers that open creamy yellow then age to white. Unfortunately no seed pods were in evidence.

Cheers,
Allen

Sunday, October 18, 1998

Dear Allen,

Thanks for your reaction to our work to save the land on which we live. We believe the Triangle Land Conservancy is an appropriate recipient for the development rights. The current director is a responsible, serious person who cares about the land as we do. She even came to one of our gardening seminars in September and, although not a gardener, seems interested in what we are doing here.

Wouldn't it be a fine coincidence if, in our undergraduate days, we had both been in Hillsborough on the same day? My family thought a trip here was a grand thing to do on a Sunday afternoon. I, too, went past St. Matthew's Church, sometimes stopping to investigate the old tombstones.

Montrose

Fall is here, and I believe our first frost and freeze will come next weekend. For one thing, we have a new moon coming in on Tuesday, and with it we may, I hope, get a little rain—but behind that we have a major cold front approaching from Canada. Craufurd, formerly a Canadian citizen, has never objected to the way our weather people exclaim about the fronts coming down from Canada, but we have Canadian friends who consider it an insult.

The instructions for your television debut are intriguing. My goodness, I haven't seen any parachute-type material in a long time. During the war that was the finest pure silk. Somehow I don't think that is what your producers have in mind, but I can't imagine what it is. Perhaps it is something that flaps in the wind or something that might make you soar above the crowd, Chagall style, like a balloon.

The large sugar maple at the edge of the school grounds is coloring beautifully. The entire top of the tree is scarlet while the lower two-thirds remains mostly green but slightly tinged with yellow. The dogwoods are burgundy and their berries bright red. Best of all, our views into the woods expand daily as the leaves fall. I can hear every creature moving about. I can identify some of them, including people, squirrels, and deer. The pecans are falling, and the trees beside the house bring blue jays, crows, and squirrels to feast. This will be a bumper crop, and I will send you the first shelling.

Mother used to say they weren't any good until after a freeze, so I won't begin picking them out until then.

The field between the house and the school is dotted with humps of puff balls. They are over a foot in diameter and probably at least five inches high. In the other direction, I saw another fantastic fungus on the way to the pond. I thought at first it was bitter melon, the fruit of *Momordica charantia*. You probably remember seeing the vine growing on the old wood splitter, but I don't know if it was ever in fruit during one of your visits. When ripe, its golden-yellow, warty, cucumberlike shell splits open to reveal seeds coated in scarlet pulp. Well, my fungus in the woods was pumpkin yellow with bright scarlet bits. I had never seen this one before.

Chrysanthemums seldom excite me, but there are some fine ones this year, including 'Celo Pink', which is bright fuchsia pink, and 'Innocence', a pink-tinged white that combines well with artemisia 'Powis Castle'. We also have some apricot and rusty brown daisy types in the color garden, and a number of clear yellow forms blooming throughout the sunny garden. Glory be, the cats have agreed to let me have plants in the laundry room. I have one of each of my forms of coleus, impatiens, and plectranthus there, as well as my one and only *Acalypha godseffiana* 'Heterophylla'. The new radiator makes this the warmest room in the house.

October 20, 1998

I'm beginning to see the value in cyberspace. What an incredible search you did on *Brachyscome*! But there is no way this disagreement or even that on the relative merits of Vaughan Williams could end or tarnish our friendship. After all, you didn't do something awful, like declaring cyclamen to be tacky!

I will reserve judgment on the Vaughan Williams hymns and hymn arrangements until I hear them. You're correct that I'm basing my estimation of Williams solely on his symphonic works. And, by the way, I, too, like "The Church in the Wildwood" and another one my grandmother sang. I don't know its name but it went like this: "I went to church last Sunday, but my lover passed me by. But I knew [this might have been "knowed"] his heart was turning by the glimmer in his eye. Let him go, let him go, God bless him, he's mine wherever he may go." Now that I think of it, it probably wasn't a hymn. I can see and hear her singing it but can't remember the rest of the words. There were many verses, I believe, and the tune was beautiful.

I wish I could sing. I used to try, but I was better at playing the piano. I kept on singing even into college, although my official role was as an accompanist. My singing was good for a laugh. I was the only one not laughing. Now I sing in the car when I am alone and there is no car right beside me.

How lovely that *Crocus goulimyi* has seeded about for you. The flower has an elegant shape like a goblet on a slender stem and doesn't collapse on itself the way *C. speciosus* does. I wish you could see the rock garden now. Thanks to many seedlings of *C. speciosus*, the planting looks natural, with clumps of crocuses in expected and unexpected places. Some flowers are almost indigo blue, some white, and some pastel lavender-blue with silvery backs. *C. tournefortii* blooms beneath the cedar near the house and by the driveway. This is a splendid crocus with colors varying from near white to lavender, but its best feature is its ability to remain open in dim light, even at night. My pepper is working well against deer, but now slugs are devouring the buds of the crocus under the metasequoias. Gardeners must fight nature all the way.

It's not worth a fuss, but tell me, why don't you like *Scaevola*? It's true that *S. aemula* 'Blue Fan' looks like something ate its top half, but it's a lovely cascading plant that can take heat. I use it in urns and at the edges of sunny beds.

We continue to pack the cold frames. Today we worked in the shade, sorting out pots with dead plants in them and rearranging the live ones so that the same plants would be grouped together. Suddenly it looks as if I will have enough room. I put about ten flats of cyclamen into an entirely new section of the woods. The soil is incredibly hard and dry—not a scrap of moisture. I've heard that this drought is expected to last all winter. I'll try not to complain to you every chance I get.

I planted three side bulbs from the cardiocrinum that bloomed last summer beneath the metasequoias. I did not follow Jekyll and dig down four feet. All I could manage was a hole maybe one foot deep, in which I alternated soil and compost, placing the bulb at the top. We'll see how well it works.

I saw color on my first *Cyclamen coum* yesterday, but I have to keep reminding myself that the flowers probably won't open until Thanksgiving. The season marches on: I rejoice in the thought, only four more days of daylight saving time!

Love,
Nancy

P.S. (October 23). We had our first killing frost last night. We'd spent the day taking the final cuttings, pulled the pump out of the pool, packed the pit below the law office, and removed and potted the most spectacular plants from the urns. All of this activity came about because at noon the weather forecast called for a low in the mid-30s. We closed the deep cold frames, and then at 6:00 the forecast was for a low of 32°. Craufurd was at Duke preparing for his evening class, and I was alone, so I had to leave the shallow cold frames open. I had checked to be certain that the plants in them could stand a light freeze, and so they did. It's over—and I'm glad.

I heard the first white-throated sparrow of the season late yesterday. He sounded a little tired, with a more quavering song than usual.

Friday, October 30, 1998

Dear Nancy,

I got back from Orlando late last night, but without Hella, who flew instead, unexpectedly, to Tennessee while I flew back here. Her mother had been taken to the hospital suddenly with what was first thought to be a heart attack, but it turned out to be something less serious (not yet quite sure what).

It may surprise you—it did me!—but last Sunday afternoon when we drove into the gates of Walt Disney World I felt a very strange sense of homecoming. Orlando is a lot like Dallas, but I'd have to write a book that I don't want to write to explain the comparison, except to mention the presence of St. Augustine grass and the absence of potholes.

I was apprehensive about the television series—not only the series itself, but also how well I would do on it—so it was a good thing that we came Sunday so I could just watch the filming Monday before my own stint Tuesday.

I know much more now than I did when we got there. "Way to Grow" is brand new, with the first half-hour show premiering in January on the House & Garden cable network (HGTV). There will be seventy shows the first go-round. Filming has been going on since mid-September and will conclude today. The people involved hail, variously, from Hollywood, Orlando, Manhattan, and Knoxville.

The show was shot in the Teaching Garden of the Disney Institute. The garden is a perfect gem. A couple of classrooms flank a patio with a stone fountain in the middle. The rest of the garden is composed of parallel pathways and raised beds, also a great many large containers. The plantings are very fine and imaginative — perfect testimony to the excellence of the small staff.

A huge set has been constructed at one end of the garden, beneath a high, flat roof of canvas, to diffuse the strong sunlight and protect crew and equipment. Within the set there are several discrete locations — gazebo, potting shed, breakfast nook, and so on. The format of the show is familiar. Mayita Dinos and Dan Plausner, the co-hosts, banter back and forth like Regis and Kathy Lee, except that they are much younger and unmistakably West Coast. Each show features a six- or seven-minute interview with a guest (Felder Rushing, Ken Druse, yours truly, and so on). Disney horticulturists (an impressive bunch of folks!) are also regularly involved, mostly with how-to stuff.

I did three segments and three cameos or vignettes. The segments were roughly based on *The Inviting Garden*. In the first, the three of us walked around the courtyard and its fountain, chatting about particular plants and what we know (or do not know) about them. We had to film it twice, since an airplane flew over right at the end of the first take. I was so extemporaneous that I repeated almost nothing from the first take in the second. After a break, Mayita and I did the second segment — walking along a raised bed, mostly planted in herbs, talking about touch, taste, smell, and hearing. Segment no. 3 was also with Mayita, sitting on a garden bench on the set, as I explained what I meant in the book by "the education of the eye."

For the vignettes, I just stood there, looking directly into the camera and answering three separate questions dreamed up for me by the producer. (1) Do you have a practical tip for our viewers? ("Yes. Lighten large containers by filling them partly with plastic packing pellets or empty soda cans.") (2) How do you get children interested in gardening? ("Resist every urge to use them as slave labor.") (3) How did you get started with gardening? (Mrs. Harkey, of course . . .) Now, I did these three bits all at one time, right after the other. Although I was yards away from anyone on the set, I was miked and there were monitors everywhere. After I finished with Mrs. Harkey there was applause, and the executive producer emerged from his trailer and congratulated me.

It was all enormous fun! The crew, maybe forty people, mostly young, all knew what they were doing — something I always love to find. I didn't stammer too much on camera, scratch my groin, touch my nose, or say "uh" or "I mean." Having make-up put on was a new experience. I enjoyed it, but not enough that I want to do it all the time in my ordinary life.

Hella "did more Disney" than I, because Monday I watched the filming to find out what it was all about, Tuesday was my day on camera, and Wednesday I came back for half the session, from pure fascination with seeing how television production works. Hella roamed the Magic Kingdom and Epcot. We spent four or five hours together at Epcot, and on the first day we managed to spend two hours at the new theme park, Animal Kingdom, just before closing. It is really quite wonderful both conceptually and aesthetically. The plantings, entirely tropical material, are very, very exciting!

Wednesday afternoon we went nursery-hopping in Winter Park, to a disappointing outcome. All of the vast numbers of nurseries there are wholesale only, and the retail outfits have pretty much the same plants we can get at garden centers here—or at Home Depot.

I did come home with one really fantastic plant, however, a gift from Wayne McGonigal of the Disney Institute. Do you know cat's whiskers (*Orthosiphon stamineus*)? It's not in any of my reference books except Bailey. It's a tender, somewhat shrubby perennial. The individual flowers look like those of Japanese honeysuckle, but with even longer protuberant stamens. They are borne in handsome racemes that open from the bottom to the top. Colors range from pure white to pale lavender to fairly purple. Mine is white, but I have a hunch that if I sow its seeds, I'll get a mix. I suspect that it may bloom constantly. It's supposed to be easy from cuttings. There are other species, including *O. aristatus*, which also looks interesting. The genus comes from several tropical regions in the Southern Hemisphere. Various species have been used in traditional Chinese medicine, especially for kidney ailments. Currently these plants are undergoing a lot of pharmacological scrutiny because of a superabundance of very strange molecules. And it's my guess that *O. stamineus* is about to become a hot item in American gardening, as I saw it not only at the Disney Teaching Garden but also at a local garden center in Orlando.

Just before we left home Sunday we finished putting several pots of *Plumbago auriculata* in the greenhouse. In Orlando they landscape highways with it, great pools of sky blue flowing along the entrance ramps!

Scaevola? I never could quite put my finger on it, but yes, it does look like something nibbled its top off. It's okay, but doesn't excite me; I see too much of it in $30 hanging baskets in garden centers in spring.

Love,
Allen

Sunday, November 1, 1998

Dear Allen,

I thought of you and Hella down in Disney World, wondered how your television debut went, and how you liked the Institute. I know the House & Garden cable network has many viewers, although we don't have cable and have never seen it. Certainly you are in good company with Felder Rushing and Ken Druse. Visitors here often mention it and the gardens and gardeners they see. Perhaps you will have a new career in television.

I've been to Disney World only once, the last year I had the nursery. The nursery received an award from the American Horticultural Society, and Craufurd and I flew down one day and came back the next. I went kicking and screaming because I knew I would hate the artificiality of the place and couldn't believe that a horticultural organization would meet there. I was wrong. I came away as impressed as you are by the quality of the horticulture. The people in charge of it have taste, knowledge, and a passion for what they are doing. We were given a behind-the-scenes tour. My favorite part was the composting facility, with its mountains of organic waste, collected from the restaurants as well as the gardens. It helps explain the beauty and health of the plants growing there.

I wish you could see Piedmont North Carolina now, at our peak of fall color. Some trees are just beginning to turn, but others are at their most spectacular point. The metasequoias are still primarily green but at the tips of some branches I can see that fine, buttery caramel color I look forward to all year. *Magnolia macrophylla* is chartreuse and golden yellow. The most spectacular tree is *Nyssa sylvatica*, planted where the *Magnolia acuminata*, whose passing we still mourn, once grew. This tupelo or black gum — which do you call it? — is finally taller than the adjacent oak-leaved hydrangea that will eventually appreciate its shade. The black gum's leaves are brilliant scarlet above, apricot below, and they glisten splendidly in the sun.

This is a spectacular year for hollies. An *Ilex opaca* that was a small tree in 1977 when we moved here is loaded with bright red berries. Nearby, the leaves of *I. verticillata* have begun to turn chartreuse and yellow as its berries become brilliant red. Meanwhile, near the wood splitter, the leaves of *I. decidua* 'Pocahontas' have not changed yet, but it is glorious with clusters of huge red fruits, through which *Clematis serratifolia* clambers with ripe seed clusters that look like a dog's shaggy beard. In this part of the garden we have cleared away much of the summer growth, so the dahlias are only memories.

As I believe I wrote to you earlier, we have had frost, but, as always at the beginning of the new season, it hasn't hit everything. Near the *Magnolia macrophylla* a large patch of *Salvia coccinea*, with flowers variously white, coral, orange-red, or deep blood red, looks vigorous and untouched. Close by, the first hellebore—*Helleborus niger*—is in bloom. (This week I saw Christmas decorations at Wal-Mart, so why not a Christmas rose in my garden?) Snowdrops—the first blossoms of *Galanthus reginae-olgae*, right on time—are flowering in the rock garden. Autumn crocuses have never been better than this year. *Crocus sativus* blooms in the rock garden, and in the woods the white *C. cartwrightianus* 'Albus' that I bought years ago as the white form of *C. sativus* is in flower. My largest crocus, *C. nudiflorus*, blooms without leaves, just as its name promises, but with violet purple flowers and a showy, well-branched style. *C. tournefortii* has just about finished, but *Cc. longiflorus, goulimyi, thomasii,* and *caspius* continue producing flowers. Near all the fall-blooming cyclamen I scratched in ripened seeds of crocuses in spring, and it is a joy now to see them blooming in unexpected places.

Amsonia hubrichtii is my most spectacular perennial for fall foliage color, growing at a corner of the big greenhouse. Its leaves now combine brilliant chartreuse, tan, golden yellow, and beige in a lovely blend. Other perennials are in full bloom. One of my favorites, *Tagetes lucida*, has tarragon-scented, edible leaves and small, single, golden yellow flowers. We have a few chrysanthemums, one a pale yellow single that came as a gift from a visitor last summer and epitomizes primrose yellow. I grow a few doubles, including 'Mei-kyo' and its sport, 'Bronze Elegance'. Almost all the others are my mother's. She wanted only singles, mostly with flowers of apricot or shades of beige or reddish brown. No pompoms. Verbenas are still good, continuing to bloom as they did in midsummer, not seeming to care that we've had frosts. Despite the ongoing absence of rain, some rain lilies manage a few flowers. Both *Habranthus robustus* and *Zephyranthes* sp. 'Labuffarosea' have about a dozen freshly opened blossoms each day. And asters are fine, especially 'Raydon's Favorite' and *Aster puniceus*. Both have flowers in shades of lilac blue, and the latter is about as tall as *A. tataricus*, but with large heads of flowers.

Roses have regained their fresh, bright colors of spring. My favorite old China rose, 'Louis Philippe', covers itself with double blossoms of deep rose-pink, their color intensified by the companion planting of *Artemisia* 'Powis Castle'. That is my best artemisia, used in many different sections of the garden, where it performs a variety of functions. Most often it is a peacemaker, providing not only a neutral color but also a soft and gentle form.

At this time of the year the lath house comes into its own. *Clematis cirrhosa* is blooming atop it, with fragrant bells of the palest yellow hanging from the rafters, making me wish I were twenty-one feet tall. On the south side and above the top slats *Rosa* 'Mme Alfred Carrière' blooms with pale pink double flowers, kept from looking too sweet by a magenta-berried callicarpa at its base. Across the path, the fragrant, almond-scented climbing aster *Aster carolinianus* blooms behind another callicarpa, *C. shikokianum*, with its masses of tiny fruits. The fresh new feathery leaves of bronze fennel look like dark, nearly black, smoke. We cut it back when it became ratty and new growth came quickly.

Fragrance in the garden is one of the best things about fall. Some of the scents are expected, such as those of *Osmanthus × fortunei* and *O. heterophyllus*, also the spicy perfume of *Elaeagnus pungens*, which travels far on the air. Other scents are surprises, such as those of the ripe fruits of chaenomeles or flowering quince, *Poncirus trifoliata*, and *Maclura pomifera* (a.k.a., osage orange or horse apple in some parts of the country). The crushed, new-fallen leaves of *Cercidiphyllum japonicum* smell like ripe plums, but I will not even try to describe the scent of our native witch hazel, *Hamamelis virginiana*. I also love the fragrance of plants blackened by frost, like the leaves of African basil and lemon balm and pineapple sage when I cut them back.

As for *Orthosiphon stamineus*, I've neither seen nor heard of it. It sounds like you've found an extraordinary new plant, so I hope you will root a bit for me.

Love,
Nancy

Tuesday, November 10, 1998

Dear Nancy,

I went to New York early Thursday, coming back Sunday. Inasmuch as the original plan for the trip was for Hella and me to play tourists in the big city and she ended up in Tennessee instead, my schedule was sparse—a reading at the New York Horticultural Society Thursday evening, an hour Sunday morning on Ralph Snodsmith's radio show, "Gardening Hotline," and nothing in between.

The reading went well, and afterward I signed about fifty books. It was especially pleasant to have my old friend Carol Hall and her husband, Leonard Majslin, in the audience, right on the front row. Carol and I grew up together, sang in the same church choir, and went to the same high school. We dated, inconclusively, over the years, right up till I met Hella. Carol is a fine songwriter, best known for the lyrics and score of "The Best Little Whorehouse in Texas." I hadn't seen Carol or Leonard for a couple of years, so after the reading I ditched the horticultural tribe to go out with them for supper. I've seen Carol perform many times, but she's never heard me talk or give a reading. In tribute to Texas days, before I got down to excerpts from *The Inviting Garden*, I read "Weighty Matters," an essay on watermelons and family affairs from fifteen years back. The response was very warm, including laughter in the right places. If only one piece of my work should survive, I wouldn't mind it being this one.

Because of heavy tourist trade at this time of year, I had to split my stay between two hotels. The experience was pretty much prince and pauper, but in reverse order. I started with two nights at the Pickwick, on 51st between 2nd and 3rd Avenues—$115 a night. The rooms were clean but tiny, but better that than dirty and big—and anyway, what could I expect in NYC at that price? The third night I was still on 51st Street, but at the New York Palace, just behind St. Pat's. It was over $300. I enjoyed it but felt like I shouldn't leave the room. At that price, every minute cost a chunk of coin.

Sunday I went over to WOR on Broadway for the Ralph Snodsmith Show—my first experience in years with an in-person radio interview instead of one over the phone. It went well, I think. Ralph is a nice man, and talking with him was like having a chat with a friend over a back fence. Radio has a much more intimate feel to it than television. I've got a tape—will try to make a duplicate for you.

After the show I took the Metroliner to Philadelphia and then the slow train home—and tidied up the house for Hella's much-desired return Monday.

Our first frost came while I was gone, but it was a partial affair. In a really general frost, our paulownia loses all its leaves at once, but so far only a few have blackened and fallen. The top leaves of castor beans are scorched, but not the lower ones. When I pulled into the driveway, Ed Plantan was here, moving hoses and sprinklers. We haven't had rain in almost a month, and it is desperately dry, although not as bad as it would be with summer's warmth.

Friday, November 20, 1998

The date above and the hiatus between this and the first part of my letter tell their tale. What with the trips to Orlando and New York and Hella's unexpected visit to her mother (whose medical problems turned out to involve her inner ear and sense of balance), we are behind on almost everything. Thanksgiving is almost upon us, but it seems only a couple of weeks have passed since Labor Day. We didn't get around to the garden chores most characteristic of autumn—cutting back perennials and raking leaves—until this week. The flowering season is almost at its end. In bloom now are only *Cyclamen hederifolium*, *Gentiana saponaria*, salvia 'Purple Majesty', and some Korean chrysanthemums. (Other mums are over and done with. I raised the Korean ones, which are singles, from seed, and plan to plant more next year.) Oh yes, one more plant is blooming, and it's a strange sight. We've got a couple of big brugmansias and some rooted cuttings safe in the greenhouse, but left six other big ones to their fate outdoors. Their foliage blackened, shriveled, and dropped off at the first real frost, but the flower buds on a plant of 'Jamaica Yellow' just outside the greenhouse weren't affected, and there are now seven gorgeous flowers hanging on the skeletal-looking trunk and branches.

Today it really feels like winter, and I hate it! (You've heard this song before!) The temperature at 4:30, near sunset, when I came in for the day, wasn't actually cold, just 48°, but there was a brisk, steady breeze. We've reached that time of the year when we must start talking about the windchill factor.

The greenhouse now plays a much more significant part in my life as a gardener than it did last year. It wasn't finished until almost Christmas (also I had some other concerns). It's now loaded with plants, and wonderfully displays Ed Plantan's ingenuity. When we went down to Florida, we already had a good many hanging baskets up, but only on the main aluminum supports running from the front to the back of the greenhouse. We bumped our heads on almost all of them. During our absence, Ed cut bamboo poles from the grove out front and wired them together in a side-to-side arrangement that (a) makes room for many more baskets and (b) permits placing them out of our way. The result is great! The greenhouse certainly makes winter easier to take.

I feared, by the way, that in the greenhouse flowering would slow way down or halt entirely with the diminishing hours of daylight, but that hasn't happened. We have abundant flowers on several Chinese hibiscuses and some brugmansias, on brachyscomes and diascias, on impatiens, and on mandevillas. Cape plumbagos are back in bud. Red shield or *Hibiscus acetosella*, which seldom produces more than a couple of flowers outdoors before frost takes it down, is loaded with flower buds. And what is really exciting is that a couple of orchids, oncidium hybrids from last year, are in full spike. Before we got the greenhouse I never had much luck with getting orchids to rebloom, so I'm very pleased. I'm also gratified by almost complete success in rooting the cuttings that were stuck back in early October.

Speaking of cuttings, as I recall it, last May you may have taken some from the *Strobilanthes isophyllus* I got at Big Bloomers in Sanford. If so, I wonder if it's blooming for you now as it is for me. Were it not for its label, which seems to be accurate, I would never guess that it was the slightest kin to *S. dyerianus*, or Persian shield. The leaves of the two plants do not resemble each other the least bit in color or in texture. The foliage of *dyerianus* is pebbly and of course has that wonderful purple and pewter iridescence (in warm weather, anyway), while that of *isophyllus* is smooth and so dark a green as to veer toward black. I've never seen *dyerianus* in flower, but *isophyllus* is now covered with many little tubular lavender flowers. The plant is on a front bench, just below a plate glass window, and here is another of Ed Plantan's wonderful contrivances wrought while we were in Florida. With bamboo and twine he has fashioned a complicated trellis for several climbing plants, including *Mandevilla boliviensis* and *M.* 'Red Riding Hood', a clerodendron of unknown further identity, and the variegated potato vine, *Solanum jasminoides* 'Aureum'. The latter, which I had in a mixed container on the deck this summer to not much effect, has now come into its own.

There's another plant acquired in Florida to mention. I finally got the genuine "Cuban oregano," *Plectranthus amboinicus* 'Variegatus'.

It is really quite different from *P. forsteri* 'Marginatus'. The real *P. a.* 'Variegatus' has considerably smaller leaves that are more waxy than downy. Their margins are a clean, not a dirty, white, and their centers have two different shades of green in them instead of just one.

It will not appear until the March issue of *Horticulture*, but Tom Cooper sent me the enclosed, extremely positive review of *The Inviting Garden* by Jane Barker Wright.

Love,
Allen

Sunday, November 22, 1998

Dear Allen,

This week the needles fell from the metasequoias, laying a light blanket over the garden beneath and part of the lawn beyond. This is the most beautiful part of the garden now, with some tufts of green grass barely showing. Also, the other evening, right at dusk, I saw patches of bright white to the west of the trees and decided they must be mushrooms. I was excited when they turned out to be snowdrops. I finally have a mass. These are *Galanthus caucasicus*, not the more common *G. nivalis*. I remember buying them nearly twenty years ago at Southern States, the farm supply store in Hillsborough we went to on your last visit. Now I'm fairly sure that the bulbs were wild collected, but I never thought of such things in those days. This species always begins to bloom around Thanksgiving and continues until the winter-flowering ones begin.

I wish you could see the garden. I love the brilliant crescendo into fall, but as you know I love even more the quiet beauty of late fall and of winter. We are in the midst of leaf work. Thus far we have received fifteen loads of ground-up leaves from the city and spread about three-quarters of them. The drought continues, so the ground is firm enough for the garbage truck to drive down the field and dump the leaves near the sunny gardens. We are just getting to the slower parts where winter annuals are germinating, so we can't come in with a cart. Except for some of our oaks, most of our trees are bare. We can see large bunches of mistletoe up in the pecans and walnuts.

I have flowers throughout the garden. The first blossom on *Iris unguicularis* hasn't opened yet, but this week I could feel fat buds on a clump near the back door. Another precocious *Helleborus niger* is in flower, but the crocuses are best of all. You may be getting tired of my telling you about them, but more open each week. Last week I had a fine patch of *Crocus serotinus* subsp. *salzmannii* with red-violet flowers. *C. longiflorus* is my longest-flowered species, continuing to send up flower after flower under the deodar cedar, where masses of *Cyclamen cilicium*, *graecum*, and *mirabile* still bloom.

The woods are peaceful now, with few flowers but new leaves on many hellebores, *Isopyrum biternatum*, and the woods orchids, *Tipularia discolor* and *Aplectrum hyemale*. In one part of the garden I saw tips of galanthus and a few buds on some primulas. I also have flowers on a very-early-flowering mahonia, *M. confusa*, perhaps so named because it blooms early.

I feel the same uncertainty about the onset of winter that I do as summer approaches. I fear we will go from warmth to temperatures in single digits — the worst of all winters. Fall has been that way. We get direct flows of very cold weather alternating with much-above-average warmth.

What are you doing in your garden? Have you had a hard freeze yet?

Love,
Nancy

Monday, December 7, 1998 (by fax)

Dear Nancy,

It was good to hear your voice, even if briefly, this morning. I was of course not surprised that we differ in our feelings about the weather now prevailing all over the East, about which more later in this letter. As regards your doubt about the plant now blooming so riotously in our greenhouse being some kind of *Ruellia* rather than *Strobilanthes isophyllus* (as I got it last summer from Big Bloomers in North Carolina), you may be right. Both plants are in the Acanthus family and have very dark green, narrow, lance-shaped leaves, but I don't find in my plant the toothing that botanical keys describe. As it happens, Martha is with us for several delightful days while Garry tends to familial duties in England, so I enclose her sketch of the plant in question. Whatever it may be, it's a wonderful plant for the greenhouse in winter, if that's the right seasonal epithet for what we are having at the moment. There must be over a hundred pale lilac, abelialike flowers on just one plant and the evidence of the buds is that many more are to follow for weeks and maybe months.

I could write much more about the pleasures of the greenhouse, but will hold off until real winter is back with us, except to mention what's going on with the pot of *Hibiscus acetosella* I brought inside in September. I love this plant for its maplelike, dark reddish leaves, but its growing season is very prolonged. I know that it bloomed sometime this summer, for I found a pod with a few seeds on it, which I planted. (They sprouted and are now growing lustily, and it turns out that the foliage color is passed on, even though some forms of the plant have green leaves.) I never saw any flowers, however, but the multiple stems of the plant in the greenhouse are loaded with buds in pairs and bloom has started. Hella and Martha agree with me that they are among the most beautiful in the whole mallow tribe—small, but a wonderful shade of old rose and intricately veined with deep maroon.

With one exception, the deciduous trees and shrubs are entirely bare, and fall foliage color has departed. The exception is a *Hydrangea quercifolia* that has finally reached respectable size and that I can see from the study window. Only sweet gums come close to it in their range of colors. It is utterly radiant on this clear and sunny day, its upper leaves blackish purple, the leaves beneath those bright cranberry and many other shades of red, and the lowest ones pale red painted with pink and gold. Another glorious sight from the study is our huge, ancient Virginia juniper. Its crop of deep turquoise berries this year is enormous. At the moment seven cardinals are feasting on them.

Now the weather. We're having the kind of December days you hate and I love. Today it will reach 76°, and tonight it won't get below 50°. Yesterday Hella and Martha and I went to Cape May for most of the afternoon, staying until nightfall so as to see the Christmas lights. We were in shirtsleeves. At 4:00 we decided to get ice cream cones, and we had to stand in line!

The garden has, of course, responded to the balmy weather. Up in our 'Arnold Promise' witch hazel Hella found a pale blue flower on a clematis. *Vinca minor* is blooming here and there. Nasturtiums have made a comeback, also gazanias. Although we have had at least one freeze, it didn't get every susceptible plant. One of our lablab vines escaped injury entirely, also many impatiens. Most amazing of all, a potted oncidium that we missed when we brought the rest of our orchids inside in September is still in perfect condition. There are a few blossoms on our small number of roses, but the climbers on a fence just down the road look like June is about to bust out all over once again. It doesn't surprise me at all that our red native honeysuckle is in flower, as it always takes a lot of harsh winter weather to discourage it, but the number of flowers now is quite remarkable. The buds of January jasmine are swelling, likewise those of hybrid witch hazels. I shall cut twigs of both plants this afternoon. It won't take more than two or three days to force them into bloom.

Yesterday was Linwood's day for touring historic houses in their holiday splendor. I didn't go, but Ed Plantan did. Enclosed is a map that was given out, showing Linwood in 1876 when it was still Leedsville and when there were just sixty houses. Ours is near the center of the map, the plot marked B. (for Benjamin) Barrett. Our house sat then on at least 150 times the acreage that it does today. In Linwood today, there are several similar instances of former farmhouses whose successive owners helped make ends meet by selling off land. Just down the road, there's even one surviving farm—a five-acre vineyard with many surviving but dilapidated outbuildings. It's been in the Krumm family since they immigrated from Stuttgart around 1848. Like ours, its land once stretched from an ocean bay to Patcong Creek.

Love,
Allen

Wednesday, December 9, 1998

Dear Allen,

Craufurd brought home your faxed letter of December 7, and I enjoyed it at the end of the day. It was interesting that Linwood and Hillsborough held their tours of historic houses on the same day. Montrose wasn't one of them, but we were involved. Craufurd was on duty at an old law office recently restored by the Preservation Fund, and I served cider and cookies on the porch of the Burwell School. I was happy there was a breeze, for the temperature was about 80°. People came in shorts and were as thirsty as if it were July. The music coming from inside was lovely. Children played and sang, and I felt peaceful and tranquil.

Thank you for sending the map of Linwood. Nothing brings a

greater sense of the transience of our existence than knowing that our houses were here before we were born and hoping that they will be there after we die. If I were in your place, I would wish for the original acreage. I wonder if you do.

Once again, we differ about the seasons. To me, December is neither fall nor winter, but a mixture of both. Nights can be in the low 50s or the low 30s. It is time to look at the shape of the garden. The leaves are all down now, and I can see across the flower beds. I look at the hollies and I remember May when they bloomed and I first began anticipating this season that I so love. The lath house, far from being stark, is draped with roses and *Clematis cirrhosa*, the latter in bloom. *Aster carolinianus* is making a comeback after severe pruning. It has climbed to about six feet and has many pink, fragrant flowers. *Galanthus caucasicus* continues to bloom, although it looked miserable and out of place in the 80° temperatures of last week. But finally it has more flowers than I can count, and the broad gray-green leaves expand daily. *Cyclamen coum* now blooms everywhere it should, although each plant as yet has only one opened flower. The first of the winter crocuses, *Crocus laevigatus*, is blooming in the rock garden and near the driveway. It has outer petals striped dark violet and inner ones in two shades of purple. *Iris unguicularis* blooms in many places. I check them every day, paying most attention to those not yet in flower. My most floriferous form is the narrow-leaved *I. u.* subsp. *angustifolia*, which is prettier than its name. I like best the flowers that are blooming now because this is when they're supposed to bloom. I worry about the freaks. We have some flowers on quinces, roses, and lingering summer bloomers such as verbenas that haven't yet felt winter's cold. I, too, have swollen buds and opened flowers on *Jasminum nudiflorum*, but it is about time for that.

About the mystery strobilanthes, thank you for having Martha draw it. My ruellia has a much longer tube, and its flowers are brilliant fuchsia, not pale lilac. You seem to have the real *Strobilanthes isophyllus*. Why not root it and send me a bit next spring?

The showiest plant in our greenhouse now is *Jasminum rex*, with large, white, unscented flowers. I have *Cyclamen persicum* in shades of pink, but no hibiscus.

You haven't mentioned the *Cardiocrinum giganteum* I sent you as the supreme Christmas present, but early. Have you planted it? How deep did you dig the hole? Oh yes, and have I mentioned that someone swiped my blooming-sized bulb last summer in the metasequoia garden? I know my garden well and when I walk through looking at plants in flower, emerging, or full of promise for next year, I feel a sense of joy. When I find a gap, it is like being assaulted. Someone who is doing a story on plant theft for the *Wall Street Journal* called me recently, and I was happy to give her my opinion. I'm delighted that someone is writing on this topic. It seems that the gardening public thinks "Thou shalt not steal" doesn't apply to plants. Many visitors who come here brag about the plants or seeds they have stolen. The more famous the garden, the greater the accomplishment. The same people probably wouldn't brag about wearing shirts stolen from Lord & Taylor. When we were in England, two seedlings of *Abies nordmanniana* were stolen — the only two that appeared during my twenty-one years here.

Galleys of Craufurd's new book, *Art and the Market*, a collection of essays by Roger Fry with Craufurd's extensive introduction, arrived this week. I enjoyed proofreading it with him and hope it will attract interested readers.

We had a glorious rain last night. It began slowly but changed to downpours. We got at least half an inch. Seasonal temperatures came with the rain, to my contentment. It looks like we won't get severe cold right away, so plants can adjust to the season before winter comes in earnest, if it ever does this year. Martha Stewart arrives on Friday, and I vowed not to do anything special. I may wear my dress-up sweat shirt, but that's all! I didn't have the nerve to invite her for lunch, but I'm comfortable showing her the garden.

Love,
Nancy

Tuesday, December 15, 1998

Dear Nancy,

Enclosed is a recording of some music I bet you've never heard of, much less listened to—Horatio Parker's oratorio, *Hora Novissima* (1893). I'm only slightly less willing to bet that you've never heard of Parker. His name is seldom mentioned now, except sometimes as having been Charles Ives's professor of harmony at Yale. Back in my choirboy days in Dallas, I noticed the work listed among other choral pieces on the cover of the edition of the *Messiah* we used at First Methodist Church. Curious about it, if my memory is correct,

I ordered a copy and showed it to Glen Johnson, the choir director at First Church who loomed so large in my life then (and still does, as an influence! No one, including my parents, gave me more good things that have stayed with me ever since.) Glen thought it looked like fun, with double choruses, lots of harp-strumming, and so on, so we performed it on a couple of occasions. I recently found the recording I'm sending. It holds up to my memories of it very well indeed. Parker had a wonderful sense of melody and a fine understanding of what choirs do best. I am very curious about your reaction, so please listen and let me know. Also, when you have listened, please return the CD. The record has had a peculiar effect on me, affording as it does the chance to revisit music not experienced for almost fifty years — and music that I have been "inside of." I don't know whether that expression means anything to you. To me, it means music that I once sang, music I once helped make, along with my fellow choristers — those hymns that have already come up, also much of the great choral repertory — the *Messiah*, *Elijah*, *Ein Deutsches Requiem*, and much, much Bach (the Magnificat in D, the *St. Matthew Passion*, the B-Minor Mass, and on and on).

At one point when I was young, I really did want to be a musician — specifically a choral director. Glen Johnson was one of my inspirations. Another was Robert Shaw. I went to two or three choral workshops he conducted. Absolutely exhilarating! It's funny that you majored in music at Duke, and I took several music courses (choral literature, conducting) without our running into one another. Listening to *Hora Novissima* has brought back some wonderful old days. One of my greatest thrills came when I was twenty. Glen Johnson wanted to hear the choir and orchestra from the back of the church during a dress rehearsal of the Mozart Requiem. He let me conduct, from the Kyrie right through the Dies Irae. It was a high moment. All that kept me from becoming a musician was a certain lack of real talent.

Enclosed also are photos taken yesterday of the greenhouse. Alarming things are suddenly going on there! Coleuses grow at a huge rate, much faster and fuller than I've ever seen in summer. I kept cuttings of five or six or more of each kind to make certain of having them next year, but I now see that one or two would be plenty. A single plant of coleus 'Inky Fingers' hogs an enormous territory on a bench, as you can see in the photo.

As regards the map of Linwood long, long ago, no, I don't regret not having the original acreage, which I reckon as half the size of

Montrose. What I do regret is that Ed Plantan and I did not buy the vacant lot next to his house, as we briefly considered shortly after Hella and I moved here. We thought the price—$4,000 split two ways—was beyond our reach. Soon afterward it sold, and a mean little rancher was plopped down on the lot. It would have been a fine place for a Plantan/Lacy vegetable patch, also a fine investment. Today the lot alone would fetch at least $80,000.

The balmy weather departed last Friday, just as Martha went back to Carolina. It rained all weekend, a good, soaking rain, and yesterday and today have been brilliantly sunny and very cold. Last night we got our first really hard frost, down to the low 20s. Castor beans and lablabs finally blackened, and all of the brilliance departed from the foliage of our oak-leafed hydrangea.

Yes, I will try to root *Strobilanthes isophyllus*, but somehow it doesn't look as easy to propagate as *S. dyerianus*. And, again yes, I have planted the precious bulb of *Cardiocrinum giganteum*, out in the back border where we can see it growing and eventually blooming. I didn't dig a huge hole, however, for in that part of the garden I don't dig huge holes, thanks to an abundance of maple roots.

A cyclamen question. Right at the easternmost edge of our deck there are several different fancy-leafed forms of *Cyclamen coum* obtained from you the last year of your nursery. It's not a good place for them, as it's too close to the foot traffic that has increased there thanks to changes in the path to our front woodland garden. Can I move the tubers? When? Any other advice? You will be pleased to know that Hella finished baking the last batch of Christmas cookies yesterday and will start mailing them tomorrow.

Merry Christmas,
Allen

Winter 1999

Wednesday, December 23, 1998

Dear Allen,

I haven't heard from you since I wrote on December 9. I wonder if my letter went astray.

Winter came at last. Cold weather arrived right on time, in tune with the calendar. We may have sleet and freezing rain tonight but not much of it. I don't look forward to it, but at least it will give plants reason to rest, with nothing tempting them into premature growth or bloom.

Crocus laevigatus continues to bloom, and it's now joined by two forms of *C. sieberi*. Both have golden bands at the base of each flower, but one is pure white and the other blue-purple. Some of the flowering quinces have swollen buds, and some, especially my old *Chaenomeles* × *superba* 'Crimson and Gold' with dark blood-red flowers, have opened. White, pink, and plum red forms of *Prunus mume* are blooming, as well as several hybrid mahonias with clusters of fragrant yellow flowers.

This afternoon we sign the papers putting conservation easements on part of Montrose. We will gradually put them on the entire property. I have no doubt that this is a wise decision and the only way we can preserve many of the qualities that make this our paradise. At the same time, I have mixed emotions about it. It is my public acknowledgment of my own mortality. I never really had any doubts about that, but there is a finality about signing these papers that makes me sad and happy at the same time.

About Martha Stewart's visit. I liked her! I did not wear my dress-up sweatshirt, nor wash the windows. She arrived with two friends. They were late, and immediately upon leaving their enormous sports utility vehicle declared they had exactly fifteen minutes in which to see the entire garden. "Fine," I said, "put on your seven-league boots and we can do it." We did! Martha introduced herself as Martha. I was impressed by her knowledge of plants. She spotted the silver-leaved *Cyclamen hederifolium* along the paths. She said she wants to do an article on cyclamen and another on the dianthus walk. At one point she asked whether Jamaica Kincaid had seen the garden and whether I had seen Kincaid's wonderful new book on various people's favorite plants. I said yes to the second question, but didn't tell her I had contributed an essay to it. Martha took away three plants: *Echeveria secunda* var. *glauca*, *Glaucium flavum*, and *Lilium formosanum*, which she loved for its standing stalks with their dried seed pods.

We treat ourselves to some of Hella's cookies morning, noon, and night, and they are almost gone now. Martha (Blake-Adams, not Stewart) told me how wonderful it was to be with you while she made them—the fragrance, the sampling, and so on. Martha's account reminded me of days when we visited my grandmother. Special thanks to you, Hella. The sprig of spruce with which you decorated the package is in water with branches of winter jasmine.

This will reach you after Christmas, but by the time you get it I hope you and Hella will have had a happy day with your family. I will think of you.

Love,
Nancy

Monday, December 28, 1998

Dear Nancy,

This year, winter arrived with winter. That is, on Tuesday, the arrival of the winter solstice coincided with a shift in temperature from balmy to unpleasantly cold. That morning we went to Ocean City to pick up some presents for our grandson at a toy shop on the boardwalk. I was wearing only a light jacket, and by the time I left the store a fierce and icy wind was already howling. On Wednesday we were hit from the south by the storm that brought you (also Tennessee westward to Texas) ice. We got snow, about four inches of the stuff, and thus the white Christmas some people profess to dream of.

We do Christmas here on its eve. For a while, it looked as if Paul and Debbie and their three wouldn't be able to drive down from Wall (about seventy-five miles), but they made it after all, so we had the pleasure of being with all five grandchildren.

Hella's family in Tennessee wasn't so lucky. It took her brother Reiner and his family two days to fly from Boston to Nashville, as they got stuck in Cincinnati. Meanwhile, electricity was out in Manchester, where Hella's mother lives, and in Tullahoma, where another brother lives. The entire crew had to drive to Murfreesboro, where they spent three nights in a motel. So much for white Christmases just like the ones we used to know! We may both be Zone 7, but my more northerly location means that a quick walk around my garden turns up little in the way of winter flowers. Perhaps there would be more to report if I were growing *Crocus laeviga-tus* and some of the other late bloomers—or if I had done more long ago to plant with this season in mind. Somewhere under the snow, which ought to melt substantially today, there may be a few blossoms on *Cyclamen coum*. We've picked a few sprigs of winter jasmine, but several nights of 16° temperatures will retard further flowering. Hybrid witch hazels haven't started yet, but we seldom if ever see much from them until the middle of January. There are three buds on a tiny camellia, one of the exceptionally winter-hardy cultivars hybridized at the National Arboretum. They might open in a couple of weeks if we get a few warm days.

I assume you went for your usual Christmas walk in search of flowers with anthers showing, that you will write me about them, so that I can enjoy them vicariously. But I do have the greenhouse, which is turning into a rain forest of luxuriant growth. I've stopped fertilizing *anything!* I've cut back night temperatures from 70° to 65° and perhaps should go lower. (I don't need to heat much in the daytime, and last Saturday afternoon, which was bright and sunny, it got up to 90°: the exhaust fans are set to come on at 75°.)

The greenhouse stars at present are abutilons, especially *Abutilon pictum* 'Thompsonii'. I had it all summer on the deck and frankly thought so little of it that I almost let it die outside instead of giving it precious greenhouse space. I didn't much like the variegated leaves—green splotched with chlorotic yellow—and it was a sparse bloomer. You should see it now! It has shot up to become a substantial shrub, with three main limbs all almost four feet tall. The flowers are small, only an inch or so across, but there are huge numbers of them. (I stopped counting yesterday at seventy-five.) Their soft orange combines very well with the variegated leaves, toning them down. My fingers are crossed, but so far I haven't seen evidence of the white fly problem that's supposed to trouble abutilons in winter in greenhouses.

But things don't stand as well with my brugmansias and their spider mites. The leaves started looking rather nasty two weeks ago, then defoliation set in. Cynthia Woodyard tells me to cut them back hard and (despite what I just said about not fertilizing) then dose them heavily with nitrogen. Perhaps I'll also stick them outside for a few hours of frosty air to cut back on their resident fauna.

The news of the progress of preserving part of Montrose—and let's hope eventually all of it—is very good.

As it happens, more history of our own patch of land has sur-

Linwood

faced. Christmas night, Ed Plantan came over for a drink, bearing a yellowed newspaper clipping. Since his wife, Jean, died right before Christmas three years ago, he couldn't quite bring himself to clean out her desk, but finally did and found there something from the local paper Jean had cut out for us in 1993 but never got around to giving us. In a column on local history, Alma Barrett Anthony reminisces about her and a sister and a brother having been born sometime after 1912 in a house at the corner of Belhaven and Shore. (That's us.) She goes on to say that her father was electrocuted while working on an electrical pole in Somers Point on March 7, 1923, widowing his wife, Amanda, at only twenty-nine and leaving her with four small children to raise. Mrs. Anthony goes on to recall the suburban trolleys that used to run up and down Shore Road, and mentions that her "Grandmom Barrett" once owned land from the bay to Patcong Creek. (That's confirmation by a reliable witness of what I wrote you in another letter recently about the shrinking of the land originally belonging to our house.)

I already knew a good bit about the ownership of our property, the kind of material that appears in deeds. In 1853 and 1854 Benjamin Barrett acquired two parcels of land, one from the Scull family, the other from Thomas Morris, who had bought it from a Captain John Somers. (All of these surnames figure prominently hereabouts.) Benjamin Barrett died in 1885, and the land passed to his widow and to his son John William Barrett in 1887. John William inherited his mother's share in 1919. He died March 7, 1923, so he was the fellow who was electrocuted.

Our property passed out of the Barrett family's hands in 1947, when William and Ethel Cannon bought it for $100. (!!) Three years later, one Clarence Owens bought it for $1. (!!!) The next year, Benjamin and Henrietta Perlstein bought it for $100. (!!!) Then in 1965, the next-to-last owners bought it for $1,000. On July 12, 1972 we entered the picture, for $26,500. The house was pretty much a wreck, with wallpaper hanging loose in all the upstairs rooms except one. But the structure was sound, and the house proved to be something we could turn into a home.

What I already knew about 1511 Shore Road was the history of a parcel of real estate. Jean's clipping gave something of a human face to part of this history. I can imagine the scene inside these walls on that March day thirteen years before I was born when the bad news came from Somers Point. And, oh yes, at that time Belhaven Avenue was Barrett Avenue.

Happy New Year!
Allen

Monday, December 28, 1998

Dear Allen,

Christmas was lovely this year. I used to long for Christmas the way it was when I was a child, but now that I have no living parents it doesn't seem to matter any more. The world seemed to stand still during this past week. The only thing that didn't stop was the weather. We had a beautiful but damaging ice storm beginning Wednesday and lingering through most of Thursday. We heard loud cracks as large branches fell, and we worried as our lights flickered. We escaped the worst of it and never lost power for any length of time. The gaps in power were just enough to leave me setting and resetting the clocks.

The large juniper behind nandinaland fell apart, and my best weeping yaupon holly broke off at the base. It must have been twenty feet high and represented years of nurturing. I have one branch that may live.

I made my Christmas walk, to the sounds of Craufurd's chain

saw, and found many flowers open. They were encased in ice but nevertheless they count. I can't count *Edgeworthia papyrifera* at the entrance to the law office because I couldn't see a single stamen even though it looked ready to open. Here's my list: *Iris unguicularis* 'Walter Butt', *I. u.* var. *angustifolia, I. u.* 'Alba'; *Camellia japonica* 'Berenice Boddy'; *Verbena canadensis, V. tenuisecta; Potentilla alba; Chaenomeles speciosa* 'Chobai White', *C.* × *superba* 'Crimson and Gold'; *Helleborus foetidus, Hh. niger,* × *hybridus, orientalis,* & *cyclophyllus; Mahonia* × *media* 'Arthur Menzies' and 'Winter Sun'; *Erica carnea* 'Springwood White' and 'Winter Beauty', *Erica* × *darleyensis* 'Arthur Johnson'; *Crocus laevigatus* and *C. sieberi* (both purple and white forms); *Cyclamen coum, Cc. mirabile, pseudibericum,* and *cilicium; Narcissus cantabricus* and *N. romieuxii; Erysimum alpinum; Chimonanthus praecox; Galanthus elwesii; Prunus mume* 'Kobai', 'Peggy Clark', and white and pink seedlings; *Jasminum nudiflorum; Phlox subulata* (several colors); *Veronica surculosa, V.* 'Goodness Grows'; *Campanula rotundifolia; Viola labradorica* (I know it now has a new name, *V. riviniana* Purpurea Group), *V. odorata* 'Madame Armandine Pages'; *Clematis cirrhosa* (both the spotted and unspotted ones); *Viburnum macrocephalum; Isopyrum biternatum; Aster carolinianus;* and *Primula* × *polyantha* (red with dark foliage). I didn't count anything in the cold frames or greenhouse. I was most excited by the pure white Algerian iris and the primroses.

Now the ice has melted, and, miraculously, *Prunus mume* still has its color. Even some of the irises, though droopy, aren't brown. The temperature dipped to 19° one night down at the cold frames, but in general I am happy with our current weather. We have temperatures about 50° during the day and in the 20s and 30s at night. That's normal for us, and that's what I want.

I saved your letter of December 15 to read on Christmas morning, and it was the nicest present of all. You are absolutely right about Horatio Parker and me. I've never heard of him. Now I have, and I have heard *Hora Novissima* twice through and return it to you before it haunts me with its beauty. Thank you for sharing it with me. I loved best the fugal sections. Craufurd and I listened to it as we drove to Warrenton on Boxing Day and had our second Christmas dinner. We heard part of the Vaughan Williams hymns on our way home. I agree with you—they're beautiful.

The pictures you sent gave me a little tour of your greenhouse. Your *Hibiscus acetosella* is wonderful—the largest flowers I've yet seen on it. Could it be a different species? *Strobilanthes isophyllus* is gorgeous and not *Ruellia makoyana,* as I thought it might be. As for

Orthosiphon stamineus, that's a great discovery! It's strange that no current encyclopedia lists it.

You asked about the fancy-leaved *Cyclamen coum* growing in the wrong place, and whether to move them or not, and if so, when and how. Don't move them unless you have to, but if you have to, it's best to do it in late summer or early fall. But if you are stomping on them—for shame!—then move them in late spring just as they go dormant. The only advantage late spring has over fall is that you can find the plants easily instead of rooting around for the tubers.

Thank you for sending Christopher Lloyd and Beth Chatto's letters. I've read good things about them (in *Homeground* and elsewhere) and will read them a bit at a time, because I believe this may be one of those books that is sad to finish. If I restrain myself, I can make the pleasure last a long time.

My best present all year has been the letters from you. Happy New Year—and keep on writing!

Love,
Nancy

Friday, January 1, 1999

Dear Allen,

Mother told me that whatever I did on New Year's Day I would do every day of the year. It used to worry me, and I would try to do only those things I really enjoyed doing. Mother also served the best New Year's dinners. We always had hoecake, sausage, black-eyed peas (a wish would come true for each pea eaten), and spinach instead of turnip greens. For dessert she served caramel pies with toasted pecans and whipped cream. I can't make most of those things and will never have them again, but I can remember how warm and happy they made me. I wish I thought I could write to you every day of 1999, but I know I can't and won't. Even more, I wish I could receive a letter from you every time I opened my mailbox, but I know I can't and won't.

Last night the temperature dropped to 19°, and this morning I found the garden covered with silver. In the sun it looked like diamond dust had been scattered over the plants. The urn at the base of the front porch contains black pansies, thus far without flowers, and their normally green leaves curled under at the edges and were nearly black. I enjoyed my walk to the end of the drive, for a silver lawn is more beautiful than a beige one.

I noticed yesterday that the *Durham Herald* gives weather forecasts for Atlantic City, so now I can see what you're facing. We have the same prediction for tomorrow—a major ice storm developing from the south and west and moving north and east. We have learned how to prepare for these things. At the first sign of ice, we lower the slatted shades on the greenhouses. We have bubble pack covering the vents for the coolers.

I'm still grieving over the beautiful yaupon holly I lost to the last ice storm. I finally took a handsaw, cut the broken trunk, and dragged it onto the lawn for Craufurd to deal with. Then I went into the woods, where I could mourn alone out of the sight of others. The woods are beautiful now, with rohdeas decorated with scarlet berries and *Ruscus aculeatus* bearing bright red ones. *Cyclamen coum* bloom in all their colors, white, pink, and crimson, and there were many flowers on *Helleborus niger*. I finally composed myself and returned to work.

We saw the new year come in last night for the first time in years, watching *Amadeus*, shelling pecans, and drinking a bottle of champagne. It was the best New Year's celebration I can remember. I was surprised to hear fireworks go off in town at midnight, but that probably happens every year.

You keep a much warmer greenhouse than I. I bring in all those plants that hate cold and put them in the basement on a couple of plant tables with fluorescent lights. Everything else must survive night temperatures of about 40°. The sun helps during daylight and I open the doors and vents if the temperature inside rises above 50°.

Happy New Year to you and Hella. I feel we have all been through an enormous transformation in 1998. You nearly left us but came back more wonderful than ever. I lost my second parent, and for the first time felt independent. Craufurd and I took the first major step to preserve this land forever, whatever that is.

From the two of us to both of you, much love!
Nancy

Wednesday, January 6, 1999

Dear Nancy,

I enjoyed your New Year's Day letter with its mention of your traditional holiday meal. Black-eyed peas! They went out of my life around the time Hella and I married. She has never considered them to be fit food for humans. For a couple of years I made sure to have them ceremonially at the outset of a new year, but I ate them alone, and where's the pleasure in that? But your version of their advantages differs from mine. In Texas I was taught only that eating black-eyed peas on New Year's brought good luck—nothing about a wish coming true for each one eaten. Perhaps if I had been indoctrinated as you were, I'd still be following the old tradition.

I also never heard the one about doing whatever you did on day 1 for the next 364. Your mother was wrong about this, by the way. Hella and I both smoked on January 1, 1998, and come next Wednesday neither of us has had a single puff for a whole year.

The old year ended for me very nicely indeed. Pat Strachan called late the afternoon of New Year's Eve to tell me that she wanted to publish the selected essays from *Homeground* that I had sent her only a couple of weeks before, now that I am no longer represented by an agent in New York. Pat, who also graduated from Duke but later than we did, was my first editor. I did three books with her when she was at Farrar, Straus & Giroux. She's a wonderful editor, and also ties with Joanne Ferguson for having the nicest telephone voice in America. It was wonderful when the phone rang and I heard her again.

I also enjoyed your earlier letter and its account of the many things blooming at your Christmas walk. Here, however, the differences between the ways we each garden become pronounced. Your much larger garden affords you room for many more plants than I have. If I had all of your winter bloomers I would have to forgo favorite plants in other seasons, for sheer lack of room. My more northerly situation also plays a part in reducing winter bloom. We may both garden in the same zone, but latitude makes a difference. Something else to consider is that you have deliberately sought out plants that show their anthers around the time of the winter solstice, and I have not, with a few exceptions. The darleyensis winter heaths flower from Thanksgiving until late April or early May. All by themselves they enable me to claim that I have something in flower 365 days a year. They're blooming now, of course, but they're solitary performers. *Cyclamen coum* has yet to open a bud. Winter jasmine was blooming before Christmas, but it's in a lull now. The 'Arnold Promise' witch hazel that delights us with its fragrant golden blossoms hasn't yet started to strut its stuff.

We escaped the ice that did so much damage to some of your trees, but it has been bitter, bitter cold since Christmas, except for last Saturday, which dawned at 16° and stayed there until midafternoon, when the temperature started rising very strangely. By nightfall it was 45° and remained there until the next day. We had heavy rain all morning, and then it cleared up and temperatures plunged again. It's been cold ever since. Today is typical—6° at sunrise, 25° now at 1:00 P.M., and not expected to get any higher. The little pool by the deck is entirely frozen, a layer of ice fifteen inches thick.

I was interested to hear your comment about the pictures I sent you, particularly about the blossoms of *Hibiscus acetosella* being the largest you've seen. It would seem that I do have a superior form; *The New RHS Dictionary* describes the blossoms as under a half inch across, and mine are larger by an inch or more. Mine don't conform in another way, either. The dictionary says that the flowers are borne solitarily in the leaf axils. Mine are in the leaf axils, all right, but they appear in pairs or trios. A closer look at my plants also shows that what I thought were flower buds turn out to be seed pods, bursting with fat white seeds, still immature. I was puzzled by this production of seeds in the absence of any insect pollinators I could detect, but my botanist friend Sandy tells me that some species of hibiscus are apomictic, just like dandelions. I had to ask her what "apomictic" meant, and she explained that apomixis is the formation of seed without benefit of sex. Every fluffy dandelion seed that sails on the wind here in America is the product of apomixis. (Europe, apparently, has both sexual and apomictic dandelions, but it was the latter that got started here, perhaps from a single seed that arrived by accident.) If Sandy is right about my hibiscus, every seed should produce plants that are genetically identical to one another and to their unwed mother.

No matter how long we live, there's always something new and often surprising for gardeners to learn.

Greenhouse problems with coleus have surfaced. A good many are wilting, not from lack of water but from too much. I have not yet mastered the art of watering plants inside, as Hella did long ago. She has made all of the important empirical discoveries: e.g. begonias thrive on amazingly small amounts of moisture. At the moment, incidentally, she is taking down the Christmas tree, removing all the ornaments we have accumulated during each of the forty years we have been married. I am not encouraged to participate in this chore. It may be that I am not gentle enough. I also think she likes to look at each ornament and bid it goodbye for another year.

You mentioned the leaf curl and the almost black color of your pansies, signs of the extreme cold. We have the same thing, not just as usual on our aucubas and on some rhododendrons around the neighborhood, but also on English ivy, photinia, *Vinca minor*, and hellebores. *Helleborus foetidus* was about to bloom when the thermometer dropped into single digits. Now it's at half-mast, and the foliage looks like black seaweed.

Tomorrow is my sixty-fourth birthday—or, as you prefer to put it, the beginning of my sixty-fifth year. The sixty-fourth was certainly eventful!

I go back to the classroom week after next, teaching my two horticulture classes. I could teach half-time for half salary in academic year 1999–2000—and how odd that date sounds! But I'm pretty sure that I'll call it quits after this coming semester, concentrating on writing, gardening, visiting gardens here and there. Perhaps I'll miss the classroom, but I think not, since I haven't missed it during the last sixteen months.

I have something surprising and splendid to tell you about Mrs. Harkey. I have long wondered what her first name was, but of course in the 1940s our Mrs. Harkeys and our Mrs. Pridgens didn't have first names, not as far as their pupils were concerned. I had some idea that Mrs. Harkey's first name started with a "G"— maybe Gladys, maybe Grace. The other day, after decades of losing track of one another, I had a telephone call from a childhood friend and playmate, Betty Dearing, from Comfort, Texas. She reminded me that I had sung at her wedding. I have no recollection of that, but hope it wasn't "O Promise Me" or "I Love You Truly." In our reminiscences about our school days in Irving, it turned out that Mrs. Harkey had been Betty's fourth grade teacher, the year after she became my gardening mentor. Betty had no idea what her first name was, but her brother still lived in Irving, and she said she would see if he could find out.

Now, in what I've written you about Mrs. Harkey so far in these letters, I left out one thing, although I may well have told you at some point. I wrote about it in my first book on gardening. It concerns how it was that I came to be working at her nursery on Saturdays, when I was in the third grade. I was in trouble. My teacher had put me under her desk to punish me for some malefaction I don't remember. She kept me there for some considerable period of time. I asked to go to the bathroom. She kicked me with a sharp tap. I bit her. After a terrible ruckus, I was expelled for the rest of the term, a couple of months. Mrs. Harkey offered to tutor me in arithmetic, grammar, and reading, in exchange for a little work at her iris nursery. I don't remember the tutoring, but I do remember vividly the magical lesson of putting pollen on the pistil of an iris and then seeing a seed pod swell—a seed pod that might or might not be pregnant with beauty.

Betty called just as I was starting this letter with news from her brother. It was Ruth—Ruth Harkey. I'm glad to know that. I wish I had a picture of her. She gave me my beginnings as a gardener. To this day, I thank her—as I thank Glen Johnson for the gift of music. These two blessed my life with grace and deep pleasure.

Love,
Allen

Index

Note: This is a selective index. Plants mentioned in passing may not be included. I have indexed mere mentions of plants only when they occur several times or have bearing on one of the persistent themes in these letters. There are no entries for Hella or Craufurd, although they appear in the text very often and are also implicit on almost every page. The nonappearance of Hella's and my children and grandchildren in the index does not mean that they are not wholly delightful beings. My parents and Nancy's are indexed, because they contributed substantially to these letters, in that had they not existed, neither would the letters. My two surviving brothers are indexed, because I know that they will check to see if they're in the book. —A.L.

Charleston (home of Vanessa Bell and Duncan Grant), 82, 87

Chatto, Beth, 144; *Dear Friend and Gardener*, 158, 161–62, 195

Chiggers, 71, 75–76

Chimonanthus praecox, 6, 194

Chiswick House, 81–82, 87

Chopin, Frédéric: "Ballade in G Minor," 129

Chrysanthemums, 174

Cigarette smoking, 20–21, 25, 47, 49, 87, 156, 197

Cimicifuga 'Hillside Black Beauty', 62

Clematis armandii, 52; *C. cirrhosa*, 6, 175, 183, 194; *C. integrifolia*, 102; *C. serratifolia*, 174; *C. terniflora*, xxii, 124, 146; *C. viticella*, 102

Coastal Gardens and Nursery, 10, 12

Cochran, Linda, 57

Colchicum, 123, 130, 141; *C. burtii*, 18; *C. kotschyi*, 110; *C. speciosum*, 130; *C.* 'Waterlily', 141

Coleus (*Solenostemon*), 38, 44, 101, 139, 144, 151–52; 'Black Duckfoot', 96, 147; 'Inky Fingers', 96, 147, 185; 'Leprechaun Lace', 147; other cultivars, 92–93; scientific name of, 93

Comptonia peregrina (sweet fern), 76

Container gardening, 36–37, 93

Copper, for controlling slugs and root growth, 151, 157

Cornus alba 'Sibirica', 31; *C. kousa*, 108

Corrigan, Maureen, 65, 80

Crabapple 'Van Eseltine', 53

Crape myrtles, dwarf, 107

Crocosmia 'Lucifer', 36; *C.* 'Solfatarre', 36

Crocus: autumn-flowering, 130; *C. cartwrightianus* 'Albus', 174; *C. caspius*, 174; *C. imperati* subsp. *suaveolens*, 18; *C. goulimyi*, 126, 166, 169, 174; *C. laevigatus*, 6, 183, 189, 191, 194; *C. longiflorus*, 6, 174, 180;

C. nudiflorus, 174; *C. sativus*, 126, 174; *C. serotinus* subsp. *salzmannii*, 180; *C. sieberi*, 189, 194; *C. speciosus*, 126, 141, 144, 169; *C. thomasii*, 174; *C. tommasinianus*, 26; *C. tournefortii*, 174

Crossvine (*Bignonia capreolata*) 'Tangerine Beauty', 52

Crug Farm Plants (nursery in Wales), 11, 13

Cryptotaenia japonica f. *atropurpurea*, 61

Cuphea ignea, 157; *C. llavea* 'Georgia Scarlet', 62

Cyclamen, xvii, 131; *C. cilicium*, 6, 141, 180, 194; *C. coum*, 6, 26, 31, 40, 51, 169, 183, 194, 195, 196, 198; *C. graecum*, 6, 90, 110, 180; *C. hederifolium*, 71, 90, 97, 101, 124, 141, 177, 189, 191; *C. intaminatum*, 141; *C. mirabile*, 180, 194; *C. persicum*, 3, 18, 183; *C. pseudibericum*, 26, 40, 51, 194; *C. purpurascens*, 90; *C. trochopteranthum*, 26

Dahlia 'Bishop of Llandaff', xxii, 18, 62; *D. imperialis*, 148

Dallas Arboretum, 88–89

Datura inoxia, *D. metel* 'Cornucopia', 87–88

Daylight saving time, 41, 48, 131

Dearing, Betty, 200

Deer at Montrose, 17–18, 42, 95–96, 98, 101, 123, 149, 153

Delius, Frederick, "Walk to the Paradise Gardens," 165

Deutzia crenata 'Nikko', 35

Diana, Princess of Wales, 15

Dianthus 'Little Boy Blue', 45, 49

Dicentra eximia 'Boothman's Variety', 61–62; *D. spectabilis*, 35

Digitalis thapsi, 85, 89

Disney Institute, 125, 163, 170–71, 172, 173